AFTER LIBERALISM

AFTER LIBERALISM

IMMANUEL WALLERSTEIN

THE NEW PRESS · NEW YORK

LIBRARY OF CONGRESS CATALOGING-IN-PUBLICATION DATA

Wallerstein, Immanuel Maurice, 1930–
    After Liberalism / Immanuel Wallerstein.
        p.   cm.
    Includes bibliographical references.
    ISBN 1-56584-304-5 (pbk.)
    1. Liberalism. 2. Post-communism. 3. Economic development.
        4. Human rights. I. Title.
JC574.W35   1995
909.82'0—dc20   95-7424 CIP

PUBLISHED IN THE UNITED STATES BY THE NEW PRESS, NEW YORK
DISTRIBUTED BY W. W. NORTON & COMPANY, INC., NEW YORK

Established in 1990 as a major alternative to the large,
commercial publishing houses, The New Press is the first full-scale
nonprofit American book publisher outside of the university presses.

The Press is operated editorially in the public interest,
rather than for private gain; it is committed to publishing
in innovative ways works of educational, cultural,
and community value that, despite their intellectual merits,
might not normally be commercially viable.

The New Press's editorial offices are located at the
City University of New York.

BOOK DESIGN BY HALL SMYTH
PRODUCTION MANAGEMENT BY KIM WAYMER
PRINTED IN THE UNITED STATES OF AMERICA

95 96 97 98 9 8 7 6 5 4 3 2 1

TO CLEMENS HELLER

WHO WORKED TO MAKE INTELLIGENT DEBATE
ABOUT THE WORLD'S FUTURE POSSIBLE

CONTENTS

ACKNOWLEDGMENTS   IX

INTRODUCTION: AFTER LIBERALISM?   1

I. THE 1990S AND AFTER: CAN WE RECONSTRUCT?   9

The Cold War and the Third World: The Good Old Days?   10

Peace, Stability, and Legitimacy, 1990–2025/2050   25

What Hope Africa? What Hope the World?   46

II. THE CONSTRUCTION AND TRIUMPH OF LIBERAL IDEOLOGY   71

Three Ideologies or One? The Pseudobattle of Modernity   72

Liberalism and the Legitimation of Nation-States:
    An Historical Interpretation   93

The Concept of National Development, 1917–1989:
    Elegy and Requiem   108

III. THE HISTORICAL DILEMMAS OF LIBERALS   125

The End of What Modernity?   126

The Insurmountable Contradictions of Liberalism:
    Human Rights and the Rights of Peoples in the Geoculture
    of the Modern World-System   145

The Geoculture of Development, or the Transformation
    of Our Geoculture?   162

America and the World: Today, Yesterday, and Tomorrow   176

IV. THE DEATH OF SOCIALISM, OR CAPITALISM IN MORTAL DANGER?   209

Revolution as Strategy and Tactics of Transformation   210

Marxism After the Collapse of the Communisms   219

The Collapse of Liberalism   232

The Agonies of Liberalism: What Hope Progress?   252

NOTES   272

ACKNOWLEDGMENTS

I am grateful to the original publishers for their kind cooperation in granting permission for publication here.

"The Cold War and the Third World: The Good Old Days?":
    Economic and Political Weekly, April 27, 1991.

"Peace, Stability, and Legitimacy, 1990–2025/2050": G. Lundestad, ed.,
    The Fall of Great Powers (Oslo: Scandinavian University Press, 1994).

"What Hope Africa? What Hope the World?": A. O. Olukoshi &
    L. Wohlgemuth, eds., *A Road to Development: Africa in the 21st Century*
    (Uppsala: Nordiska Afrikainstitutet, 1995).

"Liberalism and the Legitimation of Nation-States: An Historical
    Interpretation": *Social Justice,* Vol. 19, No. 1, Spring 1992.

"The Concept of National Development, 1917–1989: Elegy and Requiem":
    American Behavioral Scientist, Vol. 35, No. 4/5, Mar./June 1992.
    Reprinted by permission of Sage Publications, Inc.

"The End of What Modernity?": *Theory and Society,* Vol. 24, 1995.

"The Insurmountable Contradictions of Liberalism: Human Rights and the
    Rights of Peoples in the Geoculture of the Modern World-System":
    South Atlantic Quarterly, Vol. 9, No. 4, Fall 1995.

"The Geoculture of Development, or the Transformation of Our Geoculture?":
    Asian Perspective, Vol. 17, No. 2, Fall–Winter 1993.

"America and the World: Today, Yesterday, and Tomorrow":
    Theory and Society, Vol. 21, 1, Feb. 1992.

"Revolution as Strategy and Tactics of Transformation": A. Callari et al., eds.,
    Marxism in the Postmodern Age (New York: Guilford Press, 1994).

"Marxism After the Collapse of the Communisms": *Economic Review,*
    Economic and Political Weekly, Feb.–March 1992.

"The Collapse of Liberalism": R. Miliband and L. Panitch, eds.,
    Socialist Register 1992 (London: Merlin Press, 1992).

"The Agonies of Liberalism: What Hope Progress?": *New Left Review,*
    No. 204, Mar.–April 1994.

AFTER LIBERALISM?

The destruction of the Berlin Wall and the subsequent dissolution of the U.S.S.R. have been celebrated as the fall of the Communisms and the collapse of Marxism-Leninism as an ideological force in the modern world. This is no doubt correct. These events have also been celebrated as the final triumph of liberalism as an ideology. This is a total misperception of reality. Quite the contrary, these same events marked *even more* the collapse of liberalism and our definitive entry into the world "after liberalism."

This book is devoted to expounding this thesis. It is composed of essays written between 1990 and 1993. The essays were written in a period of great ideological confusion, during which a widespread, early, naive optimism began to give way to extensive, diffuse fear and dismay at the emerging world disorder.

The year 1989 has been widely analyzed as the end of the period 1945–1989, that is, as the year signifying the defeat of the U.S.S.R. in the cold war. In this book it will be argued that it is more useful to regard it as the end of the period 1789–1989, that is, the period of the triumph and collapse, the rise and eventual demise, of liberalism as the global ideology—what I call the geoculture—of the modern world-system. The year 1989 would thus mark the end of a politico-cultural era—an era of spectacular technological achievement—in which the slogans of the French Revolution were seen by most people to reflect inevitable historical truth, to be realized now or in a near future.

Liberalism was never a doctrine of the Left; it was always the quintessential centrist doctrine. Its advocates were sure of their moderation, their wisdom, and their humanity. They arrayed themselves simultaneously against an archaic past of unjustified privilege (which they considered to be represented by conservative ideology) and a reckless leveling that took no account of either virtue or merit (which they considered to be represented by socialist/radical ideology). Liberals have always sought to define the rest of the political scene as made up of two extremes between which they fall. They claimed to be equally against reactionaries and against republicans (or democrats) in 1815–1848; against Fascists and against Communists in 1919–1939; against imperialists and against radical nationalists in 1945–1960; against racists and against reverse racists in the 1980s.

Liberals have always claimed that the liberal state—reformist, legalist, and somewhat libertarian—was the only state that could guarantee freedom. And for the relatively small group whose freedom it safeguarded, this was perhaps true. But unfortunately that group always remained a minority perpetually en route to becoming everyone. Liberals have always claimed that only a liberal state could guarantee a nonrepressive order. Critics on the right have said that the liberal state, in its reluctance to appear repressive, permitted, indeed encouraged, disorder. Critics on the left, on the other hand, have always said that it was order that was in fact the primary concern of liberals in power and that they engaged in very real repression, which was only partially hidden.

The point is not once again to argue the merits or faults of liberalism as the basis of the good society. We need rather to engage in doing the historical sociology of liberalism. We need to analyze clearly its historical emergence in the aftermath of the French Revolution; its meteoric rise to triumph as the dominant ideology, first in only a few states (albeit the most powerful ones), then in the world-system as a world-system; and its equally sudden dethronement in recent years.

The origins of liberalism in the political upheavals that were launched by the French Revolution are widely argued in the literature. The assertion that liberalism became the central credo of the geoculture of the world-system is somewhat more controversial. While most analysts would agree that liberalism was triumphant in Europe as of 1914, some would argue that its decline began then, whereas I argue that its apogee was in the post-1945 period (up to 1968), the era of U.S. hegemony in the world-system. Furthermore, my view of how liberalism triumphed—its essential links with racism and Eurocentrism—would be disputed by many.

I expect however that what is most provocative is to argue that the collapse of the Communisms represents not the final success of liberalism as an ideology but the decisive undermining of the ability of liberal ideology to continue its historic role. To be sure, a version of this thesis is being argued by the troglodytes of the world Right. But many of them are either cynics manipulating slogans or hopeless romantics of a family-centered utopia that never existed historically. Many others are merely frightened by the impending disintegration of world order, which they correctly perceive to be occurring.

This rejection of liberal reformism is being implemented now in the United States under the label of the Contract With America, as it is being simultaneously force-fed to countries all over the world by the ministrations of the IMF. These overtly reactionary policies will probably stimulate a political backlash in the United States, as has been happening already in Eastern Europe, because these policies worsen rather than improve the immediate economic situation of the majority of the population. But this backlash will not mean a return to a belief in liberal reformism. It will merely mean that a doctrine that combines a fake adulation of the market with legislation against the poor and the strangers, which is what is being peddled today by reinvigorated reactionaries, cannot offer a viable substitute for the failed promises of reformism. In any case, my argument is not theirs. Mine is the view of those who uphold what I call in one of the essays the "modernity of liberation." I think we need to take a sober look at the history of liberalism in order to see what we can salvage from the wreckage, and to see how we can struggle under the difficult conditions, and with the ambiguous legacy, that liberalism has bequeathed to the world.

I am not seeking to paint doom and gloom. But neither am I preaching rosy bromides. I believe that the period after liberalism is a period of major political struggle more consequential than any other of the past five hundred years. I see forces of privilege who know very well that "everything must change in order that nothing change," and are working skillfully and intelligently to bring that about. I see forces of liberation who have literally lost their breath. They see the historical futility of a political project in which they

have invested 150 years of struggle—the project of social transformation via the obtaining of state power, state by state. And they
are very unsure whether an alternative project exists or not. But
the erstwhile project, the strategy of the world Left, failed primarily because it was infused, suffused, with liberal ideology, even
in its most purportedly antiliberal, "revolutionary" variants, such
as Leninism. Until there is clarity about what happened between
1789 and 1989, no plausible project for liberation can present itself
in the twenty-first century.

But even if we are clear about what happened between 1789
and 1989, and even if we agree that the transition of the next
twenty-five to fifty years will be a time of systemic disorder, disintegration, and acute political struggle about what kind of new
world-system(s) we shall construct, the question concerning most
people is, What to do now? People are confused, angry, fearful, *now*
—sometimes even desperate, but not at all passive. The sense that
one should act politically is still strong everywhere in the world
despite the equally strong feeling that political activity of a "traditional" type is probably futile.

The choice can no longer be presented as "reform vs. revolution." We have debated that supposed alternative for more than a
century only to discover that, in most cases, the reformers were at
best reluctant reformers, the revolutionaries were only slightly
more militant reformers, and the reforms that *were* implemented
achieved on the whole less than their proponents intended and
less than their opponents feared. This was in fact the necessary
result of the structural constraints imposed upon us by the dominant liberal consensus.

If, however, disintegration is a more apt name than revolution
for whatever will be happening now, what shall our political stance
be? I see only two things to do, and the two need to be done simultaneously. On the one hand, almost everyone's immediate concern
is how to cope with the pressing, ongoing problems of life—the
material problems, the social and cultural problems, the moral or
spiritual problems. On the other hand, fewer people, but still many,
are preoccupied with a longer-run concern—the strategy of transformation. Neither the reformers nor the revolutionaries succeeded

in the past century because neither recognized the degree to which the short-run concern and the long-run concern required simultaneous action, but of quite diverse (even divergent) kinds.

The modern state has been *par excellence* the reformer's instrument for helping people cope. This has not at all been the only function of the state, nor even perhaps its principal function. Nor has state-oriented action been the only coping mechanism. But the fact is that state action has been an ineluctable element in the process of coping, and that attempts by ordinary people to cope have been justifiably and intelligently directed toward getting the states to act in particular ways. Despite the disorder, disarray, and ongoing disintegration, this continues to be true. States can increase or diminish suffering, through their allocation of resources, their degree of protection of rights, and their interventions in social relations between different groups. To suggest that anyone should no longer bother about what their state does is folly, and I do not believe many people are going to be willing to turn away completely from an active concern with the actions of their state.

States can make things a little better (or a little worse) for everyone. They can choose between helping ordinary people cope better and allowing upper strata to thrive still more. This is, however, *all* that states can do. These things no doubt matter a lot in the short run, but they matter not at all in the longer run. If we wish to affect in significant ways the massive transition of the whole world-system through which we are living so that it goes in one direction rather than in another, the state is *not* a major vehicle of action. Indeed, it is rather a major obstacle.

The sense that the state structures have become (were always?) major obstacles to the transformation of the world-system, even when (or maybe especially when) they were controlled by reformist forces (claiming to be "revolutionary" forces), is what is behind the massive turn against the state in the Third World, in the erstwhile socialist countries, and even in the OECD "welfare state" countries. In the wreckage, the slogans of the "market," peddled by a newly aggressive array of (Western) conservative experts and political figures, have become a momentary verbal currency. Since, however, the state policies associated with the "market" as slogan make coping more difficult rather than less difficult, the swing back against market-priority governments has already begun in many countries. The swing back is not, however, toward a renewed belief in the capacity of the state to transform the world. To the extent that it is occurring, the swing back merely reflects the sober judgment that we still need to use the state in order to aid people in coping. It is therefore not inconsistent for the same people today to both turn to the state (for aid in coping) and denounce the state and policies in general as useless and even nefarious (in terms of restructuring the world in the direction they would hope it could go).

What will, what can, such people do, then, that might affect the direction of the transition? Another deceptive slogan enters here: it is the call to build, expand, and reconstruct the "civil society." This is equally vain. The "civil society" can exist insofar as states exist and are strong enough to undergird something called the "civil society," which essentially means the organization of citizens within the framework of the state to pursue activities legitimated by the state and to engage in indirect (that is, nonparty) politics vis-à-vis the state. The development of the civil society was an essential instrument in the erection of liberal states, pillars of internal and world-systemic order. The civil society was also used as a rallying symbol for the installation of liberal state structures where they did not yet exist. But most of all, the civil society historically was a mode of constraining potential destructive violence of and by the state as well as of taming the dangerous classes.

Constructing the civil society was the activity of states in Western Europe and North America in the nineteenth century. Insofar as state-building remained on the world-systemic agenda in the first two-thirds of the twentieth century, one could still talk of constructing civil societies in more states. But with the states in decline, civil society is necessarily disintegrating. Indeed, it is precisely this disintegration that contemporary liberals are deploring and that conservatives are secretly cheering.

We are living in the era of "groupism"—the construction of defensive groups, each of which asserts an identity around which it builds solidarity and struggles to survive alongside and against other such groups. The political problem for such groups is to keep from becoming simply one more agency of helping people cope (which is politically ambiguous, since it preserves order by filling in the lacunae that are being created by the collapse of the states), so that they can truly become an agency of transformation. But to be agencies of transformation, they must be clear about their egalitarian objectives. Fighting for the rights of the group as one instance of the struggle for equality is quite different from fighting for the rights of the group to "catch up" and move to the head of the line (which has in any case become for most groups an implausible objective).

During the present world transition, it is effective to work both at the local and at the world level, but it is now of limited use to work at the level of the national state. It is of use to pursue objectives for the very short run or for the long run, but the middle run has become ineffective because the middle run supposes an ongoing, well-functioning historical system. It is because such a strategy is not simple to implement since the tactics of such a strategy are so necessarily ad hoc and contingent, that the period ahead seems so confused. If, however, we accept that we now live in a world where liberal values no longer hold sway and where the existing historical system is incapable of ensuring that minimal level of personal and material security that is required for its own acceptability (not to speak of its legitimation), then we can move ahead clearly with a reasonable degree of hope and confidence, but of course without any guarantees.

The day of the arrogantly self-assured liberal ideologue is behind us. The conservatives have reemerged, after a self-abasement of 150 years, to put forth uncaring self-interestedness, masked by pieties and mysticism, as an ideological substitute. It doesn't really wash. Conservatives tend to be smug when dominant and deeply angry and vengeful when exposed or even merely seriously threatened. It is for all those who have been left out in the present world-system to push ahead on all fronts. They no longer have the easy objective of taking state power as a focus. They are required to do something far more complicated: to ensure the creation of a new historical system by acting at one and the same time very locally and very globally. It is difficult, but it is not impossible.

PART I

———

THE 1990S AND AFTER:
CAN WE RECONSTRUCT?

THE COLD WAR AND THE THIRD WORLD:
THE GOOD OLD DAYS?

Shall we be nostalgic so soon? I fear we must. We have come out of the era of U.S. hegemony in the world-system (1945–1990) and into a posthegemonic era. However difficult the position of the erstwhile Third World in that era was, I believe it is in for far more difficult times. The time just past was a time of hopes, no doubt of hopes oft deceived, but of hopes nonetheless. The time just forward is to be a time of troubles, and of struggles born more of desperation than of confidence. To use old Western symbolism, which may under the circumstances be inappropriate: it will be a time of purgatory, the outcome always uncertain.

I shall outline my views in two parts: a brief sketch of the era out of which we have come; and a projection of what it is I think we may anticipate, along with an argument as to the historical alternatives we face.

I

I believe the essential features of the period 1945–1990 may be summed up in four statements.

1. The United States was the hegemonic power in a unipolar world-system. Its power, based on an overwhelming edge in economic productivity as of 1945 and an alliance system with Western Europe and Japan, reached its apogee circa 1967–73.
2. The United States and the U.S.S.R. engaged in a highly structured, carefully contained, formal (but not substantive) conflict, in which the U.S.S.R. acted as a subimperialist agent of the United States.
3. The Third World forced itself upon the unwilling attention of the United States, the U.S.S.R., and Western Europe by demanding rights more fully and earlier than the countries of the North anticipated or desired. Both its political strength and

its ultimate weakness was its belief in, and optimism about, the twin objectives of self-determination and national development.
4. The 1970s and 1980s were a period of global economic stagnation, resistance by the United States to its impending decline, and disillusionment in the Third World with its own strategy.

Let me elaborate on each of these statements.

1. The overwhelming economic advantage of the United States in 1945—in production and productivity—was the consequence of three conjoined factors: the steady concentration of the national energy of the United States since 1865 on improving its capacity for both production and technological innovation; the freedom of the United States from serious military expenditures, at least until 1941, efficacious wartime mobilization from 1941 to 1945, and the absence of wartime destruction of its infrastructure; the enormous destruction of infrastructure and human lives over the whole of Eurasia from 1939 to 1945.

The United States was able quite rapidly to institutionalize this advantage, that is, create a hegemony that made it possible for the United States to control or dominate virtually all significant decisions in the world political and economic arenas for some twenty-five years. Its hegemony was ideological and even cultural as well.

The two key pillars on which this hegemony was consolidated were a system of alliances with the important, already industrialized countries of the world on the one hand, and a nationally integrating welfare state at home, on the other. In each case, the arrangement was economic and ideological, and nominally political.

The economic carrot for Western Europe and Japan was economic reconstruction, accompanied by a significant rise in real income of the middle strata and the skilled working classes in the United States. This guaranteed both political satisfaction and a significant market for United States productive enterprises.

The ideological package was the commitment to implementing fully for the first time the two-century-old promises of political liberalism: universal suffrage and a functioning parliamentary system. This was done within the framework of a struggle with

Communist "totalitarianism," and meant therefore a de facto exclusion of Communists from political rights.

The nominal political promise was participation of Western Europe and Japan as countries, and of the working classes as strata, in collective decision making. In reality, for some twenty-five years all major political decisions in the world-system were made by a small elite in the United States. This was called United States leadership. Western Europe and Japan were client states. The working-class movements were for the most part client movements.

2. The relationship of the United States and the U.S.S.R. was similarly one thing on the surface with another reality underneath. On the surface, the United States and the U.S.S.R. were ideological enemies, locked in a cold war not merely since 1945 but since 1917. They represented alternative visions of the social good, based on quite divergent readings of historical reality. The structures of the two countries were quite disparate, and in some aspects fundamentally different. Furthermore, they both proclaimed quite loudly the depth of this ideological cleavage and called on all nations and groups to opt for one side or the other. Remember the famous declaration of John Foster Dulles: "Neutralism is immoral." Equivalent statements were made by Soviet leaders.

Nonetheless the reality was quite different. A line was drawn in Europe, more or less where Soviet and U.S. troops met at the end of the Second World War. East of this line was a zone reserved for Soviet political dominance. The arrangement between the United States and the U.S.S.R. is well known and quite simple. The U.S.S.R. could do as it wished within its east European zone (that is, create satellite regimes). There were two working conditions. First, the two zones would observe absolute interstate peace in Europe and would abstain from any attempt to change or subvert the governments in the other zone. Secondly, the U.S.S.R. would neither expect nor obtain aid from the United States in its economic reconstruction. The U.S.S.R. might take what it could from Eastern Europe, while the U.S. government concentrated its financial resources (vast but not unlimited) on Western Europe and Japan.

This arrangement, as we know, worked marvelously well. Peace in Europe was absolute. There was never a threat of Communist insurrection in Western Europe (except in Greece, where the U.S.S.R. undermined and abandoned the Greek Communists). And the United States never gave any support to the multiple efforts of Eastern European states to loosen or end Soviet control (1953, 1956, 1968, 1980–81). The Marshall Plan was reserved for Western Europe, and the U.S.S.R. constructed a cocoon called Comecon.

The U.S.S.R. may be considered a subimperialist power of the United States because it functioned to guarantee order and stability within its zone on conditions that in fact enhanced the ability of the United States to maintain its worldwide hegemony. The very ferocity of the ultimately not very meaningful ideological struggle was a great political plus for the United States (as it was, to be sure, for the leadership of the U.S.S.R.). We shall see that the U.S.S.R. served as an ideological shield for the United States in the Third World as well.

3. The Third World was never asked, either in 1945 or since, whether it liked or approved the world order established by the United States in collusion with the U.S.S.R. It was certainly not accorded a very desirable position in this world order. In 1945, it was offered very little in the political arena, and even less in the economic arena. As the years went by, the offers improved somewhat, but always grudgingly and only because of Third World militance and rambunctiousness.

In 1945, no one took the Third World seriously as a political actor on the world scene—neither the United States nor the U.S.S.R. nor the old colonial powers of Western Europe. Any complaints were received with surprise, and the complainers were counseled patience, on the basis of a world-level version of the "trickle down" hypothesis.

To be sure, the United States had a program for the Third World. It had been proclaimed by Woodrow Wilson in 1917, and it was called the self-determination of nations. Eventually, in the fullness of time, each people was to receive its collective political rights to sovereignty, analogous to each citizen's receiving his individual political rights to suffrage. These political rights would then afford the opportunity for self-improvement, something that after 1945 acquired the name of national development.

Leninism as an ideology was presumably the antinomy of Wilsonianism. In fact, in many ways it was its avatar. The Wilsonian program for the Third World was translated by Lenin into Marxist jargon; it emerged as anti-imperialism and the construction of socialism. This obviously reflected real differences about who would control the political processes in the periphery of the world-system, but the actual program had the identical form: first a political change that would establish sovereignty (for the first time ever in colonies, for the first time *really* in already independent Third World states); then an economic change involving establishment of an efficacious state bureaucracy, the improvement of productive processes ("industrialization"), and the creation of a social infrastructure (particularly in education and health). The outcome, promised by both the Wilsonians and the Leninists, was "catching up," closing the gap between the rich countries and the poor.

The Third World countries bought this Wilsonian-Leninist package. But they were understandably impatient. Since the package involved two steps, they quite reasonably took the first step first. This was the path of anticolonial struggle in the colonies, and of analogous political revolutions in what were once called quite aptly the semicolonies. After 1945, the Third World forced the pace, everywhere. The Chinese Communists marched into Shanghai. The peoples of Indochina and Indonesia refused to welcome back their colonial overlords. The Indian subcontinent said independence immediately. The Egyptians ousted the monarchy and nationalized the Suez Canal. The Algerians refused to accept the idea that they were part of France. There was a "downward sweep" of African liberation starting in the 1950s. Political revolution was on the march in Latin America, most notably advanced by the triumph of the 26th of July Movement in Cuba in 1958. And, of course, in 1955 there was the Bandung Conference.

The essential element to observe about this whole political push is that it was, from the outset, totally indigenous in origin and in opposition to the North. The colonial powers were strongly opposed to this forcing of the pace and did all they could to stop it or slow it down. Of course, they varied in their tactics, the British being notably more flexible than the others, and the Portuguese dragging up the rear. The United States, despite its theoretical Wilsonian anticolonialism, tended to support this European slow-down as long as it could, but it eventually called for decolonization to "moderate" leaders at a moderate pace. Nor was the attitude of the U.S.S.R. very different. Leninism presumably represented a more strenuous and combative form of anticolonialism than Wilsonianism did. And of course the U.S.S.R. did give material and political support to many anti-imperialist movements. But, at very many crucial movements, it too sought to constrain or restrain the pace. Its role in Greece and its counsel to Mao Zedong are notorious. But around the world, anyone who has followed closely local struggles knows that Soviet support was never in the lead and often was obtained only with difficulty; frequently the Soviet Union refused to extend it at all.

Still, of course, as we also know, the basic political battle was won by the Third World. By the late 1960s, decolonization (or its equivalent in already independent states) had been achieved almost everywhere. It was time for the second step, national development. In fact, however, just as the moment had come for the second step, the world-system entered into a Kondratieff B-phase. The second step was never to be achieved in most places.

4. By 1970, the United States had reached the apogee and the limits of its power. Its declining gold reserves forced it off the fixed gold-dollar parity. The economic growth of Western Europe and Japan had been such that they now matched and were beginning to outstrip U.S. levels of productivity, at the very moment that the Kondratieff B-phase set in. Or rather, the global expansion of production was itself the major source of the downturn. Vietnam was demonstrating not only that the United States had to accede to its own Wilsonian credo even when it didn't approve of the group making the demands but also that the cost of not doing so was weakening the legitimacy of the U.S. government at home. And the world revolution of 1968 undermined the entire ideological consensus that the United States had constructed, including even its reserve card, the Soviet shield.

The two decades since have been United States patchwork. Each patch has been efficacious in that it slowed down the fraying, but eventually the whole framework would look tattered. Nixon went to China, a brilliant stroke, pulling the Chinese back into the world order arrangement. He cut U.S. losses by accepting defeat in Vietnam. And in another brilliant stroke, the United States connived in (perhaps even arranged) the rise in OPEC oil prices. Paraded as evidence of Third World militance, the OPEC initiative served to funnel much of the available world surplus (and surely any that the Third World had) into Western (largely U.S.) banks via the oil-producing states (who no doubt took their rent cut). The money was then sent right back to the Third World (and the Soviet-bloc states) in the form of loans to states, which enabled these states momentarily to balance their budgets and continue importing Western manufactures. The bill would come due in the 1980s.

The United States sought during the 1970s to keep everyone calm. It offered the Western Europeans and the Japanese trilateralism—that is, a promise of more consultation in world policy-making. It offered the Soviet Union détente—that is, a lowering of the ideological decibels, which served as balm for the Brezhnevian bureaucracy in the wake of the shock wave of 1968. It offered the U.S. public a relaxation of cold war tensions as well, a kind of cultural consumerism that included more liberal mores and affirmative action. And, to the Third World, it offered the post-Vietnam syndrome, which concretely meant such gestures as the Church Committee's report on the CIA, the Clark Amendment on Angola, and the withdrawal of support to Somoza and the Shah.

I believe we should see the Nixon, Ford, and Carter administrations as following a single policy, which we can term the "low posture," and which President Carter spelled out in his famous address to the U.S. public on accepting the limitations of U.S. power. These policies seemed to be working reasonably well until, once again, the Third World pulled the plug. The "low posture" foundered on the unexpected rock of the Ayatollah Khomeini. He was not to be fooled. Low posture or not, the United States was still the number one Satan (and the U.S.S.R. number two).

Khomeini's strategy was quite simple. He refused to accept the rules of the game—both the rules of the U.S. post-1945 world order and the rules of the interstate system, which had been in place for five centuries. The net result was equally simple. The United States was profoundly humiliated, Carter was ousted, and Reagan came to power on a platform of rejecting the "low posture" in every way possible. The Reagan(-Bush) strategy was to substitute fake machismo for the low posture—tough with allies, tough with the Soviet Union, tough at home, and of course tough with the Third World.

Economically, the world had to face the bill for the patchwork of the 1970s—the debt crisis, first manifested in Poland in 1980 and officially recognized in Mexico in 1982. The result was a downward economic spiral throughout the Third World and the Soviet-bloc countries, with the exception of the East Asian NICs, which managed to corner the industries devolving from core to semiperiphery because of their lower rate of profitability. Now that OPEC pump priming of the sagging world-economy had exhausted its possibilities, Reagan relied on U.S. military Keynesianism and massive borrowing from its former allies, now its economic rivals—Japan and Western Europe. It was clear by mid-decade that this bill would soon come due, as had the Third World loans of the 1970s.

Were there any patches left? The first to decide that there probably weren't was Mr. Gorbachev. The U.S.S.R. was a superpower primarily because of its special arrangement with the United States, which was called the cold war. If the United States could no longer play the role of hegemonic power, the cold war served no function, and the U.S.S.R. risked being treated as just one more semiperipheral state in the capitalist world-economy. Gorbachev sought to save the possibility of Russia/the U.S.S.R.'s remaining a world power (at the very least, a strong semiperipheral state) by a threefold program: unilateral liquidation of the cold war (highly successful); unburdening the U.S.S.R. of its now irrelevant and burdensome quasi empire in Eastern Europe (highly successful); and restructuring the Soviet state so that it could function efficaciously in the posthegemonic era (not successful).

The United States was at first stunned by this maneuver, and then decided to try to cover up this conscious dismantlement of the U.S. world order by crying victory. This last bit of advertising puff might have carried the United States for five more years had not the Third World once again pulled the plug, this time in the person of Saddam Hussein. Saddam Hussein saw the weakness of the United States, particularly as manifested in the collapse of Communist regimes in the Soviet bloc and in its inability to impose on Israel the process of regional settlements (in Indochina, southern Africa, Central America, and the Middle East) that are part of the liquidation of the cold war. Saddam Hussein decided that this was the moment for boldness. He invaded Kuwait and was quite possibly preparing to proceed further south.

I believe four variables entered into his calculation. One was the world debt crisis; Suddam Hussein knew there would be no serious relief for the Third World from the debt crisis. He at least had a solution at hand—seize the Kuwaiti accumulated rent. The second variable was Israel's ending the peace talks with the PLO. Had the talks been ongoing, an invasion would have hurt the Palestinian cause, still the focal issue of Arab popular sentiment. Once the talks were dead, Hussein would appear as the last hope of the Palestinians and harness Arab popular sentiment, as he seems to have done. But these two variables were ultimately minor.

The collapse of the Communisms was far more important. This had a double meaning from a Third World perspective. First, Saddam Hussein knew that the U.S.S.R. would *not* support him, which liberated him from the automatic constraints of the United States-Soviet settlement of all disputes that threatened nuclear escalation. And second, the collapse of the Communisms was the final collapse of the ideology of national development. If even the U.S.S.R. couldn't make it, with the full Leninist model at its disposal, surely neither Iraq nor any other Third World state was likely to catch up by a program of collective self-help within the framework of the existing world-system. The Wilsonians had lost at last the Leninist shield, which had channeled Third World impatience into a strategy that was, from the point of view of the dominant forces in the world-system, the strategy least threatening to the system the Third World would undertake.

Disabused of all alternatives, and certain of United States weakness, Saddam Hussein took into account the fourth variable. If he invaded, he had a fifty-fifty chance of succeeding. But the United States had a one hundred percent chance of losing. The United States would find itself without viable options. If it acceded, it became a paper tiger. And if it resisted, the political fallout of the carnage had to be negative for the U.S. position—in the Middle East, in Europe, at home, and ultimately everywhere.

II

Where are we heading now? Since I believe the world-system is moving into an even greater North-South polarization than heretofore, I will first present what I believe will be the restructuring of the North and its consequences for the South, and then present what I believe will be the political options of the South. Finally, I shall try to put this in the context of the future of the capitalist world-economy as such.

We are presently at the tail end of a Kondratieff B-phase that has been going on since 1967–73. We are entering the final and probably most dramatic dip down. It is analogous to the 1893–96 dip in the Kondratieff B-phase that ran from 1873 to 1896. Its impact will vary on different parts of the North, but it will probably be very great for most parts of the South. However, the world-economy, once thoroughly shaken down, will come out of it, and we shall be in for another big A-phase. It will be fueled initially, as has long been predicted, by a new product cycle of new leading industries (microchips, biogenetics, etc.); the three strong loci of such production will be Japan, the EEC, and the United States. They will be in sharp competition to gain the quasi-monopolistic control of the world market for their particular technical version of these products, and they can't all get it.

There is much talk these days of a three-way breakdown of the world market. I don't believe it, because, in this kind of acute competition, triads give way to a binary split. The stakes are high, and the weakest of the three competitors will seek an alliance with one of the other two for fear of being squeezed out altogether. Today, and surely a decade from now, the weakest of the three, in terms of efficiency of production and national financial stability, is and will be the United States. The natural alliance is with Japan. The trade-off is obvious. Japan is now strong in production processes and in capital surplus. The United States is strong in research and development capacity and potential, the service sector generally, military power, and accumulated wealth for consumption. A reunited Korea could join the Japan-United States arrangement, as would Canada. Japan and the United States would bring into the arrangement their links in Latin America and Southeast Asia. And they would make a strong bid to find the appropriate niche for China.

Europe has seen this coming for a long time. That is why the 1992 arrangements have not only never been derailed but also are surely going to be augmented, now that Germany is reunited and Thatcher has been disposed of. Europe has to work out its detailed strategy; either piecemeal expansion of the EC or wide-ranging confederation. The key is Russia, which must be included if Europe is to have any strength vis-à-vis a Japan-United States arrangement. Europe will work hard to counter a disintegration of the U.S.S.R., and since Japan, China, and the United States for other reasons are also fearful of the same process, the U.S.S.R. will probably weather the storm somehow.

The second stage will be for each of the two Norths to develop their main semiperiphery (China for the one, Russia for the other) so that it can be an adjunct producer, a major market, and a supplier of migrant labor. At the moment, the core zones are terrified of the prospects of Russian and Chinese outflow. But in 2005, with booming economies and continued demographic decline, *Gastarbeitern* will seem highly desirable, provided it is an "orderly" process.

What will happen to the erstwhile Third World? Little that is good. Of course, there will be many enclaves linked to one of the two Norths, but the overall share of the South in world production and world wealth will go down, and I believe we will see an actual reversal on the social indicator curves (that is, education and health), the one set of curves on which the South has been doing reasonably well during the 1945–90 period. Furthermore, the South will have been deprived of its major political instrument of the 1945–90 period—the national liberation movements. The ANC in South Africa will be the last great movement to have come to power. These movements have all served one historical purpose—to achieve self-determination—and they have all failed to achieve the other historical purpose—national development. The current passing fantasy that the "market" will give them what state-led industrialization could not, will not survive the acute downturn of the next five years. The fall of Mazowiecki presages the widespread impotence regimes will feel.

What choices are then available? Actually quite a few, though none of them fit in with the Weltanschauung that has governed the world in the Wilsonian-Leninist era. We may start with the choice that is the nightmare of the North precisely because they can think of no way to respond to it. This is the Khomeini option. This is usually phrased as the menace of Islamic fundamentalism but that is entirely the wrong emphasis. It is not particularly an Islamic phenomenon. And it is not particularly fundamentalist, if by that is meant some reversion to ancient religious practices.

The Khomeini option is primarily the culmination of anger at the horrors of the modern world-system, and it focuses the anger on its chief beneficiaries and instigators, the Western core of the capitalist world-economy. It is the denunciation of the West, including, and even especially, its Enlightenment values, as the incarnation of evil. If these were merely tactics, modes of popular mobilization, they could be dealt with. To the extent that they represent a genuine option, there is no avenue for communication or for resolution.

How long can such explosions last? How far can they go? It is hard to say. Khomeini's Iran seems to be on the path of passions calming down, of reentry into the cultural orbit of the world-system. If tomorrow, however, other movements erupt in other countries around the South, and more of them simultaneously, within a less stable world-system, may they not last longer or go further? Could they not substantially advance the disintegration of the current world-system, of which process they are themselves the consequence?

The second option is the Saddam Hussein option. Here again we must be clear about what it is. This is not total rejection of the values of the modern world-system. The Baath was a typical national liberation movement and a thoroughly secular one. I believe the Saddam Hussein option is nothing but the Bismarck option. It is the sense that since economic inequities are the outcome of political *rapports de forces*, economic transformation requires military strength. The Iraq-U.S. confrontation is the first genuine North-South war. The wars of national liberation (say Vietnam) all had a limited and quite clear objective: self-determination. From the South's point of view, all these wars were started by the North and could be ended by the North's letting the South alone. In the Persian Gulf crisis, the war was started by the South with the intent not of achieving self-determination but of transforming the world *rapport de forces*. This is really quite different.

Saddam Hussein may well lose the battle and be destroyed, but he has shown the way to a new option—creation of larger states, armament of these states not at the second level but at the top level, willingness to risk real warfare. If this is an option whose time has come, what will be the consequence? Terrible carnage, of course, doubtlessly including the use of nuclear warfare (and quite possibly chemical and biological). From the point of view of both North and South, the Saddam Hussein option is more dreadful than the Khomeini option. Perhaps you will wonder whether this is so different from the older wars between North and South, which were integral to the historic expansion of the boundaries of the modern world-system? The answer is, from a moral point of view, it is the same phenomenon. But, from a political and military point of view, it is quite different. The old colonial wars were one-sided militarily, and confidence lay on the side of the Northern aggressors. The new set of wars will be two-sided militarily, and confidence is now lacking in the North. It may be that the period 1945–1990 will be remembered as the period of relative North-South peace (despite Vietnam, despite Algeria, despite the multiple anticolonial struggles) between the wave of the wars of European expansion and the wave of twenty-first-century North-South wars.

The third option is what I call the option of individual resistance by physical relocation. In a world of increasing North-South polarization, with Northern demographic decline and Southern demographic expansion, how will it be politically possible to stem massive unauthorized South-to-North migration? I believe there will be no way to do this, and this South-to-North migration will come on top of authorized and unauthorized migration from Russia and China. Of course, this has been occurring already. Still, I think the scale will significantly escalate, and will thereby transform the structure of social life in the North. It is sufficient to note two things. The South within the North may well reach the thirty to fifty percent mark by 2025. And there may well be an attempt to deny them political rights, which means that after two hundred years of social integration of the working classes in the North, we would be back to the situation of the early nineteenth century—the disenfranchisement of the bulk of the lower occupational strata. This is surely not a recipe for social peace.

The triple scenario of options for the South no doubt poses political dilemmas for the ruling elites of the world-system, who will react as they will react. But it poses fundamental dilemmas for the world Left as well, the antisystemic forces both in the North and in the South.

We can already see the confusion among the movements of the Left in the North. They did not know how to react to Khomeini. They do not know how to react to Saddam Hussein. They have never had a clear position on unauthorized migration. In each case, they have not wanted to offer total support, but they have not wanted to support unconditionally Northern repression. The consequence is that the Northern Left has been voiceless and irrelevant. They were quite comfortable in engaging in solidarity with national liberation movements. In 1968 they could chant, "Ho, Ho, Ho Chi Minh." But that was because the Vietminh and the NFL appealed to Wilsonian-Leninist values. Once Wilsonianism and Leninism are both dead, once it is recognized that national development is an illusion (even a pernicious illusion), once we have given up on the basic strategy of transformation pursued for the last 150 years, is there anything remaining for the Northern Left other than patchwork?

Is it any easier for the Southern Left? Are they ready to enlist in the ranks of Khomeini or Saddam Hussein, to invest their energies in the migration option? I think it is doubtful. They have the same hesitancies as the Northern Left. They too wish to shake the world-system and recognize that these options all do shake the world-system. But they too have doubts that these options lead to the world of equality and democracy that the Southern Left stands for just as much as the Northern Left does.

The serious and quite open question before us, as we move into the first half of the twenty-first century (when the capitalist world-economy will be in full and acute crisis), is whether new transformatory movements with new strategies and agendas will in fact emerge. It is quite possible, but far from sure. The reason is that no one has put forward new strategies and agendas to replace the now defunct Wilsonian-Leninist strategies for the Third World, themselves a mere extension of the nineteenth-century strategy of achieving state power employed by both the socialist and the nationalist movements.

This, however, is the very concrete challenge for the world Left. If it does not respond seriously or soon, the collapse of the capitalist world-economy in the next fifty years will simply lead to its replacement by something equally bad. In any case, the North-South confrontation will be at the center of world political struggle from now on. It must therefore be at the center of analyses by both historical social scientists and political activists.

CHAPTER TWO

PEACE, STABILITY, AND LEGITIMACY, 1990–2025/2050

The period from 1990 to 2025/2050 will most likely be short on peace, short on stability, and short on legitimacy. In part, this is because of the decline of the United States as the hegemonic power of the world-system. But in even larger part, it is because of the crisis in the world-system as a world-system.

Hegemony in the world-system means by definition that there is one power in a geopolitical position to impose a stable concatenation of the social distribution of power. This implies a period of "peace," meaning primarily the absence of military struggle—not all military struggle, but military struggle among great powers. Such a period of hegemony requires, and at the same time engenders, "legitimacy," if by that is meant the feeling by major political actors (including amorphous groups such as "populations" of the various states) either that the social order is one of which they approve or that the world ("history") is moving steadily and rapidly in a direction they would approve of.

Such periods of real hegemony, wherein the ability of the hegemonic power to impose its will and its "order" on other major powers is without serious challenge, have been relatively short in the history of the modern world-system. In my view, there have been only three instances: the United Provinces in the mid–seventeenth century, the United Kingdom in the mid–nineteenth, and the United States in the mid–twentieth. Their hegemonies, defined in this way, lasted about twenty-five to fifty years in each case.[1]

When such periods have ended, that is, when the erstwhile hegemonic power became once again simply one major power among others (even if it continued to be for some time the strongest among them militarily), then quite obviously there ensued less stability, and correlatively less legitimacy. This implies less peace. In this sense the present period following U.S. hegemony is essentially no different from that which followed British hegemony in the mid–nineteenth century or Dutch in the mid–seventeenth.

But if this were all there were to describing the period 1990–2025, or 1990–2050, or 1990–?, then it would scarcely be worth discussing except as a matter of the technical management of a shaky world order (which is how too many politicians, diplomats, scholars, and journalists have indeed been discussing it).

There is, however, more, probably much more, to the dynamic of the coming half-century or so of great world disorder. The geopolitical realities of the interstate system do not rest exclusively, even primarily, on the military *rapport de forces* among that privileged subset of sovereign states we call great powers—those states that are large enough and wealthy enough to have the necessary revenue base to develop a serious military capability.

First of all, only some states are wealthy enough to have such a tax base, such wealth being more the source than the consequence of their military strength, though of course the process is one of circular reinforcement. And the wealth of these states relative to that of other states is a function both of their size and of the axial division of labor in the capitalist world-economy.

The capitalist world-economy is a system that involves a hierarchical inequality of distribution based on the concentration of certain kinds of production (relatively monopolized, and therefore high-profit, production) in certain limited zones, which thereupon and thereby become the loci of the greatest accumulation of capital. This concentration enables the reinforcement of the state structures, which in turn seek to guarantee the survival of the relative monopolies. But because monopolies are inherently fragile, there has been a constant, discontinuous, and limited but significant relocation of these centers of concentration all through the history of the modern world-system.

The mechanisms of change are the cyclical rhythms, of which two are the most consequential. The Kondratieff cycles are approximately fifty to sixty years in length. Their A-phases essentially reflect the length of time particular significant economic monopolies can be protected; their B-phases are the periods of the geographical relocation of production whose monopolies have been exhausted, as well as the period of struggle for control of the prospective new monopolies. The longer hegemonic cycles involve a struggle between *two* major states to become the successor to the previous hegemonic power by becoming the primary locus of the accumulation of capital. This is a long process, which eventually involves having the military strength to win a "thirty years' war." Once a new hegemony is instituted, its maintenance requires heavy financing, which eventually and inevitably leads to a relative decline of the current hegemonic power and a struggle for a successor.

This mode of a slow but certain repeated restructuring and recentering of the capitalist world-economy has been very efficacious. The rise and decline of great powers has been more or less the same kind of process as the rise and decline of enterprises: The monopolies hold for a long while, but they are ultimately undermined by the very measures taken to sustain them. The subsequent "bankruptcies" have been cleansing mechanisms, ridding the system of those powers whose dynamism is spent and replacing them with fresher blood. Through it all, the basic structures of the system have remained the same. Each monopoly of power held for a while but, just like economic monopolies, was undermined by the very measures taken to sustain it.

All systems (physical, biological, and social) depend on such cyclical rhythms to restore a minimal equilibrium. The capitalist world-economy has shown itself to be a hardy variety of historical system, and it has flourished rather exuberantly for some five hundred years now, a long time for an historical system. But systems have secular trends as well as cyclical rhythms, and the secular trends always exacerbate the contradictions (which all systems contain). There comes a point when the contradictions become so acute that they lead to larger and larger fluctuations. In the language of the new science, this means the onset of chaos (the sharp diminution of that which can be explained by deterministic equations), which in turn leads to bifurcations, whose occurrence is certain but whose shape is inherently unpredictable. Out of this a new systemic order emerges.

The question is whether the historical system in which we are living, the capitalist world-economy, has entered, or is entering into, such a time of "chaos." I propose to weigh the arguments, offer some guesses about the forms such "chaos" might take, and discuss what courses of action are open to us.

I PROPOSE NOT TO DISCUSS AT LENGTH THE ELEMENTS I consider to be the "normal" reflections of a Kondratieff B-phase or of a hegemonic B-phase; I will merely summarize them very briefly.[2] I should, however, make clear that, although a hegemonic cycle is much longer than a Kondratieff cycle, the inflection point of a hegemonic cycle coincides with that of a Kondratieff cycle (but not, of course, every one). In this case, that point was around 1967–73.

The phenomena that are symptomatic of a normal Kondratieff B-phase are: the slowdown of growth in production, and probably a decline in per capita world production; a rise in rates of active waged work unemployment; a relative shift of loci of profits, from productive activity to gains from financial manipulations; a rise of state indebtedness; relocation of "older" industries to lower-wage zones; a rise in military expenditures, whose justification is not really military in nature but rather that of countercyclical demand creation; falling real wages in the formal economy; expansion of the informal economy; a decline in low-cost food production; increased "illegalization" of interzonal migration.

The phenomena that are symptomatic of the beginning of hegemonic decline are: increased economic strength of "allied" major powers; currency instability; decline of authority in world financial markets with the rise of new loci of decision making; fiscal crises of the hegemonic state; decline of organizing (and stabilizing) world political polarization and tension (in this case, the cold war); a decline of popular willingness to invest lives in the maintenance of hegemonic power.

All this, as I've said, seems to me to have been "normal" and historically expectable. What should now happen, in the "normal" cyclical process, is the rise of replacement structures. We should enter, within five to ten years, a new Kondratieff A-phase, based on new monopolized leading products, concentrated in new locations. Japan is the most obvious locus, Western Europe the second, the United States the third (but what may prove to be a poor third).

We should also now see a new competition for hegemony beginning. As the U.S. position crumbles, slowly but visibly, two successor applicants should flex their muscles. In the current situation, they could only be Japan and the European Community. Following the pattern of the two previous successions—England vs. France to succeed to the Dutch; and the United States vs. Germany to succeed to Great Britain—we should in theory expect, not immediately, but over the next fifty to seventy-five years, that the sea/air power, Japan, would transform the previous hegemonic power, the United States, into its junior partner, and begin to compete with the land-based power, the EC. Their struggle should culminate in a "thirty years' (world) war" and the putative triumph of Japan.

I should say right off that I do not expect this to happen, or rather not quite. I think both processes of reorganization—that of the worldwide system of production and that of the distribution worldwide of state power—have already begun, and in the direction of the "traditional" (or "normal" or previous) pattern. But I expect the process to be interrupted or diverted because of the entry into the picture of new processes or vectors.

To analyze this clearly, I think we need three separate time frames: the next few years; the following twenty-five to thirty years; the period after that.

The situation in which we find ourselves today in the 1990s is quite "normal." It is not yet one that I would call "chaotic"; rather it is the final acute subphase (or the culminating moment) of the current Kondratieff B-phase—comparable to 1932–39, or 1893–97, or 1842–49, or 1786–92, etc. The worldwide rates of unemployment are high, rates of profit low. There is great financial instability, reflecting acute and justified nervousness in the financial market about short-run fluctuations. Increased social unrest reflects the political inability of governments to offer plausible short-run solutions and therefore an inability to re-create a sense of security. Both scapegoating within states and beggaring-thy-neighbor among states become more politically attractive in situations where the usual adjustment remedies seem to provide little instant alleviation of pain.

In the course of this process, a large number of individual enterprises are reducing their activity or are being restructured or are going bankrupt, in many cases never to reopen. Particular groups of workers and particular entrepreneurs will thereby lose out permanently. While all states will suffer, the degree of suffering will vary enormously. At the end of the process, some states will have risen, and others will have fallen, in comparative economic strength.

At such moments, great powers are often paralyzed militarily because of a combination of internal political instability, financial difficulties (and therefore reluctance to bear military costs), and concentration on immediate economic dilemmas (which leads to popular isolationism). The world's response to the warfare that resulted when Yugoslavia collapsed is a typical instance of such paralysis. And this, I insist, is "normal"—that is, part of the expectable patterns of the operation of the capitalist world-economy.

Normally, we should then come into a time of recovery. After a shakedown of the waste (both of luxury consumerism and ecological carelessness) and inefficiencies (whether logrolling or featherbedding or bureaucratic rigidities) should come a new dynamic thrust, lean and mean, of new monopolized leading industries and newly created segments of world purchasers to augment the total effective demand—in short, renewed expansion of the world-economy en route to a new era of "prosperity."

The three nodes, as already suggested and as is widely acknowledged, will be the United States, Western Europe, and Japan. The first ten years or so of this next Kondratieff A-phase will no doubt see an acute competition of the three centers to gain the edge for their particular product variation. As Brian Arthur has been showing in his writings, which particular variant wins out has little or nothing to do with technical efficiency, and everything to do with power.[3] One might add persuasion to power, except that in this situation persuasion is largely a function of power.

The power of which we are speaking is primarily economic power, but it is backed by state power. Of course, this constitutes a self-reinforcing cycle: A little power leads to a little persuasion, which creates more power, and so on. It's a matter of one country's propelling itself into the lead and running with it. At some point, a threshold is passed. The "Beta" products lose out, and there are "VHS" monopolies. My bet is simple: Japan will have more "VHSs" than the EC, and U.S. entrepreneurs will make deals with Japanese entrepreneurs to get a cut of the pie.

What the U.S. entrepreneurs will get out of such arrangements, as they fully commit themselves in the years between, say, 2000 and 2010, is quite obvious—not being left out altogether. What Japan will get out of it is equally obvious, three things especially: (1) if the United States is a partner, it is not a competitor; (2) the United States will still be the strongest military power, and Japan for many reasons (recent history and its impact on internal politics and regional diplomacy, plus the economic advantages of low military expenditure) will prefer to rely on a U.S. military shield for a while yet; (3) the United States still has the best R&D structure in the world-economy, even if its advantage in this area too will eventually disappear. Japanese enterprises will reduce costs by taking advantage of this structure.

Faced with this grand economic alliance, the EC members will put aside all their minor quarrels, if they haven't long since done so. The EC is incorporating the EFTA countries, but will *not* incorporate the countries of east-central Europe (except perhaps in a limited free trade area, possibly akin to the relationship between Mexico and the United States in NAFTA).

Europe (that is, the EC) will constitute a second economic megalith and a serious competitor to the Japan–United States condominium. The rest of the world will relate to the two zones of this bipolar world in multiple ways. From the viewpoint of the economic centers of power, there will be three crucial factors to consider in determining how important these other countries are: the degree to which their industries will be essential to, or optimal for, the operation of the key commodity chains; the degree to which particular countries will be essential to, or optimal for, the main-

tenance of adequate effective demand for the most profitable
sectors of production; the degree to which particular countries
will serve strategic needs (geomilitary location and/or power, key
raw materials, etc.).

The two countries not yet significantly or sufficiently integrated
into the two networks in creation, but which will be essential to
include for all three of the above reasons, will be China for the
Japan-United States condominium and Russia for the EC. In order
for these two countries to be well integrated, they will have to
maintain (or, in the case of Russia, first achieve) a certain level of
internal stability and legitimacy. Whether they can do so, and perhaps be helped to do so by interested parties, is still an open question, but I believe the odds are moderately favorable.

Suppose this picture to be correct: the emergence of a bipolar
world-economy with China part of the Japan-United States pole
and Russia part of the Europe pole. Suppose also that there is a
new, even very large, expansion of the world-economy from 2000
to 2025 or so, on the basis of new monopolized leading industries. What can we then expect? Would we have in effect a repeat
of the period 1945–1967/73, the "trente glorieuses" of worldwide
prosperity, relative peace, and above all, high optimism for the
future? I do not think so.

There will be several differences that are evident. The first and
most obvious to me is that we shall be in a bipolar, rather than a
unipolar, world-system. To categorize the world-system between
1945 and 1990 as unipolar is not a view that is widely shared. It
goes against the autodesignation of the world as one of a "cold war"
between two superpowers. But since this cold war was based on
an arrangement, made between two consenting antagonists, that
the geopolitical balance would be essentially frozen; and since
(despite all the public declarations of conflict) this geopolitical
freeze was never significantly violated by either of the two antagonists; I prefer to think of it as a choreographed (and hence
extremely limited) conflict. In reality, it was U.S. decision makers
who were calling the shots, and their Soviet counterparts must have
felt the weight of this reality time and time again.

By contrast, in the years 2000–2025, I do not expect that we will be able to say that either the Japan-United States condominium or the EC will be "calling the shots." Their economic and geopolitical real power will be too balanced. In so elementary and unimportant a matter as votes in interstate agencies, there will be no automatic, or even easy, majority. To be sure, there may be very few ideological elements to this competition. The base may be almost exclusively that of material self-interest. This will not necessarily make the conflict less acute; indeed, it will be harder to patch it over with mere symbols. As the conflict becomes less political in form, it may become more mafioso in form.

The second major difference derives from the fact that the world investment effort may be concentrated in China and Russia during the years 2000–2025 to a degree comparable to the concentration of investment in Western Europe and Japan in the years 1945–67/73. But this will mean that the amount that is left over for the rest of the world must be different in 2000–2025 than in 1945–67/73. In 1945–67/73, virtually the only "old" area where there was continued investment was the United States. In 2000–2025, continued investment will have to cover the United States, Western Europe, and Japan (and indeed a few others such as Korea and Canada as well). The question, therefore, is, After one has invested in the "old" areas plus the "new" ones, how much will remain (even in small doses) for the rest of the world? The answer will surely be much less than in the period 1945–67/73.

This in turn will translate into a situation quite different for countries in the "South" (however defined). Whereas, in 1945–67/73, the South did benefit from the expansion of the world-economy, at least from its crumbs, in 2000–2025 it risks not getting even crumbs. Indeed, the current disinvestment (of the Kondratieff B-phase) in *most* parts of the South may be continued rather than reversed in the A-phase ahead. Yet the economic demands of the South will be not less but more. For one thing, the awareness of the prosperity of the core zones and the degree of the North-South gap is far greater today than it was fifty years ago.

The third difference has to do with demography. World population continues for the time being to follow the same basic pattern it has followed for some two centuries now. On the one hand, there is worldwide growth. It is fueled primarily by the fact that, for the poorer five-sixths of the world's population, death rates have been declining (for technological reasons) while birth rates have not been or have not been declining as much (because of the absence of sufficient socioeconomic incentive). On the other hand, the percentage of world population of the wealthy regions of the world has been declining, despite the fact that the decline in their death rate has been far sharper than that of the less wealthy regions, because of the still greater lowering of their birth rate (primarily as a way of optimizing the socioeconomic position of middle-class families).

This combination has created a demographic gap parallelling (perhaps exceeding) the economic North-South gap. To be sure, this gap was there already in 1945–67/73. But it was less great then because of the still persisting cultural barriers in the North to limiting the birth rate. These barriers have now been largely swept aside, precisely during the 1945–67/73 period. The world demographic figures of 2000–2025 will reflect this far more acute disparity in social practices.

The response we can expect is truly massive pressure for migration from South to North. The push will clearly be there, not only from those prepared to take low-paid urban employment but a fortiori from the significantly growing numbers of educated persons from the South. There will also be a bigger pull than before, precisely because of the bipolar split in the core zones, as well as the consequent acute pressure this will cause employers to reduce labor costs by employing migrants (not only as low-skilled personnel but also as middle-level cadres).

There will of course be (there already is) an acute social reaction within the North—a call for more repressive legislation to limit entry and to limit the sociopolitical rights of those who do enter. The result may be the worst of all de facto compromises: an inability to prevent effectively the entry of migrants, combined with the capability to ensure second-class political status for them. This would imply that by 2025 or so, in North America, the EC, and (even) Japan, the population socially defined as being of "Southern" origin may well range from twenty-five to fifty percent, and much higher in certain subregions and within large urban centers. But since many (perhaps most) of these persons will not have voting rights (and perhaps only limited access at best to social welfare provisions), there will be a high correlation of those occupying the lowest-paid urban jobs (and urbanization will by then have reached new heights) with those who are being denied political (and social) rights. It was this kind of situation in Great Britain and France in the first half of the nineteenth century that led to well-founded fears that the so-called dangerous classes would pull the house down. At that time, the industrialized countries invented the liberal state to overcome just this danger, granting suffrage and offering the welfare state to appease the plebeians. In 2030, Western Europe/North America/Japan may find themselves in the same position as Great Britain and France were in in 1830. "The second time as farce"?

The fourth difference between the prosperity that reigned between 1945 and 1967/73 and what we can expect between the years 2000 and 2025 will have to do with the situation of the middle strata in the core zones. These were the great beneficiaries of the period 1945–67/73. Their numbers increased dramatically, both absolutely and relatively. Their standard of living went up dramatically as well. And the percentage of posts defined as "middle stratum" went up sharply as well. The middle strata became a major pillar of stability of the political systems, and they formed a very large pillar indeed. Furthermore the skilled workers, the economic stratum below them, came to dream of nothing more than to become part of these middle strata—via union-backed wage increases, higher education for their children, and government-aided improvement in living conditions.

Of course, the overall price for this expansion was a significant rise in costs of production, a secular inflation, and a serious squeeze on the accumulation of capital. The present Kondratieff B-phase is consequently spawning acute worries about "competitivity" and about the fiscal burdens of the state. This worry will not diminish, but will indeed increase, in an A-phase in which there are two acutely competing poles of growth. What one can expect therefore is a persistent effort to reduce, absolutely and relatively, the numbers of middle strata in the production processes (including the service industries). There will also be a continuation of the present attempt to reduce state budgets, an attempt that ultimately will threaten most of all these middle strata.

The political fallout of this cutback on middle strata will be very heavy. Educated, used to comfort, middle strata threatened with being *déclassé* will not take passively such a retrogression of status and income. We already saw their teeth during the world-wide revolution of 1968. To pacify them, economic concessions were made from 1970 to 1985. These countries are paying the price now, and these concessions will be difficult to renew, or, if renewed, will affect the economic struggle between the EC and the Japan-United States condominium. In any case, the capitalist world-economy will be faced with the immediate dilemma of either limiting capital accumulation or suffering the politico-economic revolt of erstwhile middle strata. It will be a bitter choice.

The fifth difference will be in the ecological constraints. Capitalist entrepreneurs have been living off the externalization of costs from the beginnings of this historical system. One major externalized cost has been the cost of renewing the ecological base of an ever-expanding global production. Since entrepreneurs did not renew the ecological base and there was also no (world) government ready to tax sufficiently for this purpose, the ecological base of the world-economy has been steadily reduced. The last and largest expansion of the world-economy, from 1945 to 1967/73, used up the remaining margin, which is what has given rise to the green movements and the planetary concern for the environment.

The expansion of 2000–2025 will therefore lack the necessary ecological base. One of three outcomes is possible. The expansion will be aborted, with the attendant political collapse of the world-system. The ecological base will be depleted more than it is physically possible for the earth to sustain, with attendant catastrophes such as global warming. Or the social costs of cleanup, limitation of use, and regeneration will be accepted seriously.

If the third, and functionally least immediately damaging, of the three is the collective path chosen, it would create an immediate strain on the operations of the world-system. Either the cleanup would be done at the expense of the South, thereby making still more acute the North-South disparity, and providing a very clearly focused source of North-South tension, or the costs would be disproportionately assumed by the North, which would necessarily involve a reduction of the North's level of prosperity. Furthermore, whichever path is taken, serious action on the environment will inevitably reduce the margin of global profit (despite the fact that environmental cleanup will itself become a source of capital accumulation). Given this second consideration, and given a context of acute competition between the Japan-United States condominium and the EC, we may expect considerable cheating and therefore inefficacy in the process of regeneration—in which case we are back to either the first or the second outcome.

The sixth difference will be in the reaching of two asymptotes in the secular trends of the world-system: geographical expansion and deruralization. The capitalist world-economy had already in theory expanded to include the entire globe by 1900. This was, however, true primarily of the reach of the interstate system. It became true of the reach of the production networks of the commodity chains only in the period 1945–67/73. It is now, however, true of both. The capitalist world-economy has equally been undergoing a process of deruralization (sometimes called, less exactly, proletarianization) for four hundred years, and for the last two hundred with increasing speed. The years 1945–67/73 saw a spectacular jump in this process—Western Europe, North America, and Japan becoming fully deruralized and the South partially but significantly so. It is probable this process will be completed in the period 2000–2025.

The ability of the capitalist world-economy to expand into new geographical zones has historically been a crucial element in maintaining its rate of profit and hence its accumulation of capital. This has been the essential counter to the creeping rise in the cost of labor engendered by the combined growth in both political and workplace power of the working classes. If now there are no longer new working strata who have not yet acquired either the political or the workplace power to increase the part of the surplus value they could retain available to be recruited, the result would be the same kind of squeeze on the accumulation of capital that is being caused by ecological exhaustion. Once geographical limits are reached, and populations deruralized, the difficulties entailed by the political process of cost reduction become so great that savings can't really be achieved. Real costs of production must rise globally, and therefore profits must decline.

There is a seventh difference between the coming Kondratieff A-phase and the last one; it has to do with the social structure and the political climate of the countries of the South. Since 1945, the proportion of the middle strata in the South has risen significantly. This wasn't hard, since it was extraordinarily small up to then. If it went from only five to ten percent of the population, then it has doubled in proportion and, given the population increase, quadrupled or sextupled in absolute numbers. Since this is fifty to seventy-five percent of the world's population, we are talking about a very large group. The cost of keeping them at the consumption level to which they feel minimally entitled will be impressively high.

In addition, these middle strata, or local cadres, were by and large quite busy with "decolonization" in the period 1945–67/73. This was obviously true of all those living in those parts of the South that were colonies as of 1945 (almost the whole of Africa, South and Southeast Asia, the Caribbean, and miscellaneous other areas). It was also almost as true of those living in the "semi-colonies" (China, parts of the Middle East, Latin America, Eastern Europe), where various forms of "revolutionary" activity comparable in psychic tonality to decolonization were occurring. It is not necessary here to evaluate the quality or the existential meaning of all these movements. It is enough to observe two characteristics of these movements: They consumed the energies of large numbers of people, especially of the middle strata. And these people were suffused with political optimism, which took a particular form, best summed up in the pithy saying of Kwame Nkrumah: "Seek ye first the political kingdom, and all things shall be added unto you." In practice this meant that the middle strata of the South (and the *potential* middle strata) were ready to be somewhat patient about their weak economic status: they felt sure that if they could achieve political power during a first thirty-year period or so, they or their children would find their economic reward in the subsequent thirty-year period.

In the period 2000–2025, not only will there be no "decolonization" to preoccupy these cadres and keep them optimistic but also their economic situation will almost certainly become worse, for the various reasons adduced above (concentration on China/Russia, expansion of numbers of cadres in the South, worldwide effort to cut back on middle strata). Some of these may escape (that is, migrate) to the North. This will only make the plight of those who remain more bitter.

The eighth and ultimately most serious difference between the last and the next Kondratieff A-phase is purely political: the rise of democratization and the decline of liberalism. For it must be remembered that democracy and liberalism are not twins but, for the most part, opposites. Liberalism was invented to counter democracy. The problem that gave birth to liberalism was how to contain the dangerous classes, first within the core, then within the world-system as a whole. The liberal solution was to grant limited access to political power and limited sharing of the economic surplus value, at levels that would not threaten the process of the ceaseless accumulation of capital or the state-system that sustained it.

The basic theme of the liberal state nationally and the liberal interstate system worldwide has been rational reformism, primarily via the state. The formula of the liberal state, as it was developed in the core states in the nineteenth century—universal suffrage plus the welfare state—worked marvelously well. In the twentieth century, a comparable formula was applied to the interstate system in the form of the self-determination of nations and the economic development of underdeveloped nations. It stumbled, however, over the inability to create a welfare state at the world level (as advocated, for example, by the Brandt Commission). For this could not be done without impinging on the basic process of the capital accumulation of capital. The reason was rather simple: The formula applied within core states depended for its success on a hidden variable—the economic exploitation of the South, combined with anti-South racism. At the world level, this variable did not exist, logically could not exist.[4]

The consequences for the political climate are clear. The years 1945–67/73 were the apogee of global liberal reformism: decolonization, economic development, and, above all, optimism about the future prevailed everywhere—West, East, North, and South. However, in the subsequent Kondratieff B-phase, with decolonization completed, the expected economic development became in most areas a faint memory, and optimism dissolved. Furthermore, for all the reasons we have already discussed, we do not expect economic development to return to the fore in the South in the coming A-phase, and we believe optimism has thus been fatally undermined.

At the same time, the pressure for democratization has been steadily growing. Democracy is basically antiauthority and antiauthoritarian. It is the demand for equal say in the political process at all levels and equal participation in the socioeconomic reward system. The greatest constraint on this thrust has been liberalism, with its promise of inevitable steady betterment via rational reform. To democracy's demand for equality now, liberalism offered hope deferred. This has been a theme not merely of the enlightened (and more powerful) half of the world establishment but even of the traditional antisystemic movements (the "Old Left"). The pillar of liberalism was the hope it offered. To the degree that the dream withers (like "a raisin in the sun"), liberalism as an ideology collapses, and the dangerous classes become dangerous once more.

THIS, THEN, IS WHERE WE SEEM TO BE HEADING IN THE NEXT A-phase, circa 2000–2025. Although it will appear to be a spectacularly expansive period in some ways, in others it will be very sour. This is why I expect little peace, little stability, and little legitimacy. The result will be the onset of "chaos," which is merely the widening of the normal fluctuations in the system, with cumulative effect.

I believe a series of things will occur, none of them new phenomena. What may be different will be the inability to limit their thrusts and thus bring the system back to some kind of equilibrium. The question is, To what degree will this lack of ability to limit the thrusts prevail?

1) The ability of the states to maintain internal order will probably decline. The degree of internal order is always fluctuating, and B-phases are notoriously moments of difficulty; for the system as a whole, however, and over four to five hundred years, internal order has been steadily increasing. We may call this the phenomenon of the rise of "stateness."

Of course, over the last one hundred years, the imperial structures *within* the capitalist world-economy (Great Britain, Austria-Hungary, most recently the U.S.S.R./Russia) have all disintegrated. But the thing to notice is rather the historic construction of states, which created their citizenry out of all those located within their boundaries. Such was metropolitan Great Britain and France, the United States and Finland, Brazil and India. And such also was Lebanon and Somalia, Yugoslavia and Czechoslovakia. The breakup or collapse of the latter is quite different from the breakup of the "empires."

One may dismiss the breakdown of stateness in the peripheral zone as either expectable or geopolitically insignificant. But it goes against the secular trend, and the breakdown of order in too many states creates a serious strain on the functioning of the interstate system. It is however the prospect of the weakening of stateness in the core zones that is most threatening. And the undoing of the liberal institutional compromise, which we have argued is occurring, suggests that this is happening. The states are deluged with demands for both security and welfare that they are politically unable to meet. The result is the steady privatization of security and welfare, which moves us in a direction out of which we had been moving for five hundred years.

2) The interstate system has also been growing more structured and regulated for several hundred years, from Westphalia to the Concert of Nations to the UN and its family. There has been a tacit assumption that we have been easing ourselves into a functional world government. In a spirit of euphoria, Bush proclaimed its imminence as a "new world order," which met with a cynical reception. The threat to "stateness" and the disappearance of reformist optimism have on the contrary shaken an interstate system whose foundations were always relatively weak.

Nuclear proliferation is now as inevitable, and will be as rapid, as expanded South-North migration will be. Per se, it is not catastrophic. Medium-size powers are probably no less "trustworthy" than big ones. Indeed they may be all the more prudent in that they may fear retaliation even more. Still, to the extent that stateness declines and technology advances, the creeping escalation of local tactical nuclear warfare may be difficult to contain.

As ideology recedes as the explanation for interstate conflicts, the "neutrality" of a weak confederal United Nations becomes ever more suspect. The ability of the UN to "peacekeep," limited as it is, may decline rather than increase in such an atmosphere. The call for "humanitarian interference" may come to be seen as merely the twenty-first-century version of nineteenth-century Western imperialism, which also affected civilizational justifications. Might there be secessions, multiple secessions, from the nominally universal structures (following the line North Korea has suggested vis-à-vis the IAEA)? Might we see the construction of rival organizations? It is not to be ruled out.

3) If the states (and the interstate system) come to be seen as losing efficacy, to where will people turn for protection? The answer is already clear—to "groups." The groups can have many labels —ethnic/religious/linguistic groups, gender or sexual preference groups, "minorities" of multiple characterizations. This too is nothing new. What is new is the degree to which such groups are seen as an *alternative* to citizenship and participation in a state that by definition houses many groups (even if unequally ranked).

It is a matter of trust. Whom shall we trust in a disorderly world, in a world of great economic uncertainty and disparity, in a world where the future is not at all guaranteed? Yesterday, the majority answered the states. This is what we mean by legitimacy, if not of the states that existed in the present, then at least of those states we could expect to create (postreform) in the near future! States had an expansive, developmental image; groups have a defensive, fearful image.

At the same time (and this is precisely the rub), these same groups are also the product of the phenomenon of democratization, of the sense that the states have failed because liberal reform was a mirage, since the "universalism" of the states involved in practice forgetting or repressing many of the weaker strata. Thus the groups are products not only of intensified fear and disappointments but also of egalitarian consciousness-raising, and thus are a very powerful rallying point. It is hard to imagine that their political role will soon diminish. But given their self-contradictory structure (egalitarian but inward-looking), the amplification of this role may be consequently quite chaotic.

4) How then will we dampen the spread of South-South wars, minority-minority conflicts in the North, that are one kind of derivation of such "groupism"? And who is in the moral, or military, position to do such dampening? Who is ready to invest their resources in it, especially given the projection of an intensified and roughly balanced North-North competition (Japan-United States vs. EC)? Here and there, some efforts will be made. But for the most part, the world will look on, as it did in the Iran-Iraq war and as it is doing in former Yugoslavia or in the Caucasus, or indeed in the ghettos of the United States. This will be all the more true as the number of simultaneous South-South conflicts grow.

Even more serious, who will limit North-South little wars, not only initiated, but deliberately initiated, not by the North but by the South, as part of a long-term strategy of military confrontation? The Gulf War was the beginning, not the end, of this process. The United States won the war, it is said. But at what price? At the price of revealing its financial dependence on others to pay for even little wars? At the price of setting itself a very limited objective—that is, one far less than unconditional surrender? At the price of having the Pentagon discuss a future world military strategy of "win, hold, win"?

President Bush and the U.S. military gambled that they could get their limited victory without much expenditure of lives (or money). The gamble worked, but it may seem wise to the

Pentagon not to push one's luck. Once again, it is hard to see how the United States, or even the combined military of the North, could handle several Persian Gulf "crises" at the same time. And, given the pattern of the world-economy and that of the evolving world social structure I have postulated for 2000–2025, who would be so bold as to argue that such multiple simultaneous Persian Gulf "crises" will not occur?

5) There is one last factor of chaos we should not underestimate —a new Black Death. The etiology of the AIDS pandemic remains a subject of great controversy. No matter, since it may have launched a process: AIDS has promoted the revival of a new deadly TB whose spread will now be autonomous. What is next? The spread of this disease not only reverses a long-term pattern of the capitalist world-economy (parallel to reversing the pattern of the growth of stateness and the strengthening of the interstate system) but also contributes to the further breakdown of stateness both by adding to the burdens of the state machinery and by stimulating an atmosphere of mutual intolerance. This breakdown in turn feeds the spread of the new diseases.

The key thing to understand is that one cannot predict which variable will be most affected by the spread of pandemic diseases: It reduces food consumers but also food producers. It reduces the number of potential migrants, but it increases labor shortages and a need for migration. In every case, which variable will be more? We shall not know until it is over. This is simply one more instance of the indeterminacy of the outcome of bifurcations.

THIS, THEN, IS THE PICTURE OF THE SECOND TIME FRAME, THE entry into a period of chaos. There is a third time frame, the outcome, the new order that is created. Here one can be most brief because it is the most uncertain. A chaotic situation is, in a seeming paradox, that which is most sensitive to deliberate human intervention. It is during periods of chaos, as opposed to periods of relative order (relatively determined order), that human intervention makes a significant difference.

Are there any potential intervenors of systemic, constructive vision? I see two. There are the visionaries of restored hierarchy and privilege, the keepers of the eternal flame of aristocracy. Individually powerful persons but lacking any collective structure —the "executive committee of the ruling class" has never held a meeting—they act (if not conjointly, then in tandem) during systemic crises because they perceive everything to be out of control. At that point, they proceed on the Lampedusan principle: "Everything must change in order that nothing change." What they will invent and offer the world is hard to know, but I have confidence in their intelligence and perspicacity. Some new historical system will be offered, and they may be able to push the world in its direction.

Against them are the visionaries of democracy/equality (two concepts I believe to be inseparable). They emerged in the period 1789–1989 in the form of the antisystemic movements (the three varieties of "Old Left"), and their organizational history was that of a gigantic tactical success and an equally gigantic strategic failure. In the long run, these movements served more to sustain than to undermine the system.

The question mark is whether a new family of antisystemic movements will now emerge, with a new strategy, one strong enough and supple enough to have a major impact in the period 2000–2025, such that the outcome will not be Lampedusan. They may fail to emerge at all, or to survive, or to be supple enough to win out.

After the bifurcation, after say 2050 or 2075, we can thus be sure of only a few things. We shall no longer be living in a capitalist world-economy. We shall be living instead in some new order or orders, some new historical system or systems. And therefore we shall probably know once again relative peace, stability, and legitimacy. But will it be a better peace, stability, and legitimacy than we have hitherto known, or a worse one? That is both unknowable and up to us.

CHAPTER THREE

WHAT HOPE AFRICA?
WHAT HOPE THE WORLD?

ANGER AND CYNICISM WELL UP IN [U.S.] VOTERS
AS HOPE GIVES WAY.
New York Times, October 10, 1994

When I first set foot in Africa, in Dakar in 1952, I came in contact with an Africa in the last moments of the colonial era, an Africa in which nationalist movements were coming into existence and rapidly flourishing everywhere. I came in contact with an Africa whose populations, and particularly its young people, were optimistic and sure that the future looked bright. They were angry about the abuses of colonialism and suspicious of the promises of the colonial powers and more generally of the West, but they had faith in their own ability to reshape their world. More than anything else, they yearned to be free of any kind of tutelage, to make their own political decisions, to provide their own personnel for public services, and to participate fully in the world polity of nations.

In 1952, Africans were not alone in such sentiments and in the expectation that they would obtain their just due. The search to regain national autonomy was common to what we began to denote collectively as the Third World. Indeed, similar sentiments pervaded the peoples of Europe. And the general optimism was shared even, perhaps especially, in the United States, where life had never seemed so good.

Here we are in 1994, and the world now looks very different. The year of Africa, 1960, seems very long ago. The United Nations development decades seem like a wan joke. And Afro-pessimism is a new and overused word in our dictionary. In February 1994, the *Atlantic Monthly* published an article about Africa that has gotten wide publicity. Its title is "The Coming Anarchy," and its subheading reads: "How scarcity, crime, overpopulation, tribalism, and disease are rapidly destroying the social fabric of our planet."

On May 29–30, 1994, *Le Monde* put on its front page an article entitled "The pillaged museums of Nigeria." The correspondent opens the article with this striking comparison:

> **Imagine that audacious thieves succeeded in getting away with the *Auriga* of Delphi or *La Primavera* of Botticelli. Such a feat would make the teleprinters of the whole world crackle and would get at least 60 seconds of prime time on CNN. During the night of April 18-19, 1993, some unknown persons stole from the collection of the National Museum of Ife in Nigeria twelve exceptional pieces—ten human heads in terra cotta and two in bronze—which are recognized as among the masterpieces of African sculpture. More than a year later, they have still not been found; the thieves are still free and, aside from a few specialists, the rest of humanity (not to speak of the Nigerian public) do not even know this has happened.**

And on June 23, 1994 a reviewer in the *London Review of Books* commented on Basil Davidson's latest book. He notes that despite the fact that, for Davidson, Africa remains "a continent of hope," even he paints a dismal picture of "the failed promises of independence." The reviewer adds that whatever Davidson "detects in the way of hopeful signs can... be very tenuous...." The reviewer then ends with this assessment: "For very many Africans, at the mercy of kleptocracies, dictatorships and derailed liberation movements—sometimes of all three—there is not much solace" in Davidson's book.

So here we have it. From the wonderful days of 1957 (the independence of Ghana) and 1960 (the year sixteen African states became independent, but also, let us remember, the year of the Congo crisis) and 1963 (the founding of the Organization of African Unity) to 1994—when, insofar as we hear anything at all about Africa in the world press, what we hear from the newspapers is that Somalia is a land of feuding clan warlords, Rwanda is a country where Hutu and Tutsi slaughter each other, and Algeria (once proud and heroic Algeria) is a land where Islamist groups cut the throats of intellectuals. To be sure, there has been one bit of wonderful news: South Africa has made an unexpectedly peaceful transition out of apartheid and into being a state where all citizens may vote. We are all celebrating, and affirming the hope that the new South Africa will not founder. But we are also holding our breath.

What has happened in thirty years, that a continent suffused with hope became a continent described by outsiders (and indeed by many of its own intellectuals) in terms almost as negative as those used in nineteenth-century discourse? There are two things to say immediately. One is that negative geocultural descriptions of Africa are not new; they are a return to the mode in which Europeans have regarded Africa for at least five centuries, that is, throughout the history of the modern world-system. The optimistic, positive language the world used in the 1950s and 1960s was exceptional and, it seems, momentary. The second thing to say is that what changed between the 1960s and the 1990s is not so much Africa as the world-system as a whole. We shall not be able to assess seriously anything about the state of Africa today or its possible trajectory until we first analyze what has been happening in the world-system as a whole in the last fifty years.

The defeat of the Axis powers in 1945 marked the end of a long struggle—a sort of "thirty years' war"—between Germany and the United States to be the successor hegemonic power to the United Kingdom, whose decline had begun in the 1870s. The colonial conquest of Africa, the so-called Scramble, was a by-product of the interpower rivalry that dominated the scene once Great Britain was no longer in a position to decree unilaterally the rules of world order and world commerce.

The United States, as we know, won this thirty years' war "unconditionally," and in 1945 stood alone in the world-system with an enormous productive apparatus that had become not only the most efficient of the time but also the only one that was physically intact (untouched by wartime destruction). The story of the next quarter century was that of the consolidation of the hegemonic role of the United States by appropriate measures in the three geographic arenas of the world, as the United States came to define them—the Soviet sphere, the West, and the Third World.

While the United States was unquestionably way out in front of its nearest competitors in the economic arena, this was not the case in the military arena, where the U.S.S.R. was a second superpower (although, be it said, at no point matching fully the power of the United States). The U.S.S.R., in addition, presented itself as incarnating the ideological opposition to dominant Wilsonian liberalism in the form of Marxism-Leninism.

However, at the ideological level, Marxism-Leninism had become more a variant of Wilsonian liberalism than a genuine alternative. The two ideologies shared in fact a commitment to the basic presumptions of the geoculture. They agreed on at least six major programs and worldviews, if sometimes they expressed this agreement in slightly different language: (1) they stood for the principle of the self-determination of nations; (2) they advocated the economic development of all states, meaning by that urbanization, commercialization, proletarianization, and industrialization, with prosperity and equality at the end of the rainbow; (3) they asserted a belief in the existence of universal values, applying equally to all peoples; (4) they asserted their faith in the validity of scientific knowledge (essentially in its Newtonian form) as the only rational basis of technological improvement; (5) they believed that human progress was both inevitable and desirable, and that for such progress to occur there must be strong, stable, centralized states; 6) they stated a belief in the rule of the people—democracy —but they defined democracy as a situation in which rational reforming experts were in fact allowed to make the essential political decisions.

The degree of subliminal ideological accord greatly facilitated the division of world power on the terms of Yalta, which essentially were three: (a) The U.S.S.R. could have de facto suzerainty in a *chasse gardée* in Eastern Europe (and by further amendment in a divided Korea and China), provided it in effect restricted its real (as opposed to rhetorical) claims to this zone alone; (b) the two sides would guarantee total absence of warfare in Europe; (c) each side could and would suppress groups in radical opposition to the existing geopolitical order ("leftists" in the U.S. zone; "adventurers" and "nationalists" in the Soviet zone). This agreement did not render impossible or implausible an ideological struggle, even one conducted with great fanfare. On the contrary, it presumed and even encouraged it. But this ideological struggle was to be pursued within strict limits, barring full-scale military involvement of one or the one great power outside its designated domain. Of course, a further element of this "legal separation" of the wartime allies was that the U.S.S.R. was not to expect any sort of postwar economic assistance from the United States in its reconstruction. It was on its own.

This is not the place to review the history of the cold war. Suffice it to note that between 1945 and 1989, the accord (as outlined here) was essentially carefully observed. Each time its terms seemed threatened by forces outside the immediate control of the two superpowers, they managed to rein in these forces, and renew their tacit accord. For Africa, what this meant was very simple. By the late 1950s, both the U.S.S.R. and the United States had taken a formal position in favor of decolonization, deriving from their theoretical commitment to universal values. To be sure, it was often the case in practice that they gave covert (and even overt) political and financial support to different political movements in particular countries. The fact is, however, that Africa was inside the U.S., and outside the Soviet, zone. Hence, the U.S.S.R. always severely limited its involvement, as may be seen both in the Congo crisis of 1960–65 and in the postindependence destabilization attempts in southern Africa in the post-1975 period. In any case, African liberation movements had first to survive on their own before they were able to get even moral support from the U.S.S.R. and a fortiori from the United States.

The policy of the United States toward its major allies in the world arena—Western Europe and Japan—was rather straightforward. It sought to aid their economic reconstruction massively (notably via the Marshall Plan). This was crucial for the United States both economically and politically. Economically, it was not difficult to understand. There was little point in creating the most efficient economic machinery in the world-economy, if there were no customers for the products. U.S. enterprises needed an economically restituted Western Europe and Japan to serve as the principal external outlets for its production. No other zones could have played this role in the postwar period. Politically, the two alliance systems—NATO and the U.S.-Japan Defense Treaty—guaranteed the United States two crucial additional elements in the structure it was erecting to maintain its world order: military bases across the world, and a set of automatic and powerful political allies (for a long time, serving more as clients than as allies) in the geopolitical arena.

This alliance structure of course had implications for Africa. The west European states were not only the main allies of the United States but were also the principal colonial powers in Africa. The colonial powers were hostile to any U.S. involvement in what they persisted in regarding as their "internal affairs." The United States was therefore cautious about offending its allies, especially in the period 1945–60, when the U.S. government still largely shared the views of the colonial governments—that precipitate decolonization was dangerous. African liberation movements were nonetheless able to force the pace. And by 1960, the "downward sweep of African liberation" was already half completed. The year 1960 marks a turning point, since this "downward sweep" had now reached the Congo, and thus the zone of political and economic hard-core resistance to decolonization, the settler-cum-mining zone of southern Africa. The so-called Congo crisis erupted. Within a year, there were two (in fact, two and a half) sides not only within the Congo, but among the independent African states and indeed in the world as a whole. We all know the outcome. Lumumba was assassinated and the Lumumbists suppressed. The secession of Tshombe's Katanga was also put down. Colonel Mobutu came to preside over Zaire; he is still there. The Congo crisis also transformed the geopolitical stance of the United States in Africa. It pushed the United States into thenceforth playing a direct role in Africa, deciding to defer no longer in any important way to the (ex-)colonial powers.

The scenario that the United States hoped would occur in the colonial world after 1945 (and more generally in the non-European

world) was one of slow, gentle political change that would bring
to power so-called moderate leaders with nationalist credentials
who would continue, and work to augment, their country's involvement in the commodity chains of the capitalist world-economy.
The U.S.S.R.'s official position was that it favored the coming to
power of progressive forces that would be "socialist" in orientation.
In practice, as we have already said, the U.S.S.R. was lukewarm
in its support of such forces, as can be seen in their go-slow advice
to the Chinese Communist Party in 1945, in their long delay in
supporting the independence movement in Algeria, and in
the support the Cuban Communist Party gave to Batista right up
to 1959.

What neither the United States nor the U.S.S.R. expected was
the intensity of the national liberation movements in the extra-
European world at this time. To be sure, all kinds of radical nationalist outbreaks were suppressed—in Malaya, the Philippines, and
Iran; in Madagascar, Kenya, and Cameroon; in multiple countries
of the Americas. Even where such uprisings were suppressed,
however, they pushed forward the calendar of decolonization.

And in four countries, there were extremely strong, ultimately
victorious, wars of liberation that left a major mark. They were
China, Vietnam, Algeria, and Cuba. In all four cases, the movements refused to accept the rules of the game as the United States
defined them, and as the U.S.S.R. tacitly endorsed them.

The details of each case were different because the geography,
the history, and the array of internal social forces were different. But
all four movements shared certain features: (1) they imposed their
arrival in power on the world-system's great powers, by the fierce-
ness with which they pursued their political autonomy; (2) they
proclaimed a belief in modernity and national development; (3)
they sought power in the state as the necessary prerequisite of
social transformation, and once in power they sought to achieve full
legitimation by the populace of the strong state they were erecting;
(4) they were sure that they were riding the wave of historical
progress.

By 1965, the spirit of Bandung seemed to have conquered the
world. The national liberation movements had come to power

everywhere, except in southern Africa, and armed struggle had begun there as well. It was, if you will, a strange situation. Never had the United States seemed so in control of the situation, so on top of everything. Yet never had antisystemic movements seemed so strong. It was the calm in the eye of the hurricane. There were early warning signals in Africa. The year 1965 saw the fall of some of the symbolic figures of the so-called Casablanca group, the group of more "militant" states: Nkrumah in Ghana and Ben Bella in Algeria. It was also the year the Rhodesian settlers proclaimed UDI, the Unilateral Declaration of Independence. And in the United States, it was the year of the first Vietnam teach-in. In 1966, the Chinese Cultural Revolution started. The momentous year of 1968 was in sight.

Early in 1968 the Tet offensive signaled the incapacity of the United States to win the war in Vietnam. In February, Martin Luther King Jr. was assassinated. And in April, the worldwide revolution of 1968 began. Over three years it occurred everywhere—in North America, Europe, and Japan; in the Communist world; and in Latin America, Africa, and South Asia. The local manifestations were, to be sure, each different from the other. But two themes were common, making of these multiple uprisings a worldwide event. The first was antagonism to U.S. hegemony (symbolized by opposition to its role in Vietnam) and to Soviet collusion with the United States (as evoked in the theme of the "two superpowers"). The second was a deep disillusion with the so-called Old Left, in all its three major variants: Social-Democratic parties in the West; Communist parties; and national liberation movements in the Third World. The revolutionaries of 1968 saw the Old Left as insufficiently and ineffectively antisystemic. Indeed, one might argue that, even more than the United States, the Old Left was the prime villain of the piece for the revolutionaries of 1968.

As a political event, the world revolution of 1968 flared up quickly and then was extinguished. By 1970, there were only embers—mostly in the form of Maoist sects. By 1975, even the embers had been extinguished. Nonetheless, the revolution left a lasting impact. It delegitimized reformist centrist liberalism as the reigning ideology of the geoculture, reducing liberalism to merely one competing ideology in the arena, with strong forces both to its right and to its left. It soured people everywhere on the state as the instrument of social transformation. And it destroyed the optimism about the inevitability of progress, especially when the last avatar of such optimism, its own meteoric career, fizzled out. The mood had turned.

The events in 1968 took place at just the moment that the world-economy was entering into the Kondratieff-B downturn in which we still find ourselves today. Once again, as has happened repeatedly in the history of the capitalist world-economy, the high profitability of the leading sectors came to an end, primarily because the relative monopoly of a few firms had been undermined by persistent entry into the market of new producers attracted by the high rates of profit, and usually supported by governments of semiperipheral states. The acute decline in worldwide rates of profit from productive activities resulted, as one could expect, in reduction of production and unemployment in the loci of leading sectors; consequently in the reduction of purchases of raw material imports coming from peripheral zones; further relocation of industries to semiperipheral zones in search of lowered labor costs; acute competition between states in the core zone seeking to shift the negative burdens to each other; and a significant shift of investors from seeking profits in production to seeking profits in financial (speculative) activities.

In this particular B-phase, the two major events that brought the economic stagnation to the world's attention (but by no means could be said to have caused the stagnation) were the rise in OPEC oil prices in the 1970s and the debt crisis of the 1980s. Both of course had particularly negative consequences for the South in general, not least of all for Africa. It is worth discussing their significance as politico-economic mechanisms of adjustment.

In 1973, the Organization of Petroleum Exporting Countries, or OPEC—a group that had been in somnolent and obscure existence for more than a decade—suddenly announced a spectacular price rise. Notice several things about this event. Oil prices had been remarkably low during the whole Kondratieff A-phase, when world production was expanding. Yet it was precisely at the moment when the world-economy began to be in trouble, and when producers were everywhere beginning to seek ways in which they could sell their products in a tighter market by either reducing their prices or reducing their costs, that the oil producers raised their prices, and not by a small amount. The effect, of course, was to raise the costs of production of almost every industrial process worldwide, since oil is a direct or indirect component of almost all of this production.

What was the rationale of such an action? One might argue that it was a syndical action by the oil-exporting states seeking to take advantage of an economically weakened Western world to alter the distribution of world surplus value in their favor. This might explain why members of OPEC who had politically radical governments at the time, such as Algeria or Iraq, were pushing for such action. But why would the two closest allies of the United States in the oil region—Saudi Arabia and Iran (the Iran of the Shah)—have not merely gone along but actually taken the lead in obtaining the OPEC accord on a joint price rise? And if the action was intended to rectify the distribution of world surplus value, how is it that the immediate effect was actually to increase the amount of world surplus value in the hands of U.S. corporations?

Let us look at what happens when you raise oil prices suddenly and drastically. Since it is hard to reduce the need for oil very quickly, several things follow. The revenues of the oil producers go up, indeed go way up. This is so despite the fact that the quantity of oil sold is reduced, since it has become so expensive. A reduction in the quantity of oil sold means a reduction in world current production; that, however, is actually a plus, given the fact that in the 1960s there had been overproduction in the erstwhile leading sectors. Indeed, it makes more legitimate the laying off of industrial workers.

For non-oil-producing states in the peripheral zone—for example, most African states—the oil price rise was a very severe blow. The price of importing oil went up. The price of importing industrial products in whose production oil played a significant role, which is almost all production as we have already noted, went up.

And this occurred at a time when the quantity and often the per-unit price of exports was going down. Of course, African states (except for a few) found themselves in severe balance of payments squeezes. The populations found themselves confronted with reduced standards of living and deteriorating governmental services. They could scarcely be content with this apparent outcome of the independence for which they had successfully struggled a decade or so earlier: They turned against the very movements they had previously supported so strongly, especially whenever they saw signs of corruption and high living among their elites.

Of course, oil prices did not rise for Africans alone; they rose everywhere, including in the United States. It was part of a long inflationary thrust, which was generated by many other factors. What the oil price rise (itself not a cause but a consequence of the world-economic stagnation) did was to create a big funnel that channeled a remarkably large portion of world surplus value through its cash registers. What happened to this revenue? Some of it was kept by the oil-producing states as rent and served to permit luxury consumption for a small minority. It also for a short while improved levels of income for a larger segment of the citizenry. It permitted these states to improve their infrastructures and conduct arms purchases on a large scale. The latter was socially less useful than the former, especially since it would permit such spectacular wastage of lives and accumulated capital stock as the Iran-Iraq war of the 1980s. But both kinds of expenditure—infrastructure and arms purchases—helped resolve part of the economic difficulties of the states in the North, from which the goods were imported.

Still, expenditures within the oil-producing states account for only part of the revenue. Another large part went to the Seven Sisters, that is, the Western petroleum corporations who no longer controlled oil production but who continued to control worldwide oil refining and oil distribution. What did they in turn do with their extraordinary profit windfalls? In the absence of enough profitable production outlets, they placed a good portion of this money in the world financial markets, fueling the incredible currency roller coaster of the past two decades.

All this activity did not exhaust the coffers of this concentration of world surplus value. The rest was placed as accounts in banks, primarily in the United States but also in Western Europe. Bank profits come from lending the money that is deposited with them. And the banks now had huge additional sums deposited—at a time where new productive enterprise was slowing down, as compared with the Kondratieff A-phase. To whom could the banks lend the money? The answer seemed obvious: to governments in balance of payments difficulties, which meant almost all African states, large portions of Latin America and Asia, and almost all the so-called socialist bloc as well (from Poland to Romania to the U.S.S.R. to North Korea). In the mid–1970s, world banks pressed these loans upon these governments, which seized the opportunity to balance their accounts in this way and reduce somewhat the immediate political pressures of unhappy ordinary citizens. Similar loans were made even to the oil-producing states who did not need to balance their accounts but who were anxious to spend quickly on what they perceived (and misperceived) as "development." These loans in turn helped the Western countries by counteracting the inability of the rest of the world to purchase their exports.

The situation in Western countries must be analyzed carefully. There are three different ways to assess what happened in the 1970s and continued in the 1980s. One is to see how countries fared globally. Globally, their rates of growth went down considerably from the Kondratieff A-phase of 1945–circa 1970, although in absolute terms they of course kept growing. Second, one can assess them in relation to each other. Here we can see that, despite the best efforts of the United States (and its early advantage from the OPEC action deriving from the fact that it was less dependent on oil imports than Western Europe or Japan were), the U.S. economic position has declined overall in relation to Western Europe and especially Japan, despite constant short-term reversals of fortune.

Third, one can assess the Western countries in terms of internal distribution of surplus value. While it could be said that the pattern of the A-phase had been one of overall improvement of income levels and some convergence of extremes, the pattern of the B-phase has been rather one of considerable increase in internal polarization of revenue. A small percentage has done quite well, at least for a long time; we have even invented a term for them—yuppies. But, aside from this small group, there has been a marked increase in internal poverty, a fall from middle-class status for a considerable group, and a decline in real income for most of the rest of the middle strata. This internal polarization has been particularly marked in the United States and Great Britain, but is also true of continental Western Europe, and even of Japan.

A word should be said at this point about East Asia, especially since it is constantly thrown in the face of Africans as a model of successful development. Whenever there is a stagnation of the world-economy and a squeeze on profits in general and profits from productive activities in particular, one geographic zone, previously not at the top of the profit-making hierarchy, tends to do very well. It becomes the locus of considerable worldwide relocation of production, the beneficiary of the difficulties of the world-economy as a whole. In the 1970s and since, this zone has been East Asia—Japan, primarily, with its immediate rim of the so-called Four Dragons benefiting next, and tertiarily (and more recently), a series of countries in Southeast Asia. How East Asia was able to become this beneficiary region is not the point of this discussion, except for two remarks. A key role was played by governmental involvement in the construction of the necessary economic frameworks and state protection of the internal markets. Furthermore, there was no way that a second zone could have achieved the same economic returns simultaneously. It could have been the case that some region other than East Asia achieved this growth, but it could not have been both East Asia and a second region. Hence, East Asia presents no relevant model for Africa in any near future.

I have spent so much time on the OPEC oil price rise not because it was a key cause of economic distress. It was not; it was merely one intervening process by which the world-economic stagnation had its effect. But it was very visible, and looking at the mechanism in detail makes clearer the process. It also helps to illuminate the 1980s, when the world forgot about oil prices as they came down again, if not, however, quite to their 1950 levels. The loans to governments came home to roost in the 1980s. Loans solve balance of payments in the present, to create them down the line, as the costs of debt repayment as a percentage of national income go up. The decade of the 1980s started out with the so-called debt crisis and ended with the so-called collapse of the Communisms. They are not unrelated.

The term debt crisis appeared in 1982 when Mexico, an oil-producing country, announced its inability to keep up with debt repayments and sought renegotiation of its debt. Actually the debt crisis initially surfaced in 1980 in Poland, a heavy borrower in the 1970s, when the Gierek government, faced with debt repayment problems, tried to reduce wage levels as a partial solution. Result: Solidarność. The Polish Communist government got in trouble because it began to implement the IMF remedy for the situation without even having the IMF ask it to do this. What the IMF began to recommend to all countries in this situation (not least to African states) was that they reduce expenditures (fewer imports and less welfare for the population) and increase exports (by keeping wages low or lowering them, by diverting production from goods for internal consumption to whatever was sellable immediately on the world market). The weapon the IMF had for ensuring adoption of this unpalatable advice was the withholding of short-term aid by all Western governments should a given state fail to implement the IMF policy; hence (given the debt crisis) the prospect of governmental insolvency. One African state after another would yield to the pressure, though none did as well as the only country that fully repaid a large debt in the 1980s, which was Ceaușescu's Romania, to the great joy of the IMF and the great anger of the Romanian people.

The "debt crisis" in Africa translated into much that was nasty: famines, unemployment, massive deterioration of infrastructure, civil wars, and the disintegration of state machineries. In southern Africa, the difficulties were compounded by the destabilization programs of the apartheid regime of South Africa, which was fighting its rear-guard action against the downward sweep of African liberation—which was able to reach Johannesburg only in

1994. We will distort our understanding of Africa's serious plight of the 1980s, however, if we do not place it in the larger picture of the world-economy. The debt crisis of course occurred elsewhere as well, and indeed, in terms of total sums, occurred most notably in Latin America. The debt crisis of the Third World (plus the socialist bloc) meant the end of lending these countries new money. Indeed, the flow of money in the 1980s was decidedly from South to North, not in the other direction.

However, the problem of placing surplus value profitably did not disappear, since the absence of sufficient lucrative outlets for productive investment continued. The collapse of the borrowers of the 1970s (including the African states) was no doubt a problem for these borrowers, but it was also a serious problem for the lenders, who needed to lend money to someone. In the 1980s they found two important new borrowers, and not minor ones: the major corporate enterprises of the world, and the government of the United States.

The 1980s is an era that will be remembered in the world of corporations as the era of junk bonds and corporate takeovers. What was going on? Essentially, a lot of money was being invested in the process of buying corporations, largely in order to chop them up, sell off profitable chunks, and allow the other parts to rust away (in the process, laying off workers). The outcome was not at all increased production but rather enormous debts for such corporations. As a result, many industrial corporations and banks went bankrupt. If they were big enough, as bankruptcy approached, the states intervened to "save" them because of the negative political and economic consequences. The result, as in the case of the savings-and-loan-associations scandal in the United States, was huge profits to the junk-bond dealers and a huge bill for the U.S. taxpayer.

The huge bill deriving from corporate debts was compounded, in the case of the United States, by the huge debt of military Keynesianism. The Reagan nonrevolution meant first of all, contrary to its own very loud rhetoric, a vast expansion of state involvement in the U.S. economy and in the size of its bureaucracy. Economically, what Reagan did was to reduce federal tax levels for the wealthier segments of the population (which resulted in further internal polarization) while simultaneously massively increasing military expenditures (which held back unemployment ratios). But as the 1980s went on, the United States was experiencing, as a result of its borrowing, the same problems that Third World debt had caused for the Third World. There was, however, one difference: The IMF was in no position to impose IMF policies on the United States. And politically, the United States was unwilling to impose them on itself. But in the process, the U.S. economic position vis-à-vis its now strong competitors (Western Europe and Japan) was constantly deteriorating, precisely because of the military focus of U.S. investment.

It is at this point that the so-called collapse of the Communisms intervened. We have already noted that its accepted starting point, the rise of Solidarność in Poland, was a direct outcome of the debt crisis. Essentially, the socialist countries faced the same negative consequences of the world-economic stagnation as did the African states: end of the impressive growth rates of the A-phase; decline in real standards of living, if not in the 1970s, then in the 1980s; deterioration of infrastructure; decline of governmental services; and above all, disillusionment with the regimes in power. The disillusionment focused on political repression, but its motor was the failure of the promise of "development."

In the case of the U.S.S.R., the general problem of all the socialist states was compounded by the contradiction of the Yalta accord. The Yalta accord was, we have argued, a quite precise arrangement. It allowed for rhetorical struggle about the distant future but presumed a deal about the present, a bargain that was sedulously respected. To do this, both sides had to be strong, strong enough to control all their satellites and allies. The ability of the U.S.S.R. to do its part was now compromised by the economic difficulties of the 1980s as well as, of course, by the deterioration of ideological coherence that started in 1956 with the XXth Party Congress. Its problems were made worse by the military Keynesianism of the United States, which increased pressure on the U.S.S.R. to expend funds it didn't have. However, the biggest dilemma of all was not U.S. military strength but the growing economic and political *weaknesses* of the United States. The United States-U.S.S.R. relationship was held together like a taut rubber band. If the United States weakened its hold, the link was untenable. The result was Gorbachev's desperate attempt to save the situation by forcing an end to the cold war, disengaging from Eastern Europe, and relaunching the U.S.S.R. internally. It turned out not to be possible—at least not the third part—and the U.S.S.R. is no more.

The collapse of the U.S.S.R. has created enormous difficulties, perhaps insurmountable ones, for the United States. It has eliminated the only political control the United States had over its now quite strong economic rivals, Western Europe and Japan. While it kept the U.S. debt from further increasing by ending military Keynesianism, it created as a consequence a massive problem of economic deployment, with which the United States has not coped very well. And ideologically, the collapse of Marxism-Leninism has eliminated the last credence that state-managed reform could bring about significant economic development of the peripheral and semiperipheral zones of the capitalist world-economy. That is why I have argued elsewhere that the so-called collapse of the Communisms was really the collapse of liberalism as an ideology. But liberalism as the dominant ideology of the geoculture (already undermined in 1968, and mortally wounded by the events of 1989) has been a political pillar of the world-system, having been the main instrument by which the "dangerous classes" (first the European working classes in the nineteenth century, then the popular classes of the Third World in the twentieth) were "tamed." Without a belief in the efficacy of national liberation, dosed with Marxism-Leninism, the popular classes of the Third World have little reason to be patient, and they will cease to be so.

Finally, the economic consequences of the end of military Keynesianism has been very bad news for Japan and East Asia. Their expansion in the 1980s was strongly fueled by both the ability to lend money to the U.S. government and the ability to participate in the now dormant process of corporate takeovers. Thus the East Asian miracle, still real insofar as we look at it in terms relative to the United States, is now in trouble in absolute terms.

These dramatic transformations of the late 1980s were marked in Africa (as in Latin America and in Eastern Europe) by the rise of two leitmotivs: the market and democratization. Before we can look at the future, we must spend a moment dissecting them. The popularity of the "market" as organizing mantra is the counterpart of the disillusion with the "state" as organizing mantra. The problem is that the market conveys two quite different messages. For some, particularly younger elite elements, erstwhile bureaucrats and/or socialist politicians, it is the great cry of pre-1848 France—"Messieurs, enrichissez-vous!" And, as has been true for some five hundred years now, it is always possible for some new group to become "nouveaux riches."

But, for most people, the turn to the "market" does not signify any change in objective at all. Over the past decade, people in Africa (and elsewhere) have turned to the "market" for exactly the same thing as they had previously turned to the "state." What they hope to get is that elusive pot of gold at the end of the rainbow, "development." By "development" of course they really mean equality, living as well as, as comfortably as, people do in the North, probably in particular as people do in American movies. But this is a profound illusion. Neither the "state" nor the "market" will promote egalitarian "development" in a capitalist world-economy, whose guiding principle of the ceaseless accumulation of capital requires and generates ever-greater polarization of real income. Since most people are reasonably intelligent and reasonably aware, it will not take too long for whatever magic attaches to the "market" as medicine to dissipate, leaving a stunning hangover.

Is "democratization," and its annexed slogan of "human rights" very different from the market? Well, yes and no. First of all, we have to be clear about what is meant by "democratization." Since 1945, there has been virtually no state in which there have not been regular elections of the legislature, with near-universal suffrage. Such procedures we all recognize can be meaningless. We seem to mean something more. But what is this more? Elections in which two or more parties contest? Contest really and not nominally, contest with votes counted correctly and not fraudulently, contest fairly and not have the results annulled? If adding such requirements is what it takes to move us in the direction of "democratization," then I suppose we have been making a little progress. But in an era when the *New York Times* reveals that the governing party of Japan over the last forty-odd years, the Liberal Democratic Party, has been receiving regular subsidies from the CIA, we may be allowed to doubt whether the formality of holding freely contested elections is enough to talk of democratization.

The problem, as we know, is that democracy, like the market, has two quite different affective connotations. One goes with the market as locus of enrichment; the other goes with the objective of egalitarian development. The first meaning of "democracy" appeals to a small, albeit powerful, group. The second appeals to a much larger, but politically weaker, group. The efforts to achieve democratization in recent years in such bellwether African situations as Togo, Nigeria, and Zaire have not been terribly encouraging. Perhaps, however, real democracy can only be possible with real development, and if development is an illusion in the present world-system, democratization may not be much better.

Am I then preaching a doctrine of hopelessness? Not at all! But before we can have useful hope, we must have lucid analysis. The world-system is in disarray. Africa is in disarray, but not really more so than the rest of the world-system. Africa has emerged from an era of perhaps exaggerated optimism into a mood of pessimism. Well, so has the world. From 1945 to the late 1960s, everything seemed to be getting better and better everywhere. From the late 1960s to the late 1980s things started to go sour in various ways almost everywhere, and people began at the very least to rethink their easy optimism. Today we are frightened, diffusely angry, unsure of our verities, and in disarray. This is simply the reflection in collective consciousness of a deep crisis in our existing world-system, in which the traditional mechanisms of resolving normal cyclical downturns are no longer working so well, in which the secular trends of the world-system have led the system "far from equilibrium." We are therefore approaching a "bifurcation" (to use the language of the new science) whose outcome is inherently indeterminate, which can push us in possible alternative directions that are quite different from each other.

If one wants to face up to Africa's dilemmas, the first thing to see is how they are not special to Africa. Let me take four that are frequently discussed about Africa, and try to put each in a wider context. The first is the collapse of the national liberation movements. In almost every country, a movement emerged during colonial times that incarnated Africans' demands for autonomous control of their own destiny and that led the political battle to achieve this goal. These movements were a nationally integrating force, mobilizing the populations in the name of a better life and a more equal world. They were against divisive particularisms within the state, but in favor of the assertion of national and African culture within the world-system. They were modernizing and democratizing movements, and they purveyed hope.

Yesterday, these movements achieved their primary objective of national independence. Today, none of these movements has survived intact; most have not survived at all. The only real exception is the ANC of South Africa, and it achieved its primary objective only in 1994. Wherever these movements have crumbled in the post-independence era, no other political force has filled the vacuum or has been able to mobilize national consciousness in similar ways, nor are any such forces in sight.

This may be dismaying, but is this so special to Africa? Have national liberation movements fared better in South and Southeast Asia, in the Arab world, in Latin America and the Caribbean? Certainly the Communist movements that took power in a geographic stretch from the Elbe to the Yalu seem not to have fared any better. And if we look at Western Europe, and the extra-European world of White settlement, is the picture really different? The movements there comparable to the national liberation movements of Africa are the Social-Democratic movements (*latō sensū*), which also mobilized popular opinion in modernizing, democratizing directions, and which also, in most cases, were able after long decades of struggle to come to power. But are not these movements also now in disarray, renouncing old slogans, unsure of what they stand for, and incapable of obtaining the kind of mass affective support that had been their force? Personally I do not see much difference.

The second of Africa's dilemmas derives in part from the collapse of these movements. What we mean by their collapse is the withdrawal of mass support. They can no longer mobilize anyone. But what about the mobilizers, the cadres of all these movements, the strata whose upward mobility was made possible by the success of these movements—the politicians, the bureaucrats, the intellectuals? It was they who propagated the national project, and in many ways it was they who profited most by it.

As the movements began to collapse, as the objectives for which the movements' struggle seemed to recede into the horizon, these cadres seemed to scramble to shore, seeking individual salvation. The ideological commitments faded into the background, the selflessness of the period of nationalist struggle was abandoned, and many entered into a competitive scramble in which the line between the legitimate and the illegitimate became difficult to distinguish.

This is no doubt true of the Africa of the 1990s. But is venal corruption of cynical elites an African specialty? I doubt it. We see the same phenomenon at work in Latin America and Asia. It is graphic in the ex-Communist world. And one needs only to read the headlines to realize that the corruption in Africa pales before that which daily comes to light in Italy and Japan, in France and the United States. Nor is this new, of course.

What created the disarray is not the corruption in high places but the fact that, of all those who benefited from the worldwide expansion of the middle strata in the period 1945–1970, so large a percentage has fallen off the Ferris wheel on its downward turn in the post-1970 period. This group that rose socially and economically, and then fell (while others did not) is an acutely destabilizing force politically, harboring deep resentments and turning to all kinds of antistate, moralistic, and moralizing movements to secure their personal safety and express their aggressions. But here, too, Africa is not special. If anything, this problem is far more serious in Europe and North America than it is in Africa.

The third problem with which Africa is said to be faced is the disintegration of the state structures. Certainly Liberia or Somalia presents extreme examples of this phenomenon. But once again we need to go beyond the glaring examples to look at the problem. The withdrawal of legitimation of the states resulting from the collapse of the national liberation movements is the first part of the problem. The new antistate disposition of erstwhile cadres threatened with downward mobility is another part. But the most fundamental problem is the structural inability to provide egalitarian development, while the demand for democratization is ceaselessly growing. We have already discussed the strain in state resources that world economic stagnation has caused. States have been increasingly unable to provide services even at the inadequate levels at which they previously supplied them. This started a circular process. States have found it more difficult to raise revenues. Their ability to ensure order has declined. As the ability to ensure order has declined, people have turned to other structures to provide security and welfare, which in turn has further weakened the states.

But here, too, the only reason this is so visible in Africa is that this decline in stateness has set in so soon after the states themselves were established. If we look at this worldwide, we can see that for over five hundred years there was a secular trend of strengthening state structures, a trend that seems to have reached its peak in the late 1960s and has started moving in the other direction everywhere. In the North, it gets discussed under various rubrics: the fiscal crisis of the states; the rise of urban crime and the creation of self-defense structures; the inability of the states to contain the influx of persons; the pressure to dismantle welfare state structures.

Finally, many point to the collapse in Africa of physical infrastructure and the dangerous trends in epidemiology. This is, of course, true. Highway systems, educational systems, hospitals are in bad shape and getting worse, and the money to rectify the situation doesn't seem to be there. The spread of AIDS is proverbial. And even if its spread can be contained, there looms the danger of new maladies spread by drug-resistant bacteria or viruses coming into existence.

Here again, the problem is dramatic in Africa but scarcely restricted to it. Just as we seem to have hit a peak in the strengthening of state structures some twenty-five years ago, we may also have hit a peak in the two-century-long worldwide attack on infectious and contagious diseases. The self-confident utilization of dramatic solutions may have undone some protective ecological mechanisms, making possible new kinds of terrible, previously unknown, epidemic diseases. The breakdown in physical infrastructure cannot help in this regard. In any case, at a time when new strains of tuberculosis are emerging in U.S. cities, it is hardly the moment to deem this an African problem.

If, however, the problem is not that of Africa but that of the world-system as a whole, is Africa destined merely to be a bystander in a world crisis, suffering its fate but not being able to do anything about it? My belief is quite the contrary. The crisis of the world-system is the opportunity of the world-system in general, and perhaps of Africa in particular. While we can expect in theory that the very processes of our present world-system will exacerbate, and not eliminate, the crisis, we know that this involves a disarray, a great world disorder over twenty-five to fifty years, out of which will come some new kind of order.

What we all do in this transitional period in which we are living will determine whether the historical system(s) that will emerge at the end of this process will in fact be better or worse than the modern world-system though whose demise we find ourselves living. There is not merely room in this period for action at the local level: Action at the local level is the critical variable that will determine how we come out of the crisis.

There are no simple formulas. We need to analyze more clearly the existing world situation and divest our minds of categories and concepts that have closed our vision to the real historical alternatives that are, or can become, available. We need to organize and revitalize local solidarities that turn outward and not inward. Above all, we must become very aware that protecting our own group *at the expense of* some other group is self-destructive.

I think above all we need to keep our eye on the ball. A more equal distribution of goods, services, and power has got to be the basis on which we create our new historical system(s). Our time horizons must be longer than they have been, in terms of the use of our resources, both natural and human. In this kind of reconstruction, Africa is well placed to take a lead. Africa has been a zone of exclusion in our modern world-system, and we may expect that over the next twenty-five to fifty years the ongoing political, economic, and cultural mechanisms of the world-system will operate to exclude Africa and Africans still more.

If Africans stay mired in the claim for inclusion within the world-system in its present definition, they will tilt at windmills. If Africans show the way in combining short-run local meliorations with a middle-run transformation of values and structures, they will help not only Africa; they will help the rest of us as well. Do not ask me or other non-Africans to draw up a specific agenda for action. We cannot do it. The ball is very much in Africa's court.

Let me say one last thing. I do not say Africa will inevitably succeed as it tries. Africa has—we all have—at best a fifty-fifty chance of coming out of this transition with something better. History is not necessarily on our side, and if we think it is, this belief will work against us. But we are all very much an important and integral part of this process. And if we engage in it in the right way, we may indeed achieve the kind of world-system we want. It is around this realization that we must organize our collective efforts, though the road is hard and the outcome uncertain, the struggle is worth it.

PART II

THE CONSTRUCTION AND TRIUMPH
OF LIBERAL IDEOLOGY

THREE IDEOLOGIES OR ONE?
THE PSEUDOBATTLE OF MODERNITY

The story line of modern times, in terms of the history of ideas or of political philosophy, is a familiar one. It can be briefly stated in this way: There emerged during the nineteenth century three great political ideologies—conservatism, liberalism, and socialism. Ever since, the three (in ever-changing guises) have been in constant struggle with each other.

Virtually everyone would agree to two generalizations about these ideological struggles. One, each of these ideologies represents a response to the fact that new collective outlooks had been forged in the wake of the French Revolution, which gave rise to the feeling that specific political strategies were necessary to cope with a new situation. Two, none of the three ideologies has ever been encrusted in one definitive version. Quite the contrary; each has seemed to appear in as many forms as there have been ideologists.

No doubt, most people believe that there are some essential differences among these ideologies. But the closer one looks either at the theoretical statements or at the actual political struggles, the more disagreement one finds about exactly what these presumably essential differences are.

There is even disagreement about how many different ideologies there are. There are quite a few theoreticians and quite a few political leaders who have argued that there are in reality only two, and not three, ideologies, although the pair to which it is possible to reduce the trio is itself debated. That is to say, there are conservatives who see no essential difference between liberalism and socialism, socialists who say the same thing about liberalism and conservatism, and even liberals who argue that there is no serious distinction between conservatism and socialism.

This is in itself strange, but the story does not stop there. The term *ideology* in its many usages has never been a word that people or groups have liked to use about themselves. Ideologists have always denied being ideologists—except for Destutt de Tracy, who is said to have invented the word. But Napoleon quickly used the word against him, saying that political realism was to be preferred to ideology (by which he meant a theoretical doctrine), a sentiment shared by quite a few politicians then and since.

A half-century later, in *The German Ideology*, Marx used the word to characterize a worldview that was both partial and self-serving, the view of a class (the bourgeoisie). Ideology, said Marx, was destined to be replaced by science (reflecting the views of the working class, which was the universal class). Mannheim, in the period between the two world wars, went still further. He agreed with Marx about the partial and self-serving nature of ideologies, but added Marxism to the list of such ideologies. He wanted to replace ideologies with utopias, which he saw as the creation of classless intellectuals. And after the Second World War, Daniel Bell expressed the weariness of Mannheim's intellectuals with both ideologies and utopias. When Bell proclaimed the end of ideology, he was thinking primarily of Marxism, which he saw giving way to a sort of gentle, nonideological liberalism, based on an awareness of the limits of politics.

Thus, for the two centuries of its existence, the concept of ideology has been perceived negatively, as something one had to reject or to supersede. But does this allow us to understand what an ideology is, what people have intended to accomplish by means of ideologies? I shall treat this subject via five queries, none of which I shall answer totally, but all of which represent an attempt to understand the concept of modernity and its links with the concept of ideology:

1) What is the difference between an an ideology and a Weltanschauung (or worldview)?
2) Who is the "subject" of an ideology?
3) What is the relation of ideologies to the state(s)?
4) How many different ideologies have there really been?
5) Is it possible to supersede ideology, that is, can one operate without one?

WELTANSCHAUUNG AND IDEOLOGY

There is an anecdote, probably apocryphal, about Louis XVI, who, upon hearing from the Duc de Liancourt about the storming of the Bastille, is said to have asked, "Is it a riot?" Came the reply, "No, Sire, it's a revolution" (Brunot, 1937, 617). This is not the place to discuss once again the interpretation of the French Revolution, except to indicate that one of its principal consequences for the world-system was that it made acceptable for the first time the idea that change, novelty, transformation, even revolution, were "normal," that is, not exceptional, phenomena of the political arena, at least of the modern political arena. What at first appeared as statistically normal quickly became perceived as morally normal. This is what Labrousse was referring to when he said that Year II was "a decisive turning point," after which "the Revolution took on a prophetic, annunciatory role, bearing within it an entire ideology that would eventually fully emerge" (1949, 29). Or, as Watson said: "The Revolution [was] the shadow under which the whole nineteenth century lived" (1973,45). To which I would add—the twentieth century as well. The revolution marked the apotheosis of seventeenth-century Newtonian science and eighteenth-century concepts of progress; in short, what we have come to call modernity.

Modernity is the combination of a particular social reality and a particular Weltanschauung, or worldview, which has replaced, even buried, another pair that, precisely to indicate how outdated it is, we now designate as the Ancien Régime. No doubt not everyone reacted in the same way to this new reality and this new worldview. Some welcomed them, some rejected them, others were unsure how to react. But very few were unaware of the degree of change that had occurred. The anecdote about Louis XVI is very telling in this regard.

The way in which people within the capitalist world-economy reacted to this "turning point" and dealt with the enormous discombobulation resulting from the shock of the French Revolution—the "normalization" of political change, which now came to be seen as something inevitable, occurring regularly—is an essential component of the cultural history of this world-system. Might it not be useful therefore to think of "ideologies" as one of the ways in which people coped with this new situation? In this sense, an ideology is not itself a Weltanschauung but rather one response among others to the coming of this new Weltanschauung we call modernity.[5]

It is obvious that the first ideological reaction, an almost immediate one, had to come from those who were most profoundly shocked, even repelled, by modernity, by the cult of change and progress, by the persistent rejection of whatever was "old." Thus it was that Burke, Maistre, and Bonald invented the ideology we have come to call "conservatism." A great British conservative, Lord Cecil, in a booklet written in 1912 and intended to be a popular statement of the doctrine of conservatism, specifically emphasized the role of the French Revolution in the birth of the ideology. He asserted that there had always existed a sort of "natural conservatism," but that before 1790 there was nothing "resembling a consciously held body of Conservative doctrine" (1912, 39).

Certainly, in the view of conservatives,

. . . the French Revolution was but the culmination of the historical process of atomization that reached back to the beginning of such doctrines as nominalism, religious dissent, scientific rationalism, and the destruction of those groups, institutions and intellectual certainties which had been basic in the Middle Ages. (Nisbet, 1952, 168–169)

Conservative ideology was thus "reactionary" in the immediate sense that it was a reaction to the coming of modernity, and set itself the objective either (the hard version) of reversing the situation entirely or (the more sophisticated version) of limiting the damage and holding back as long as possible the changes that were coming.

Like all ideologies, conservatism was first and foremost a political program. Conservatives knew full well that they had to hold on to or reconquer state power, that the institutions of the state were the key instruments needed to achieve their goals. When conservative forces returned to power in France in 1815, they baptized this event a "Restoration." But as we know, things did not really go back to the *status quo ante*. Louis XVIII had to concede a "Charter," and when Charles X tried to install a true reaction, he was ousted from power; in his place was put Louis-Philippe, who assumed the more modern title of "King of the French."[6]

The next stage in the story was the construction of liberalism, which defined itself as the opposite of conservatism, on the basis of what might be called a "consciousness of being modern" (Minogue, 1963, 3). Liberalism always situated itself in the center of the political arena, proclaiming itself universalist.[7] Sure of themselves and of the truth of this new worldview of modernity, liberals sought to propagate their views and intrude its logic into all social institutions, thereby ridding the world of the "irrational" left-overs of the past. To do this, they had to fight conservative ideologues, whom they saw as obsessed with fear of "free men,"[8] men liberated from the false idols of tradition. In other words, liberals believed that progress, even though it was inevitable, could not be achieved without some human effort, without a political program. Liberal ideology was thus the belief that, in order for history to follow its natural course, it was necessary to engage in conscious, continual, intelligent reformism, in full awareness that "time was the universal friend, which would inevitably bring greater happiness to ever greater numbers" (Schapiro, 1949, 13).

Socialism was the last of the three ideologies to be formulated. Before 1848, one could hardly yet think of it as constituting a distinctive ideology. The reason was primarily that those who began after 1789 to call themselves "socialists" saw themselves everywhere as the heirs and partisans of the French Revolution, which did not really distinguish them from those who had begun to call themselves "liberals."[9] Even in Great Britain, where the French Revolution was widely denounced, and where "liberals" therefore laid claim to a different historical origin, the "radicals" (who were more or less the future "socialists") seemed to be primarily somewhat more militant liberals.

In fact, what particularly distinguished socialism from liberalism as a political program and therefore as an ideology was the conviction that the achievement of progress needed a big helping hand, without which it would be a very slow process. The heart of the socialist program, in short, consisted in accelerating the course of history. That is why the word "revolution" appealed to them more than "reform," which seemed to imply merely patient, if conscientious, political activity, and was thought to incarnate mostly a wait-and-see attitude.

In sum, three postures toward modernity and the "normalization" of change had evolved: circumscribe the danger as much as possible; achieve the happiness of mankind as rationally as possible; or accelerate the drive for progress by struggling hard against the forces that were strongly resisting it. It was in the period 1815–1848 that the terms *conservatism, liberalism,* and *socialism* began to be used to designate these three postures.

Each posture, it should be noted, located itself in opposition to something else. For conservatives, this was the French Revolution. For liberals, it was conservatism (and the Ancien Régime whose revival they were thought to seek). And for socialists, it was liberalism that they were rejecting. It is this fundamentally critical, negative tone in the very definition of the ideologies that explains why there are so many versions of each ideology. In terms of what they stood *for*, many varied, even contradictory, propositions were put forward in each camp. The true unity of each ideological family lay only in what they were *against*. This is no minor detail, since it was this negativity that succeeded in holding together the three camps for 150 years or so, at least until 1968, a date to whose meaning we shall return.

THE "SUBJECT" OF IDEOLOGY

Since ideologies are in fact political programs for dealing with modernity, each one needs a "subject," or a principal political actor. In the terminology of the modern world, this has been referred to as the question of sovereignty. The French Revolution asserted a crystal clear position on this matter: against the sovereignty of the absolute monarch, it proclaimed the sovereignty of the people.

This new language of the sovereignty of the people is one of the great achievements of modernity. Even if for a century thereafter there were lingering battles against this new idol, the "people," no one has since been able to dethrone it. But the victory was hollow. There may have been universal agreement that the people were sovereign, but from the outset there was no agreement on who the "people" were. Furthermore, on this delicate question, none of the three ideologies has had a clear position, which has not stopped them from refusing to admit the murkiness of their respective stances.

The position that seemingly was least equivocal was that of the liberals. For them, the "people" was the sum of all the "individuals" who are each the ultimate holder of political, economic, and cultural rights. The individual is par excellence the historic "subject" of modernity. As it is impossible to review here the vast literature on individualism, I confine myself to noting the three conundra around which the debate has been waged.

1. All individuals are said to be equal. But can one take such a declaration literally? Obviously not, if one is speaking of the right to make autonomous decisions. No one would dream of authorizing a newborn to take autonomous decisions. But then how old does one have to be to have such a right? The answers have at all times been multiple. But if we agree to leave "children" (however defined) out of the exercise of these rights on the grounds of the immaturity of their judgment, it follows that an autonomous individual is someone whom others believe has the capacity to be autonomous. And thereupon, once the possibility exists of someone else's making a judgment as to whether an individual has the capacity to exercise his/her rights, other categories may be designated as incapable: the senile aged, imbeciles, psychotics, imprisoned criminals, members of dangerous classes, the poor, and so forth. This list is quite obviously not a fantasy. I am not here taking a position on whether each of these groups should or should not be eligible, say, to vote, but I am simply pointing out that there is no self-evident dividing line that separates those who ought to be eligible for the exercise of their rights from those who might legitimately be denied this exercise.

2. Even if we limit the discussion to those persons socially recognized as being "responsible" and therefore legitimately eligible for the full exercise of their rights, it may be that one individual

exercising his/her rights may prevent another from doing the same. What are we to think about this possibility? That it represents the inevitable consequence of social life with which we have to live, or that it involves an assault on the rights of the second person which we must prevent or penalize? A very knotty question that has never received more than a partial and imperfect answer both at the level of political practice and at the level of political philosophy.

3. Even if all individuals who are eligible for the full exercise of rights (the "citizens") never impinge on the rights of other citizens, they still might not all be in agreement about some collective decision. Then what? How can we reconcile the differing positions? This is the great debate concerning political democracy.

One can credit the liberals at least with having debated extensively this question of who the individual is in whom sovereignty is vested. Conservatives and socialists ought in principle to have been debating this issue as well, since each proposed a "subject" quite different from the individual, but their discussion was far less explicit. If the "subject" is not the individual, who, then, is it? It is a bit difficult to discern. See, for example, Edmund Burke in *Reflections on the Revolution in France*:

> **The nature of man is intricate; the objects of society are of the greatest possible complexity; and therefore no simple disposition or direction of power can be suitable either to man's nature, or to the quality of his affairs.**
> **(cited in White, 1950, 28)**

If one didn't know that this was a text attacking French revolutionaries, one might have thought it was intended to denounce absolute monarchs. The matter becomes a bit clearer if we look at something Burke stated ten years earlier in his "Speech on Economic Reform": "Individuals pass like shadows, but the Commonwealth is fixed and stable" (cited by Lukes, 1973, 3).

Bonald's approach is quite different, because he insists on the crucial role of the Church. His view shares, however, one element common to all the varieties of conservative ideology—the importance they confer on social groups such as the family, corporations, the Church, the traditional "orders"—which become for them the "subjects" that have the right to act politically. In other words, conservatives gave priority to all those groups that might be considered "traditional" (and thus incarnating continuity) but rejected identifying conservatism with any "totality" as a political actor. What has never in fact been clear in conservative thought is how one can decide which are the groups that incarnate continuity. After all, there have always been arguments around contending royal lineages.[10]

For Bonald, the great error of Rousseau and Montesquieu had been precisely to "imagine . . . a pure state of nature antecedent to society . . . ." Quite the contrary, "the true nature of society . . . is what society, public society, is at present . . ." (1988 [1802], 87). But this definition was a trap for its author, because it so legitimated the present that it virtually forbade a "restoration." But precise logic has never been the forte or main interest of conservative polemics. Rather, they were concerned about issuing warnings about the likely behavior of a majority that was created by adding up individual votes. Their historical subject was a far less active one than that of the liberals. In their eyes, good decisions were taken slowly and rarely, and such decisions had largely already been taken.

If conservatives refused to give priority to the individual as historical subject in favor of small, so-called traditional groups, socialists refused to give the individual priority in favor of that large group which is the whole of the people. Analyzing socialist thought in its early period, G. D. H. Cole remarked:

> The "socialists" were those who, in opposition to the prevailing stress on the claims of the individual, emphasised the social element in human relations and sought to bring the social question to the front in the great debate about the rights of man let loose on the world by the French Revolution and by the accompanying revolution in the economic field. (1953, 2)

But if it is difficult to know which individuals constitute the problem, and even more difficult to know which "groups" constitute the "people," the most difficult thing of all is to know how to define the general will of the whole people. How could one know what it is? And to begin with, whose views should we take into account—those of the citizens, those of the persons resident in the country? Why limit the people in this way? Why not take into account the views of all humanity? By what logic can a restriction be justified? What is the relationship in actual practice between the general will and the will of all? In this set of knotty questions we find the source of all the difficulties encountered by socialist movements once they came to power.

In short, what the three ideologies offered us was not a response to the question, Who is the appropriate historical subject? but simply three starting points in the quest for who incarnates the sovereignty of the people: the so-called free individual, for the liberals; the so-called traditional groups, for the conservatives; the entire membership of "society," for the socialists.

THE IDEOLOGIES AND THE STATE

The people as "subject" has as its primary "object" the state. It is within the state that the people exercise their will, that they are sovereign. Since the nineteenth century, however, we have also been told that the people form a "society." How might we reconcile state and society, which form the great intellectual antinomy of modernity?

The most astonishing thing is that when we look at the discourses of the three ideologies in this regard, they all seem to take the side of society against the state. Their arguments are familiar. For staunch liberals, it was crucial to keep the state out of economic life and to reduce its role in general to a minimum: "*Laissez-faire* is the nightwatchman doctrine of state" (Watson, 1973, 68). For conservatives the terrifying aspect of the French Revolution was not only its individualism but also, and particularly, its statism. The state only becomes tyrannical when it questions the role of the intermediate groups who command the primary loyalty of people—the family, the Church, the corporation.[11] And we are familiar with the famous characterization by Marx and Engels in the *Communist Manifesto*:

> The bourgeoisie has at last, since the establishment of modern industry and of the world market, conquered for itself, in the modern representative state, exclusive political sway. The executive of the modern state is but a committee for managing the common affairs of the whole bourgeoisie. (1973 [1848], 69)

These negatives views of the state did not stop each of the three ideologies from complaining that this state, which was the object of their critique, was out of their control and said to be in the hands of their ideological opponents. In point of fact, each of the three ideologies turned out to be in great need of the services of the state in order to promote its own program. Let us not forget that an ideology is first and foremost a political strategy. Socialists have long been under attack for what has been said to be their incoherence; most of them, despite their antistatist rhetoric, have always striven in the short run to increase state activity. Anarchism has always been a very minority viewpoint among socialists.

But surely conservatives were more seriously antistate? Haven't they been regularly opposed to achieving reforms by state action? Not at all, in reality. For we must take into account the question of the "decline of values" that conservatives see as one of the central consequences of modernity. To struggle against the current decadence of society, to restore society as it was before, they have needed the state. What has been said of one of the great English conservatives of the 1840s, Sir Robert Peel—"he believed that a constitution issuing in a strong executive was essential to the anarchic age in which he lived" (Gash, 1951, 52)—in fact appplies more generally.

Note the way in which Halévy explains the evolution of the conservative position vis-à-vis the state during the "Tory reaction" in England at the beginning of the nineteenth century:

> In 1688 and in the years following, the King regarded himself, and was regarded by public opinion, as the

> Sovereign. It was always to be feared that he would make
> his sovereignty absolute, and the independence of his
> authority enjoyed by all the powers of the State constituted
> a deliberate limitation of the prerogative, a system of con-
> stitutional guarantees against royal despotism. At the
> opening of the nineteenth century it was the people who in
> America, in France, in England even, had asserted, or were
> about to assert, the claim to be supreme; it was therefore
> against the people that the three powers now maintained
> their independence. It was no longer the Whigs, it was the
> Tories who supported institutions whose significance had
> changed, while their form remained the same. And now the
> King presided over the league formed by the three powers
> for the defence of their autonomy against the new claimant
> for sovereignty. (1949, 42–43)

The analysis is limpid. Conservatives were always ready to
strengthen the state structure to the degree necessary to control
popular forces pushing for change. This was in fact implicit in what
was stated by Lord Cecil in 1912: "As long as State action does
not involve what is unjust or oppressive, it cannot be said that the
principles of Conservatism are hostile to it" (1912, 192).

Well, at least the liberals—champions of individual freedom
and of the free market—remained hostile to the state? Not at all!
From the outset, liberals were caught in a fundamental contradiction. As defenders of the individual and his rights vis-à-vis the
state, they were pushed in the direction of universal suffrage, the
only guarantee of a democratic state. But thereupon, the state
became the principal agent of all reforms intended to liberate the
individual from the social constraints inherited from the past. This
in turn led the liberals to the idea of putting positive law at the
service of utilitarian objectives.

Once again, Halévy pointed clearly to the consequences:

> The "utilitarian" philosophy was not solely, nor even
> perhaps fundamentally, a liberal system; it was at the same
> time a doctrine of authority which looked to the deliberate

and in a sense scientific interference of Government to produce a harmony of interests. As his ideas developed, Bentham, who as a young man had been an advocate of "enlightened despotism," was converted to democracy. But he had reached that position by what we may call a long jump, which carried him at a bound over a number of political doctrines at which he might have been expected to halt —aristocracy, a mixed constitution, the balance of powers, and the doctrine that the statesman's aim should be to free the individual by weakening the authority of the Government and as far as possible dividing its powers. In Bentham's view, when the authority of the state had been reconciled by a universal or at least a very wide suffrage with the interests of the majority there was no further reason to hold it suspect, it became an unmixed blessing.

And thereupon, the Conservatives

were now the upholders of the genuine Liberal tradition, the old system of aristocratic self-government with its unpaid officials against a new system of bureaucratic despotism administered by salaried officials. (Halévy, 1950, 100, 99)

You may think that Benthamism was in fact a deviation from liberalism, whose optimal expression is to be found in the classical economists, the theoreticians of laissez-faire. Let us then remember that when the first Factory Acts were passed in Great Britain, all the leading classical economists of the time supported the legislation, a phenomenon spelled out (and approved) by none other than Alfred Marshall (1921, 763–764). Since that time, the great bureaucratic state has never stopped growing, and its expansion has been sponsored by successive liberal governments. When Hobhouse wrote his book on liberalism as an answer to that of Lord Cecil on conservatism, he justified this expansion in this way: "The function of State coercion is to overcome individual coercion, and, of course, coercion exercised by any association of individuals within the State" (1911, 146).

No doubt the justifications each ideology invoked to explain its somewhat embarrassing statism were different. For socialists, the state implemented the general will. For conservatives, the state protected traditional rights against the general will. For liberals, the state created the conditions permitting individual rights to flourish. But in each case, the bottom line was that the state was being strengthened in relation to society, while the rhetoric called for doing exactly the opposite.

HOW MANY IDEOLOGIES?

All this muddle and intellectual confusion involved in the theme of the proper relation of state and society permit us to understand why it is that we have never been entirely sure how many distinct ideologies came into existence in the nineteenth century. Three? Two? Only one? I have just reviewed the traditional arguments that claim there were three. Let us now look at how one can reduce the three to two.

In the period from the French Revolution to the revolutions of 1848, it seems clear that for contemporaries the "only clear cleavage" was between those who accepted progress as inevitable and desirable, and thus "were globally favorable" to the French Revolution, and, on the other hand, the Counter-Revolution, which took its stand against this disruption of values, considering it as profoundly wrong (Agulhon, 1992, 7). Thus the political struggle was between liberals and conservatives, while those who called themselves radicals or Jacobins or republicans or socialists were regarded as simply a more militant variety of liberals. In *The Village Cure*, Balzac has a bishop exclaim:

We are compelled to perform miracles in a manufactory town where the spirit of sedition against religious and monarchical doctrines has put forth deep roots, where the idea of close scrutiny, born of Protestantism and today known as Liberalism, with liberty to adopt another name tomorrow, extends to everything. (1898, 103)

Tudesq reminds us that in 1840 a Legitimist newspaper,

l'Orléanais, denounced another newspaper, *Le Journal de Loiret*, as a "liberal, Protestant, Saint-Simonian, Lamennaisian paper" (1964, 125–126). This was not completely wild since, as Simon notes: "The Idea of Progress, in fact, constituted the core and central inspiration of Saint-Simon's entire philosophy of thought" (1956, 330; cf. Manning, 1976, 83–84).

Furthermore, this liberal-socialist alliance has roots in liberal and egalitarian thought of the eighteenth century, in the struggle against absolute monarchy (see Meyssonier, 1989, 137–156). It continued to be nourished in the nineteenth century by the ever increasing interest of both ideologies in productivity, which each saw as the basic requirement for a social policy in the modern state.[12]

With the rise of utilitarianism, it might have seemed that the alliance might become a marriage. The conservatives did not fail to argue this:

> When the Tories wished to discredit Utilitarianism, they denounced it as an unpatriotic philosophy, inspired by foreign ideas, and especially by French ideas. Were not the political principles of the Benthamites the democratic principles of the Jacobins? Did they not derive their ethics and their jurisprudence from Helvétius and Beccaria, their psychology from Condillac, their philosophy of history and their political economy from Condorcet and Jean-Baptiste Say? Were they not irreligious Voltairians? Had not Bentham composed in French and published at Paris his *Traités de Législation*? But the Utilitarians could reply with truth that all these so-called French ideas, of whose importation they were accused, were in reality English ideas which had found a temporary home abroad. (1949, 583)

Once again, the conservative view was not incorrect. Brebner speaks with sympathy of the "collectivist" side of Bentham, concluding, "What were the Fabians but latter-day Benthamites?" And he adds that John Stuart Mill was already in 1830 "what might be called a liberal socialist" (1948, 66).

On the other hand, after 1830 a clear distinction begins to

emerge between liberals and socialists, and after 1848, it becomes quite deep. At the same time, 1848 marks the beginning of a reconciliation between liberals and conservatives. Hobsbawm thinks that the great consequence of 1830 was to make mass politics possible, by allowing the political triumph in France, England, and especially Belgium (but even partially in Switzerland, Spain, and Portugal) of a "moderate" liberalism, which consequently "split moderates from radicals" (1962, 117). Cantimori, analyzing the issue from an Italian perspective, thinks that the question of a divorce was open until 1848. Until then, he notes, "the liberal movement . . . had rejected no path: neither a call for insurrection nor reformist political action" (1948, 288). It was only after 1848 that a divorce between these two tactics was consummated.

What is crucial to note is that, after 1848, socialists stopped referring to Saint-Simon. The socialist movement began to organize itself around Marxist ideas. The plaint was no longer merely poverty, susceptible to repair by reform, but the dehumanization caused by capitalism, whose solution required overturning it completely (see Kolakowski, 1978, 222).

At this very time, conservatives began to be conscious of the utility of reformism for conservative objectives. Sir Robert Peel, immediately following the Reform Act of 1832, issued an electoral manifesto, the Tamworth Manifesto, which became celebrated as a doctrinal statement. It was considered by contemporaries as "almost revolutionary" not merely because the manifesto announced the acceptance of the Reform Act as "a final and irrevocable settlement of a great constitutional question" but because this position was announced to the people rather than to Parliament, which caused a great "sensation" at the time (Halévy, 1950, 178).[13]

In the process, conservatives noted their convergence with liberals on the importance of protecting property, even though what interested them about property was primarily the fact that it represented continuity and thus served as the foundation for family life, the Church, and other social solidarities (see Nisbet, 1966, 26). But beyond this philosophical convergence, there was the concrete menace of real revolution, a fear they shared, as Lord

Cecil noted: "For it is an indispensable part of the effective resistance to Jacobinism that there should be moderate reform on conservative lines" (1912, 64).

Finally, we should not entirely neglect the third possible reduction of three to two: conservatives and socialists joining hands in opposition to liberals, even if this seems the least likely theoretically. The "conservative" character of Saint-Simonian socialism, its roots in Bonaldian ideas, has often been remarked upon (see Manuel, 1956, 320; Iggers, 1958, 99). The two camps could come together around their anti-individualist reflex. Equally, a liberal like von Hayek denounced the "socialist" character of the conservative Carlyle's thought. This time, it was the "social" side of conservative thought that was in question. Lord Cecil did not in fact hesitate to declare this affinity openly:

> It is often assumed that Conservatism and Socialism are directly opposed. But this is not completely true. Modern Conservatism inherits the traditions of Toryism which are favourable to the activities and the authority of the State. Indeed Mr. Herbert Spencer attacked Socialism as being in fact the revival of Toryism . . ." (1912, 169)

The consequence of liberal-socialist alliances was the emergence of a sort of socialist liberalism. The consequence of liberal-conservative alliances was a sort of conservative liberalism. In short, we ended up with two varieties of liberalism. The conservative-socialist alliances, more improbable, were originally merely passing tactics. But one might wonder whether one might not think of the various "totalitarianisms" of the twentieth century as a more lasting form of this alliance, in the sense that they instituted a form of traditionalism that was both populist and social. If so, these totalitarianisms were yet another way in which liberalism remained center stage, as the antithesis of a Manichean drama. Behind this facade of intense opposition to liberalism, one finds as a core component of the demands of all these regimes the same faith in progress via productivity that has been the gospel of the liberals. In this way we might conclude that even socialist conservatism (or conservative socialism) was, in a way, a variant of liberalism, its diabolical form. In which case, would it not be correct to conclude that since 1789 there has been only one true ideology, liberalism, which has displayed its colors in three major versions?

Of course such a statement has to be spelled out in historical terms. The period 1789–1848 stands out as a great ideological struggle between a conservatism that failed in the end to achieve a finished form and a liberalism in search of cultural hegemony. The period 1848–1914 (or 1917) stands out as a period in which liberalism dominated the scene without serious opposition, while Marxism was trying to constitute a socialist ideology as an independent pole, but not being entirely able to succeed. One might then argue (and this assertion would be the most controversial) that the period 1917–1968 (or 1989) represented the apotheosis of liberalism at the world level. In this view, although Leninism was making the claim that it was an ideology violently opposed to liberalism, it was actually being one of its avatars.[14]

BEYOND IDEOLOGIES?

Is it now at last possible to go beyond ideologies, that is, to go beyond the dominant liberal ideology? The question has been explicitly put, and repeatedly, since the world revolution of 1968. For what were the revolutionaries of 1968 attacking if not liberalism as an ideology, as that ideology among the three which served as the ideology of the capitalist world-economy?

Many of those engaged in the confrontations in 1968 no doubt clothed their demands in a Maoist discourse, or that of some other variant of Marxism. But that did not stop them from putting the Marxists into the same liberal pot, rejecting both official Soviet Marxism and the great Communist parties of the industrialized world. And when, in the period after 1968, the most "conservative" elements sought to formulate a response to the revolutionaries of 1968, they gave themselves the name of "neoliberals."

Recently, *Publisher's Weekly,* reviewing a book by Kolakowski, summarized his thoughts in the following way: "'Conservatism,' 'liberalism' and 'socialism' are no longer mutually exclusive political positions" (*New York Review of Books*, March 7, 1991,

20: advertisement). But if our analysis is correct, we may wonder if there ever was a moment when these ideologies were mutually exclusive. What is new is not that confusion reigns concerning the meaning and validity of liberalism, the great hegemonic ideology of the capitalist world-economy: This has always been the case. What is new is that for the first time in its history as a dominant ideology since 1848, liberalism, which is at heart nothing but modernity, has been once again fundamentally questioned. What we should conclude from this will go beyond what we can deal with here. I believe, however, that liberalism as an effective political project has had its day, and that it is in the process of collapsing under the impact of the structural crisis of the capitalist world-economy.

This may not be the end of all ideology. But now that it is no longer so clear that political change is necessary, inevitable, and therefore normal, one no longer needs to have an ideology to deal with the consequences of such a belief. We are entering a period of transition, which may go on for some fifty years, and which can be described as a major "bifurcation" (*vide* Prigogine) whose outcome is uncertain. We cannot predict the worldview(s) of the system(s) that will emerge from the ruins of our present one. We cannot predict what ideologies will be born or how many there will be, if any.

BIBLIOGRAPHY

AGULHON, MAURICE. 1992. *1848, ou l'apprentissage de la République, 1848–1852*, nouv. éd. révisée et complétée. Paris: Ed. du Seuil.

BALZAC, HONORÉ DE. 1898. *The village cure*. Philadephia: George Barrie and Sons.

BASTID, PAUL. 1953. "La théorie juridique des Chartes." *Revue internationale d'histoire politique et constitutionelle*. n.s. 3:63–75.

BONALD, LOUIS DE. 1988 (1802). *Législation primitive considérée par la raison*. Paris: Ed. Jean-Michel Place.

BREBNER, J. BARTLETT. 1948. "Laissez-faire and state intervention in nineteenth-century Britain" *The Tasks of Economic History* (a supplemental issue of the *Journal of Economic History*). 8:59–73.

BRUNOT, FERDINAND. 1937. *Histoire de la langue française des origines à 1900*, IX: *La Révolution et l'Empire*, 2e Partie: *Les événements, les institutions et la langue*. Paris: Lib. Armand Colin.

CANTIMORI, DELIO. 1948. "1848 en Italie." In F. Fejtö, dir., *Le printemps des peuples: 1848 dans le monde*. Paris: Ed. du Minuit. I: 255–318.

CECIL, LORD HUGH. 1912. *Conservatism*. London: Williams & Northgage.

COLE, G. D. H. 1953. *A history of socialist thought*. Vol. 1. *Socialist thought: The forerunners, 1789–1850*. New York: St. Martin's Press.

CONDLIFFE, J. B. 1951. *The commerce of nations*. London: George Allen & Unwin.

GASH, NORMAN. 1951. "Peel and the party system, 1830–50." *Transactions of the Royal Historical Society*, 5th ser.. I: 47–70.

HALÉVY, ELIE. 1949. *A history of the English people in the nineteenth century*. 2nd rev. ed. Vol 2. *England in 1815*. London: Ernest Benn.

———. 1950. *A history of the English people in the nineteenth century*, 2nd rev. ed. Vol. 3. *The Triumph of Reform, 1830–1841*. London: Ernest Benn.

HAYEK, FREDERICK A. VON. 1952. *The counter-revolution of science: Studies on the abuse of reason*. Glencoe, IL: Free Press.

HOBHOUSE, L. T. 1911. *Liberalism*. London: Oxford Univ. Press.

HOBSBAWM, ERIC J. 1962. *The age of revolution, 1789–1848*. New York: World Publishing, A Mentor Book.

IGGERS, GEORG G. 1958. *The cult of authority: The political philosophy of the Saint-Simonians. A chapter in the intellectual history of totalitarianism*. The Hague: Martinus Nijhoff.

KOLAKOWSKI, LESZEK. 1978. *Main currents of Marxism: Its rise, growth, and dissolution*. 3 vols. Oxford: Clarendon Press.

LABROUSSE, ERNEST. 1949. "1848–1830–1789: Comment naissent les révolutions." In *Actes du Congrès historique du Centenaire de la Révolution de 1848*. Paris: Presses Univ. de France. 1–20.

LUKES, STEVEN. 1973. *Individualism*. Oxford: Basil Blackwell.

MANNING, D. J. 1976. *Liberalism*. London: J. M. Dent & Sons.

MANUEL, FRANK E. 1956. *The new world of Henri Saint-Simon*. Cambridge: Harvard Univ. Press.

MARSHALL, ALFRED. 1921. *Industry and trade*. London: Macmillan.

MARX, KARL, AND FREDERICK ENGELS. 1973 (1848). *Manifesto of the Communist Party*. In Karl Marx, *The revolutions of 1848: political writings*. Vol. I. Harmondsworth, UK: Penguin. 62–98.

MASON, E. S. 1931. "Saint-Simonism and the rationalisation of industry." *Quarterly Journal of Economics*. 45:640–683.

MEYSSONIER, SIMONE. 1989. *La balance et l'horloge. La genèse de la pensée libérale en France au XVIIIe siècle*. Montreuil: Ed. de la Passion.

MINOGUE, K. R. 1963. *The liberal mind*. London: Methuen.

NISBET, ROBERT A. 1944. "De Bonald and the concept of the concept of the social group." *Journal of the History of Ideas*. 5:315–31.

———. 1952. "Conservatism and sociology." *American Journal of Sociology*. 58:167–75.

———. 1956. *The sociological tradition*. New York: Basic Books.

PLAMENATZ, JOHN. 1952. *The revolutionary movement in France, 1815–1870*. London: Longman, Green.

SCHAPIRO, J. SALWYN. 1949. *Liberalism and the challenge of fascism: Social forces in England and France (1815–1870)*. New York: McGraw-Hill.

SIMON, WALTER M. 1956. "History for utopia: Saint-Simon and the idea of progress." *Journal of the History of Ideas*. 17:311–331.

TUDESQ, ANDRÉ-JEAN. 1964. *Les grands notables en France (1840–1849): Etude historique d'une psychologie sociale*. 2 vols. Paris: Presses Univ. de France.

WALLERSTEIN, IMMANUEL. 1991. "The French revolution as a world-historical event." In *Unthinking social science: The limits of nineteenth-century paradigms*. Cambridge: Polity Press. 7–22.

WATSON, GEORGE. 1973. *The English ideology: Studies in the language of Victorian politics*. London: Allan Lane.

WHITE, R. J., ed. 1950. Introduction to *The conservative tradition*. London: Nicholas Kaye. 1–24.

CHAPTER FIVE

LIBERALISM AND THE LEGITIMATION OF NATION-STATES:
AN HISTORICAL INTERPRETATION

The ideological cement of the capitalist world-economy from 1789 to 1989 was liberalism (along with its correlative, albeit not derived, partner, scientism). The dates are quite precise. The French Revolution marks the entry onto the world political scene of liberalism as a significant ideological option. The fall of the Communisms in 1989 marks its exit.

The plausibility of these statements hinges, of course, on what we believe to be the essence of liberalism. Dictionaries are of little help in deciding this, and the library of books on liberalism not much more, for *liberalism* has been a rubber term. It is not merely that it has had many definitions; this is normal for any important political concept. It is that these definitions have varied so extensively that the term has been given directly opposite meanings. To take only the most current and obvious of examples, while Presidents Reagan and Bush fulminated against liberalism in their political diatribes in the United States, they were quite frequently referred to in European writings as "neoliberals."

To be sure, some would say that this linguistic reversal comes from the fact that we ought to regard political liberalism and economic liberalism as two separate intellectual positions, or even two separate streams of thought. How is it, then, that we have used the same word for both? And what are we to do with the category of cultural liberalism? Are countercultural hippies liberals? Are libertarians liberals? One could go on; there would be no point. This explanation of linguistic confusion is far too easy an out, since in fact liberalism has always expressed itself in all arenas of human activity. If the term liberalism is to be intelligently used, we must locate its core.

Liberalism must be situated in its historical context, and that context, I contend, is bounded by the dates 1789 to 1989. I am interested in liberalism as an ideology and use ideology to mean a comprehensive, long-term political agenda intended to mobilize large numbers of people. In this sense, as I have argued previously,[15] ideologies were neither needed nor possible before the transformation of the geoculture of the capitalist world-economy that was brought about by the French Revolution and its Napoleonic aftermath.

Prior to the French Revolution, the dominant Weltanschauung of the capitalist world-economy, as of other historical systems, was the normality of political stability. Sovereignty resided in the ruler, and the ruler's right to govern derived from some set of regulations concerning the acquisition of power, usually inheritance. Rulers were of course frequently challenged and even overthrown, but the replacement rulers always preached the same belief in the normality of stability. Political change was exceptional, to be justified exceptionally; when it occurred, it was not thought to set a precedent for further change.

The upheaval launched by the French Revolution—an upheaval felt all over Europe and beyond—transformed this mentality. The people had become the sovereign. All the efforts of the "reactionaries" from 1815 to 1848 would make little dent on the new mentalities. After 1848, no one would even seriously try again,[16] at least until today. Indeed, change—all kinds of change, including political change—had become "normal." It is precisely because this worldview took hold so rapidly that ideologies arose. They were the political agendas to be pursued *in the light of the normality of political change* and the correlative belief in popular sovereignty.

It was logical that conservatism would be the first response. Two of the classic works that are today considered progenitors of conservative thought, *Considérations sur la France* (1789) by Joseph de Maistre, and *Reflections on the Revolution in France* (1790) by Edmund Burke, were written in the very heat of the first days of the revolution. In general, opponents of the French Revolution argued that only social ills could result from legitimating the normality of change. Yet they soon realized that an intransigent position had become socially impossible. During the period 1789 to 1848, there was an evolution of the conservative position from one of total rejection of the new Weltanschauung to what might be called the dominant conservative ideology of the past 150 years: "normal" change ought to be as slow as possible and ought to be encouraged only when carefully justified as necessary to prevent the greater breakdown of social order.

Liberalism was the ideological response to conservatism. The very term *liberal* (in noun form), as we know, emerged only in the first decade of the nineteenth century. Generally speaking, in the period before 1848, there was a blurred field of persons who overtly (or covertly, in the case of the English) supported the ideals of the French Revolution. The field included persons with such diverse labels as republicans, radicals, Jacobins, social reformers, socialists, and liberals.[17]

In the world revolution of 1848, there were really only two camps, the Party of Order and the Party of Movement, representing, respectively, conservative and liberal ideology, or, if one wishes to use another terminology with origins in the French Revolution, the Right and the Left. It was only after 1848 that socialism emerged as a truly distinctive ideology different from, and opposed to, liberalism. The world-system then entered into the period of the trimodal ideological spectrum with which we are all familiar. Liberalism came to represent the center of the political hemicycle and thus came into the position of occupying center stage as well (to shift metaphors slightly, but deliberately).

The essential distinction between liberalism and socialism, at the moment of disjuncture between the two streams, was not over the desirability or even the inevitability of change (or progress). As a matter of fact, this view of change formed their common trunk. The difference was, rather, ideological; that is, the difference was one of political agenda. Liberals believed that the course of social amelioration was, or ought to be, a steady one, based on both a rational assessment made by specialists of existing problems and a continuing conscious attempt by political leaders, in the light of that assessment, to introduce intelligent social reforms. The agenda of the socialists was fueled by skepticism over whether reformists could accomplish significant change through intelligent good will and largely on their own. Socialists wished to go further faster, and argued that without considerable popular pressure the process would not result in progress. Progress was inevitable only because popular pressure was inevitable. The specialists by themselves were impotent.

The world revolution of 1848 was a turning point in the political strategies of all three ideological currents. From the failures of 1848 the socialists learned that it was doubtful that anything much could be accomplished by relying either on spontaneous political uprising or communication withdrawal. State structures were too strong, and repression was too easy and too efficacious. It was only after 1848 that socialists began seriously to organize parties, trade unions, and workers' organizations in general, with an eye on long-term political conquest of the state structures. In this post-1848 period the two-stage socialist strategy was born. This strategy was common to the two main wings of the socialist movement, the Second International Social-Democrats and the Third International Communists, that would later emerge. The two stages were quite simple: first, obtain state power; second, use the state power to transform the society (or arrive at socialism).

The conservatives also learned a lesson from 1848. Workers' insurrections had become a real political possibility, and, while they were put down with comparative ease in 1848, the future was more cloudy. Furthermore, conservatives noticed that social revolutions and nationalist revolutions, while not at all the same thing, might develop a dangerous tendency to overlap and to reinforce each other on the world-systemic stage. It followed that something concrete had to be done to avert such uprisings at a point in time earlier than the uprisings themselves. This something might be called the construction of more integrated national societies.

If one looks carefully at these new socialist and conservative strategies, each in effect was coming closer to the liberal notion of ongoing, managed, rational normal change. What was liberal strategy at this time? The liberals were groping with two main ideas as the keys to managed, rational, normal change. The principal problem, it was plain for everyone to see, was that the industrialization of Western Europe and North America involved a necessary process of urbanization and long-term transformation of previously rural populations into an urban proletariat.[18] The socialists proposed to organize this proletariat, and it was clear already from what had happened in the 1830s and 1840s that they were organizable.

The solution that liberalism could offer to this danger to social order, and therefore to rational social development, was to make concessions to the working classes: some participation in political power, and some share of the surplus value. The problem, however, was how to give the working classes enough to make them hesitate to be disruptive, but not so much as to threaten seriously the ceaseless and expanding accumulation of capital that was the raison d'être of the capitalist world-economy and the prime consideration of the ruling strata.

What one can say about Liberals between 1848 and 1914— capital "L" Liberals being the political incarnation of small "l" liberalism as an ideology—is that they dithered for all that time, never quite sure how daring to be, never quite knowing how many concessions were too much, or how few were too little. The political result of the dithering was that the political ball was taken away from capital "L" Liberals as part of the process in which small "l" liberalism triumphed definitely as the dominant ideology of the world-system.[19]

What occurred from 1848 to 1914 was doubly curious. First, the practitioners of all three ideologies turned from a theoretical antistate position to one of seeking to strengthen and reinforce in practice the state structures in multiple ways. Second, the liberal strategy was in fact put into effect by the combined effort of conservatives and socialists.

The shift from ruler to people as the locus of theoretical sovereignty had opened the question of whether any particular state reflected the people's will. This was the existential basis of the classic antinomy—state versus society—that so dominated nineteenth-century political theory. There could be no doubt that the logic of popular sovereignty meant that one was obliged to favor society over state in any conflict. Society and the people's will were in effect synonymous. It is indeed a measure of the degree to which popular sovereignty was (implicitly and explicitly) accepted by all three ideological streams that they all claimed to defend primarily the interests of society, and invoked, therefore, hostility toward the state.

Of course, the three schools of thought offered different explanations for hostility to the state. For conservatives, the state seemed to be an actor of the present that, if it took any innovative positions, would be going against the traditional bastions of society and social order—the family, the community, the Church, and, of course, the monarchy. The presence of the monarchy on this list was itself a tacit admission of the dominance of the concept of popular sovereignty; if a king were truly sovereign, he would be able to legislate in the present. Indeed, the opposition of the Legitimists to Louis XVIII, not to speak of their opposition to Louis-Philippe, was based precisely on this premise.[20] The Legitimists saw these two kings, by virtue of their acceptance of the concept of the Charter, as having yielded to the thesis that the state could legislate against tradition. Hence, in the name of the · traditional authority of the king, they opposed the contemporary real authority of the king and the state.

The theoretical hostility of liberalism to the state is so fundamental that most writers regard the defining characteristic of liberalism to be the night-watchman doctrine of the state. The presumed *mot d'ordre* is laissez-faire. There is no doubt that liberal ideologists and politicians have spoken regularly and frequently on the importance of removing the state's hand from the market, and quite often, but perhaps less frequently, of keeping the state from impinging upon decision making in the social arena. The reification of the individual, and the view that the sovereign people is composed of individuals with "inalienable rights," constitute the foundation of this deep suspicion of the state.

Finally, we know that socialists of all persuasions found their justification in the needs and will of society, against what they considered the oppressive (and class-biased) actions of the state. Yet, it is equally crucial to note, all three ideologies pushed *in practice* toward that real increase in state power and efficacy in decision making and intrusiveness that has been the historical trajectory of the modern world-system in the nineteenth and twentieth centuries.

It is commonplace that socialist ideology in practice led to the reinforcement of state structures. The *Communist Manifesto* is quite specific in this regard:

> We have seen . . . that the first step in the revolution by the working class is to raise the proletariat to the position of ruling class, to establish democracy.

> The proletariat will use its political supremacy to wrest, by degrees, all capital from the bourgeoisie, to centralize all instruments of production in the hands of the state, i.e., of the proletariat organised as the ruling class, and to increase the total of productive force as rapidly as possible.

Furthermore, on the road to the "first step," the *Manifesto* adds: "The Communists fight for the attainment of the immediate aims, for the enforcement of the momentary interests of the working class." This latter intention translated itself in the actions not only of Marxist social-democratic parties but also of non-Marxist socialists (such as the Labour Party): a constant pressure for state intervention to regulate conditions of the workplace, the establishment by the state of income transfer structures, and both the legalization and the legitimation by the state of working-class organizational activities.

Were conservatives less likely to support in practice an expansion of the role of the state? We may leave aside the historic link of conservative political forces with landed proprietors and their consequent defense of varieties of state protection of agrarian interests, which had been inherited from earlier times. In their response to the new industrialism and its social consequences, did conservatives feel the state should play no role in counteracting what they saw as social disintegration? Of course not. Lord Cecil expressed with prudence the heart of the conservative ideology toward the state: "[A]s long as State action does not involve what is injust or oppressive, it cannot be said that the principles of Conservatism are hostile to it."[21] The conservative problem was very simple. To get society nearer to the social order they found preferable, especially given the post-1789 rapid evolution of societal structures, they needed the intervention of the state.[22]

As for liberals, have they ever taken the night-watchman state concept seriously, as opposed to rhetorically? Have they not from the beginning instead viewed the state as the optimal instrument of rationality? Was this not the essence of Jeremy Bentham's philosophic radicalism?[23] Did John Stuart Mill, epitome of liberal thought, argue differently? In Great Britain, at the very moment that the liberals sought to get the state out of agricultural protectionism they simultaneously sought to get the state into factory legislation. It is L. T. Hobhouse who, in my view, summarized best the actual practice of liberals concerning the state:

> It appears then that the true distinction is not between self-regulating and other-regulating actions, but between coercive and noncoercive actions. The function of State coercion is to overcome individual coercion, and, of course, coercion exercised by any association of individuals within the State.[24]

This convergence of the three ideologies on the reinforcement of state structures is what eliminated a separate political role for capital "L" Liberals. In the second half of the nineteenth century, the conservatives became liberal-conservatives and the socialists became liberal-socialists. What place was there, then, for liberal-liberals?

The evolving political reality is quite visible not merely in the evolution of the rhetoric but also in the political process itself. The liberal objective of increasing political participation of the working classes pointed toward universal suffrage. The liberal objective of allowing workers' participation in the distribution of surplus value pointed toward the welfare state. Yet the greatest breakthroughs in these two fields—which served as models for all of Europe—were the doing of two "enlightened Conservatives,"

Disraeli and Bismarck. It was they who were willing to make the great leap that the Liberals never dared to make.

No doubt, the enlightened conservatives made the leap under socialist pressure. The working classes demanded the suffrage, and they demanded the benefits we today call the welfare state. Had they never demanded these changes, it is unlikely the conservatives would have conceded them. To tame the working classes, the enlightened conservatives pushed for timely concessions, since this would integrate and deradicalize the proletariat. It is an historic irony that socialist tactics fed into this correct perception of the enlightened conservatives.

A final liberal theme was implemented by their rivals. The liberals were the first to attempt to realize popular sovereignty via the building of a national spirit. Conservatives and socialists were in theory more recalcitrant. The nation was not a traditional conservative communal category, and the socialists affected an anti-nationalist internationalism. In theory, only the liberals saw the nation as the appropriate summation of individual wills.

Yet, as the nineteenth century progressed, it was the conservatives who seized the banners of patriotism and imperialism. It was the socialists, moreover, who first and most effectively integrated the "outlying" zones into their respective nation-states. Witness the strength of the British Labour Party in Wales and Scotland, the strength of French socialists in Occitania, and the strength of Italian socialists in the south. The nationalism of the socialist parties was finally confessed and confirmed by their rallying to the flags in August 1914. The European working classes rewarded with their loyalty the liberal states that had made concessions to them. They legitimated their states.

As Schapiro says, "when the nineteenth century ended historically in 1914, liberalism had become the accepted way of political life in Europe."[25] But Liberal parties were dying out. The core countries of the capitalist world-economy were all moving toward a de facto ideological split: on the one side were liberal-conservatives and on the other liberal-socialists. This split was usually reflected, more or less directly, in the party structures.

The liberal agenda had achieved a great success. The working classes of the core countries had indeed been integrated into the ongoing national political process in such a way that they posed no threat to the functioning of the capitalist world-economy. Of course this refers only to the working classes of the core countries. The First World War reopened the whole question on a world scale, where the whole scenario would be repeated.

On a world scale, conservatives were back to their pre-1848 position. Imperial rule of the lands of others was considered beneficent for the natives and desirable both for world society and for the particular metropole. Furthermore, there was no reason why it should ever end. Empire in the conservative vision was eternal, at least for barbarous zones. Should there be any doubt about this, we need merely to refer to the concept of class-C mandates in the League of Nations structure.

Socialist ideology as antiliberalism was renewed by the Russian Revolution and the construction of Marxism-Leninism as a new political agenda. The heart of Leninism was the denunciation of other social-democrats for having become liberal-socialists, and hence for no longer being antisystemic. This perception, as we have argued, was quite correct. Leninism was therefore basically a call for the return to the original socialist agenda—going further faster by using popular pressure in the process of inevitable social change. This was translated concretely into a set of revolutionary tactics espoused by the Third International and incarnated by the "Twenty-One Demands."

Liberalism, having largely lost its political function as an autonomous political grouping on the national scene of the core countries, renewed its role as the expression of an agenda for dealing with the popular classes of the noncore countries, what today we call the South. Its heralds were first Woodrow Wilson and then Franklin Roosevelt. Wilson and Roosevelt took the two main proposals of mid-nineteenth-century liberals—universal suffrage and the welfare state—and adapted them to the world level.

Wilson's call for the self-determination of nations was the world equivalent of suffrage. As every individual should have an equal vote within states, so every state should be sovereign and equal in the world polity. Roosevelt renewed this call during the Second

World War and added to it the need for what would come to be called the "economic development of underdeveloped countries," to be furthered by "technical assistance" and "aid." This was intended to be the functional equivalent on the world scene of the welfare state, an attempt to achieve a partial and limited redistribution of surplus value, now *world* surplus value.

History would now repeat itself more or less. The liberals proclaimed the agenda, but they dithered. The agenda was finally implemented by a coalescence of socialist popular pressure (primarily the national liberation movements) and the bold leaps of enlightened conservatives like, for example, de Gaulle. In the process, from 1917 to the 1960s, the conservatives were transformed into liberal-conservatives on the world scene. They embraced the need for decolonization and "development." It was Harold Macmillan who lectured the South African parliament in 1960 on bending with "the wind of change." Meanwhile, the Leninists were transformed into liberal-socialists, a process culminating in Gorbachev, but one that had already started with Stalin and Mao Zedong. There were two crucial elements in the deradicalization of Leninism: the acceptance of the objective of socialism within one country, defining it as a catching-up industrialization; and the search for national power and advantage within the interstate system.

Thus, both conservatives and socialists accepted the world-scale liberal agenda of self-determination (also called national liberation) and economic development (sometimes called construction of socialism). However, on a world scale, the liberal agenda could not possibly have had the same success it had had on a national scale in the core countries in the 1848 to 1914 period, and even more in the period following the end of the Second World War. And this for two reasons.

First, it was not possible on a world scale to provide the third element in the national "historic compromises"—national solidarity—that had held in check the class struggle. This third element had provided the final seal to the national liberal programs of suffrage and the welfare state in Western Europe and North America. A world nationalism is precisely theoretically impossible, since there is no one against whom to profess it.[26] Second, however, and more important, the transfer of income involved in instituting the welfare state in core countries was possible because the total sum thereby transferred was not so large as to threaten the accumulation of capital on a world scale. This would not be true were the transfers to be replicated worldwide, especially given the inherently polarizing nature of capitalist accumulation.

Some time was to pass before the reality of the impossibility of closing the North-South gap on a world scale fully entered the consciousness of people around the world. Indeed, the post-1945 period initially created an aura of optimism that was very bracing. Worldwide decolonialization, plus the incredible expansion of the world-economy and its dribble-down benefits, led to the flourishing of a rosy vision of reformist transformation (all the sweeter in that revolutionary rhetoric masked the reformist tactics). It is crucial to see that, in this period, the so-called socialist bloc served as the fig leaf of world capitalism by containing intemperate discontent and holding out the promise, in Khrushchev's unforgettable worlds, that "we will bury you."

In the 1960s, triumphalism still prevented a sober assessment of capitalist reality. The world revolution of 1968, for all its euphoria, intruded the first note of realism. The world revolution of 1968 continued for two decades, we shall argue, culminating in the collapse of the Communisms in 1989. On a world-historical stage, 1968 and 1989 constituted a single grand event.[27] The meaning of this event is the disintegration of liberal ideology, the end of a two-century era.

What was the note of reality that 1968 intruded? It was exactly the theme we are arguing here, that the history of the world-system for more than a century had been the history of the triumph of liberal ideology and that the Old Left antisystemic movements had become what I have been calling "liberal-socialists." The revolutionaries of 1968 presented the first serious intellectual challenge to the trimodal model of ideology—conservative, liberal, and socialist—by insisting that it was liberalism alone that was being preached, and that it was liberalism that was the "problem."

Ironically, the first consequence of this break in the legitimacy of the liberal consensus was the seeming revival of both conservative and socialist ideologies. All of a sudden, neoconservative ideologues seemed to attract a serious audience, as did neosocialist ones (for example, the numerous Maoist sects of the 1970s). The effervescence of 1968 soon died down and was repressed. Yet the Humpty Dumpty of a liberal consensus could not be put together again. Furthermore, the times were against liberal optimism. The world-economy entered the long B-phase of stagnation that began in 1967–1973 and is not yet completed. This is not the place to review in detail the economic history of the world-system in the 1970s and 1980s—the oil shock and the consequent recentralization of capital, the debt crisis first of the Third World (plus the socialist bloc), then of the United States, and the shift of capital from productive enterprises to financial speculation.

The cumulative effect of the shock of the 1968 revolution, plus the very negative consequences of the long downturn in the world-economy for over two-thirds of the countries of the world, had an immense impact on the mentalities of the world's peoples. In the 1960s, optimism reigned so high that the United Nations proclaimed that the 1970s would be the "Development Decade." It turned out to be exactly the opposite. For most of the Third World, it was a period of retrocession. One by one, states succumbed to the reality that the gap would not be closed in any foreseeable future. State policies concentrated on begging, borrowing, and stealing to keep budgets from collapse.

The general economic difficulties were even a bigger blow ideologically than they were economically or politically. Hardest hit were those who preached the ideology of liberal reformism most loudly—first the radical national liberation movements, then the so-called Communist regimes. Today in many (perhaps most) of these countries, the slogans of the free market are on everyone's lips. Yet these are slogans of desperation. Few really believe (or will believe for very long) that this will make much difference, and those few are likely to be disappointed. Rather, there has been a tacit claim on world sympathy and charity and, as we well know, such claims have rarely had serious historical consequences.

The politicians and publicists of the core countries are so bemused by their own rhetoric that they believe that something called Communism has collapsed, and seem blind to the fact that it is the liberal promise that has collapsed. The consequences will not take long to be upon us, for liberalism as an ideology in fact depended on an "enlightened" (as opposed to a cramped) view of the interests of the upper strata. This, in turn, depended on pressure from popular forces that was both strong and tamed in form. Such contained pressure in turn depended on the credibility of the process for the lower strata. It is intermeshed. If you lose credibility, you lose pressure in a tamed form. If you lose pressure in a tamed form, you lose the readiness for concessions from the upper strata.

A certain set of ideologies formed on the ground of the new mentalities created by the French Revolution. The world revolution of 1848 set in motion an historical process that led to the triumph of liberalism as an ideology and the integration of the working classes. The First World War renewed the issue on a world scale. The process was repeated but could not be fulfilled. The world revolution of 1968 unraveled the ideological consensus, and the twenty years that followed saw the undoing of the credibility of liberalism, of which the collapse of the Communisms in 1989 was the culmination.

We have entered a new era in terms of mentalities. On the one hand, there is the passionate call for democracy. This call is not a fulfillment of liberalism, however, but its rejection. It is a statement that the present world-system is undemocratic because economic well-being is not equally shared, because political power is not in fact equally shared. Social disintegration, not progressive change, is now coming to be seen as normal. Further, when there is social disintegration, people look for protection.

As people onced turned to the state to secure change, they are now turning to group solidarities (all kinds of groups) to provide protection. This is a different ball game altogether. How it will be played over the next fifty years or so is very unsure, both because we haven't seen how it works and because the possible fluctuations of a disintegrating world-system are very great. We shall surely not be able to navigate this period very well if we are unclear about the fact that none of the ideologies—that is, the agendas for political action—that have governed our actions for the last two hundred years are very serviceable for the coming period.

The Persian Gulf crisis marked the onset of the new world disorder. Disorder is not necessarily worse (or better) than order. However, it requires a different mode of action and reaction. It is scarcely sensible to call it order, or the triumph of liberalism, which is the same thing.

CHAPTER SIX

THE CONCEPT OF NATIONAL DEVELOPMENT, 1917–1989: ELEGY AND REQUIEM

Since at least the sixteenth century, European thinkers have been discussing how to augment the wealth of the realm, and governments have sought, or were adjured to take steps, to maintain and enhance this wealth. All the debates about mercantilism centered around how to be certain that more wealth entered a state than left it. When Adam Smith wrote *The Wealth of Nations* in 1776, he attacked the notion that governments could best enhance this wealth by various restrictions on foreign trade. He preached instead the notion that maximizing the ability of individual entrepreneurs to act as they deemed wisest in the world market would in fact result in an optimal enhancement of the wealth of the nation.

This tension between a basically protectionist stance and a free trade stance became one of the major themes of policy-making in the various states of the world-system in the nineteenth century. It often was the most significant issue that divided the principal political forces of particular states. It was clear by then that a central ideological theme of the capitalist world-economy was that every state could, and indeed eventually probably would, reach a level of national income that was high; and it was believed that conscious, rational action would make it so. This fit in very well with the underlying Enlightenment theme of inevitable progress and the teleological view of human history that it incarnated.

By the time of the First World War, it was also clear that a series of countries in Western Europe, plus the White settler countries in the rest of the world, had indeed become, in our contemporary parlance, "developed," or at least were well on their way to doing so. Of course, by the standards of 1990, all these countries (even Great Britain) were far less "modern" and wealthy than they became later in the century, but by the standards of the time they were doing magnificently. The First World War was the shock it was precisely because, among other things, it seemed a direct menace to this generalized prosperity of what we today call the core zones of the world-economy.

The year 1917 is often taken to be an ideological turning point in the history of the modern world-system. I agree that it was, but not quite in the way it is usually argued to be. On April 2, 1917, President Woodrow Wilson addressed the Congress of the United States and called for a declaration of war against Germany. He argued, "The world must be safe for democracy." That same year, on November 7, the Bolsheviks assaulted the Winter Palace in the name of the workers' revolution. The great ideological antinomy of the twentieth century, Wilsonianism vs. Leninism, may be said to have been born in 1917. I shall argue that it died in 1989. I shall further argue that the key issue to which both ideologies addressed themselves was the political integration of the periphery of the world-system. And finally I shall argue that the mechanism of such integration was, both for Wilsonianism and for Leninism, "national development," and that the essential dispute between them was merely about the path to such national development.

I

Wilsonianism was based on classical liberal presuppositions. It was universalist, claiming that its precepts applied equally everywhere. It assumed that everyone acted on the basis of rational self-interest, and that therefore everyone in the long run was reasonable. Hence, peaceful and reformist practice was plausible. It placed great emphasis on legality and on form.

Of course, none of these precepts were new. In 1917, in fact, they seemed quite old-fashioned. Wilson's innovation (not invention, but innovation) was to argue that these precepts applied not only to individuals within the state but also to nation-states or peoples within the international arena. The principle of self-determination, the centerpiece of Wilsonianism, was nothing but the principle of individual freedom transposed to the level of the inter-state system.

Taking a theory that had been intended to apply only at the level of individuals and applying it to the level of groups is a very tricky proposition. A harsh critic, Ivor Jennings, said of Wilson's doctrine of self-determination: "On the surface it seemed reasonable: let the people decide. It was in fact ridiculous because the people cannot decide until somebody decides who are the people."[28] Ay, there is the rub, indeed!

Still, it was obvious that, when Wilson was talking about the self-determination of nations, he was not worrying about France or Sweden. He was talking about the liquidation of the Austro-Hungarian, Ottoman, and Russian Empires. And when Roosevelt picked up the same theme a generation later he was talking about the liquidation of the British, French, Dutch, and other remaining imperial structures. The self-determination of which they were speaking was the self-determination of the peripheral and semiperipheral zones of the world-system.

Lenin pursued very similar policy objectives under the quite different slogans of proletarian internationalism and anti-imperialism. His views were no doubt based on other premises. His universalism was that of the world working class, the soon-to-be singular class that was slated to become literally identical with the "people." Nations or peoples had no long-run place in the Marxian pantheon; they were supposed eventually to disappear, like the states. But nations or peoples did have a short-run, even middle-run, reality, which not only could not be ignored by Marxist parties but also were potentially tactically useful to their ends.

The Russian Revolution denounced the Russian Empire in theory, and provided for the same self-determination of nations/peoples that did Wilson's doctrines. If much of the "empire" was retained, the Bolsheviks scrupulously insisted that this took the form of a voluntary federation of republics—the U.S.S.R.—with plenty of room for formal autonomy of peoples, even within each of the republics. And when all hope was abandoned for the mythical German revolution, Lenin turned at Baku to proclaiming a new emphasis on the "East." Marxism-Leninism in effect was moving from its origins as a theory of proletarian insurrection against the bourgeoisie to a new role as a theory of anti-imperialism. This shift of emphasis would only grow with time. In the decades to come, it is probable that more people read Lenin's

Imperialism: The Last Stage of Capitalism than the *Manifesto*.

Wilsonianism and Leninism emerged thus as rival doctrines for the fealty of the peoples of the peripheral zones. Because the doctrines were rivals, each placed in its propaganda great emphasis on its differences with the other. And of course there were real differences. But we should not be blind to the deep similarities as well. The two ideologies not only shared the theme of the self-determination of nations; they also believed it was immediately (if not always urgently) relevant to the political life of the peripheral zones. That is, both doctrines favored what later came to be called "decolonization." Furthermore, by and large, even when it came to the details of who precisely the people were who had this hypothetical right to self-determination, the proponents of both doctrines came up with very similar lists of names. There were, to be sure, minor tactical scuffles related to passing considerations of the world *rapport de forces*, but there was no important example of fundamental empirical disagreement. Israel was on both lists, Kurdistan on neither. Neither was to accept the theoretical legitimacy of the Bantustans. Both found no theoretical reason to oppose the eventual realities of Pakistan and Bangladesh. It could not be said that fundamentally different measuring rods were being used to judge legitimacy.

To be sure, there were differences about the road to self-determination. Wilsonians favored what was termed a "constitutional" path, that is, a gradual, orderly transfer of power arrived at by negotiations between an imperial power and respectable representatives of the people in question. Decolonization was to be, as the French would later put it, *octroyée* (given). Leninism came of a "revolutionary" tradition and painted a more insurrectional path to "national liberation." Independence was not to be *octroyée* but *arrachée* (taken). This would be incarnated in the later Maoist injunction of the need for "protracted struggle," which came to be widely repeated and, more important, which came to be part of the fundamental strategy of movements.

One should not exaggerate even this difference. Peaceful decolonization was not unacceptable in Leninist doctrine—merely improbable. And revolutionary nationalism was not inherently inconsistent with Wilsonian ideas—merely dangerous and thus to be avoided whenever possible. Still, the debate was real because it masked another debate: who was to lead the struggle for self-determination. And this was important, in turn, because it would presumably determine the "postindependence" policies. Wilsonians saw the natural leadership of a national movement to lie in its intelligentsia and bourgeoisie—educated, respectable, and prudent. They foresaw a local movement that would persuade the more "modern" sectors of the traditional leadership to join in the political reforms and accept a sensible, parliamentary mode of organizing the newly independent state. Leninists saw the leadership to lie in a party/movement modeled on the Bolshevik party, even if the national movement did not accept the whole Leninist ideological canon. The leaders could be "petty bourgeois," provided they were "revolutionary" petty bourgeois. When it came to power, the party/movement was supposed to become a party/state. Here too one should not exaggerate the difference. Often, the respectable intelligentsia/bourgeoisie and the so-called revolutionary petty bourgeoisie were in reality the same people, or at least cousins. And the party/movement was almost as frequent a formula of "Wilsonian" movements as of "Leninist" ones. As for the postindependence policies, neither the Wilsonians nor the Leninists worried too much about them as long as the struggle for self-determination was ongoing.

II

What, then, of the postdecolonization practice? Surely here the Wilsonian-Leninist antinomy would reveal its importance. In one major respect, there was no question that the two paths to independence tended to correlate with opposite postindependence policies. This was in the domain of foreign policy. In all world issues in which the United States and the U.S.S.R. were locked in cold war battle, the states outside the core zones tended to lean in one direction or the other. Some states were considered and considered themselves "pro-Western," and other states considered themselves to be part of a world progressive camp that included the U.S.S.R.

There was, of course, a long continuum of positions, and not all states were consistent over time. Nonalignment was itself a major movement. Still, when the chips were down, on unimportant matters like voting for resolutions in the General Assembly of the United Nations, many votes were easily predictable. The United States and its allies on the one hand and the U.S.S.R. and the so-called socialist bloc on the other hand spent much diplomatic energy on trying to push wavering states in one direction or the other. Wilsonian vs. Leninist propaganda was incessantly purveyed, directly through government media and indirectly through scholarly discourse.

A close look at the internal realities of the various states reveals, however, that, both in the political and in the economic arenas, there was less difference than the theory or the propaganda would suggest. In terms of the actual political structures, most of the states most of the time were either one-party states (de facto or de jure) or military dictatorships. Even when states had a multiparty system in formal terms, one party tended in reality to dominate the institutions and to be impervious to change of regime other than by military coup d'état.

Nor was much more difference to be located in the economic arena. The degree to which private local enterprise was permitted has varied, but in almost all Third World states there has been a large amount of state enterprise and in virtually no state has state ownership been the only property form. The degree to which foreign investment has been permitted has no doubt varied more. In the more "pro-Western" states it has been encouraged, indeed solicited, albeit quite frequently in the form of joint ventures with a state corporation. In the more radical, or "progressive," states, foreign investment has been dealt with more cautiously, although seldom totally repudiated. Rather it has been the case that investors from OECD countries have themselves been reluctant to invest in such countries because of what they considered higher political risk.

Finally, the aid picture has not been too different. Virtually all Third World countries have actively sought to obtain aid in the form of both direct grants and loans. To be sure, the aid-giving donors tended to correlate their assitance with the foreign policy stance of the potential recipients. A long list of countries received aid primarily from OECD countries. A smaller list received aid primarily from socialist bloc countries. A few countries self-consciously sought to emphasize the Nordic countries (plus the Netherlands and Canada) as aid sources. A large number of countries were ready to accept aid from multiple sources. In the end, most of the aid took the same form: personnel and tied grants, intended to support military structures and to fund so-called development projects.

What was most alike in all these countries was the belief in the possibility and urgent importance of "national development." National development was operationally defined everywhere as "catching up." Of course, it was assumed by everyone involved that this was a long and difficult task. But it was also assumed that it was doable, provided only that the right *state* policies were pursued. These covered the whole ideological gamut from facilitating the unrestricted flow of capital, commodities, and labor across the national frontiers (on one extreme) to total state control of productive and exchange operations within largely closed frontiers (on the other extreme). There were, of course, a very large variety of in-between positions.

What was common, however, to the programs of all the noncore state members of the United Nations—from the U.S.S.R. to Argentina, from India to Nigeria, from Albania to St. Lucia—was the overall state objective of increasing the wealth of the nation and "modernizing" its infrastructure. What was also common was an underlying optimism about this objective. What was further common was the sense that this objective could be best pursued by full participation in the interstate system. When any state was excluded even partially, as was the People's Republic of China for many years, it worked very hard to regain its unquestioned status of full membership.

In short, the Wilsonian-Leninist ideology of the self-determination of nations, their abstract equality, and the developmentalist paradigm incarnated in both variants of the ideology, was overwhelmingly and virtually unfailingly accepted as the operational program of the political movements of the peripheral and semi-peripheral zones of the world-system.

In this sense, the U.S.S.R. itself was the first test case of the validity of the analysis and the workability of the recommendations. The postrevolutionary state was formally structured— a federation of states, each of which contained autonomous subunits—to respond precisely to the juridical formula of self-determination. When Lenin launched the slogan "Communism equals the Soviets plus electricity," he was putting forward national (economic) development as the prime objective of state policy. And when Khrushchev, decades later, said that the Soviet Union would "bury" the United States by the year 2000, he was venting supreme optimism about "catching up."

These themes grew stronger in the interwar years—in eastern and central Europe, in Latin America, in India, and elsewhere.[29] The original great boast of the U.S.S.R. was that in the 1930s, at a time of world economic depression, there was not only no unemployment in the U.S.S.R. but there was also a program of rapid industrialization.

After 1945, the world chorus on the possibilities of national development grew stronger. The relatively rapid reconstruction of Western Europe and Japan (after massive wartime destruction of infrastructure) seemed to demonstrate that, with will and investment, it was possible to rapidly upgrade technology and thus to raise the overall standard of living. All of a sudden, the theme of economic development became pandemic—among politicians, journalists, and scholars. The forgotten corners of already industrialized states (the South in the U.S., southern Italy, etc.) were targeted for "development." The Third World was to develop as well—partly through self-help, partly with the assistance of the more advanced "developed" countries. The United Nations would officially proclaim the 1970s the Development Decade.

In the universities of the world, development became the new intellectual organizing theme. A liberal paradigm, "modernization theory," was elaborated in the 1950s, to be countered by a *marxisant dependista* counterparadigm elaborated in the 1960s. This was of course essentially the updating of the Wilsonian-Leninist antinomy. Once again, in practice, the specific recommendations for state policy may have been polar opposites, but both sets of theories involved specific recommendations for state policy. Both sets of applied practitioners, who advised the governments, were confident that, if their recommendations were implemented, national development would in fact follow and the countries in question would eventually catch up.

We know what happened in the real world. From roughly 1945 to 1970, there was considerable practical effort to expand the means and level of production around the world. It was in this period that GNP and GNP per capita became the principal measuring tools of economic growth, which itself had become the principal indicator of economic development.

This period was a Kondratieff A-phase of exceptional amplitude. The amount of growth varied considerably around the world, but on the whole the figures were upward everywhere, not least of all in the so-called socialist countries. This same period was a period of the political triumph of a large number of movements in the Third World, which had evolved the strategy of struggling for state power in order thereby to implement policies that would guarantee national development. Everything therefore seemed to be moving in the same positive direction: worldwide economic expansion; the fulfilment state-by-state of the Wilsonian-Leninist vision; the almost universally upward growth rates. Developmentalism was the order of the day; there was a worldwide consensus about its legitimacy and its inevitability.

This consensus, however, suffered two shocks from which it has not recovered and, I am arguing, will not recover. The first shock was the worldwide revolution of 1968. The second shock was the worldwide economic stagnation of the period 1970–1990, the economic failure of almost all the governments of the peripheral and semiperipheral zones, and the collapse of regimes in the so-called socialist states. The ideological crust was broken by the world revolution of 1968. The 1970s and 1980s removed the rest of the ideological covering. The gaping sore of the North-South polarization was uncovered and exposed to view. At the moment, in desperation, the world is muttering incantations about the market as remedy, as though this could solve anything. But market medicine is Mercurochrome and will not prevent further deterioration. It is highly unlikely that most states now abandoning "socialist" slogans in favor of "market" slogans will see a significant improvement in the 1990s in their standard of living. After all, the vast majority of noncore states who adhered to market slogans in the 1980s did quite poorly. Reference is always made to the rare "success" stories (the current hero is South Korea), neglecting the much larger number of failures and the fading of earlier so-called success stories such as Brazil.

The main issue, however, is not whether or not specific state policies have or have not led to economic development. The main issue is whether or not there will continue to be widespread belief in the likelihood of economic development as the result of any particular state policies.

III

The worldwide revolution of 1968 grew out of a sense that national development had not occurred; it was not yet the consequence of feeling that the objective itself was an illusion. There were two main themes that were common to all the uprisings (east and west, north and south), whatever the local details. The first theme was a protest against U.S. hegemony in the world-system (and the collusion of the U.S.S.R. in that hegemony). The second was a protest against the inefficacy of the so-called Old Left movements that had come to power in multiple versions throughout the world—social democracy in the West, Communism in the East, national liberation movements in the South. These movements were attacked for not having truly transformed the world, as they had promised in their mobilizational days. They were attacked for being too much a part of the dominant world-system, too little antisystemic.[30]

In a sense, what those who participated in the various uprisings were saying to the "Old Left" political movements is that their organizational activities had achieved the formal political objectives they had historically set themselves—most notably state power—but that they had distinctly not achieved the greater human equality that was supposed to be the reason for achieving the state power. On the other hand, the worldwide attraction during this period to "Maoism" was due to the fact that it expressed in the most vigorous possible way this double rejection: of U.S. hegemony (and Soviet collusion); and of inefficacious "Old Left" movements in general. However, Maoism represented the argument that the fault lay in the poor leadership of the "Old Left" movements, those who were in Maoist terminology the "capitalist roaders." Hence it was implied that, were the movements now to reject the "capitalist roaders," were they to have a "cultural revolution," then at last the objective of national development would in fact be achieved.

The significance of the worldwide revolution of 1968 was not in the political change it brought about. By 1970, the uprisings had been suppressed or had fizzled everywhere. Nor was the significance in the new ideas it launched. Maoism had a short career in the 1970s but disintegrated by middecade, and first of all in China. The themes of the new social movements—cultural nationalism of "minorities," feminism, ecology—have had somewhat more staying power than Maoism, but have yet to find a firm ideological footing. The significance of 1968 was rather that it punctured the consensus around Wilsonianism-Leninism by questioning whether the developmentalist ideology had in fact achieved anything of lasting importance. It sowed ideological doubt, and corroded the faith.

Once the faith was shaken, once the consensus viewpoint was reduced to the status of merely one viewpoint amidst others in the arena (even if still the one most widely held), it was possible for day-by-day reality to have the effect of stripping that ideology bare. This is what has happened in the 1970s and 1980s. The world-economic stagnation, the Kondratieff B-phase, has thus far been played out in two major dramas. The first was the OPEC oil price rise of the 1970s. The second was the debt crisis of the 1980s.

The OPEC oil price rise was thought at first to give renewed credence to the possibilities of national development. It seemed to be a demonstration that primary producers in the South, by concerted action, could significantly affect the terms of trade.

An initial hysteria in Western public opinion abetted such an interpretation. It was not long before a more sober assessment took hold. What had really happened? The OPEC countries, under the leadership of the Shah of Iran and the Saudis (the leading friends of the United States among OPEC nations, be it noted), raised the price of oil dramatically, thereby drawing a significant percentage of world surplus into their hands. This represented a very significant drain on national accounts for all Third World and socialist countries that were not themselves oil producers, at a time when the world market for their own exports was weakening. The drain on the national accounts of the major industrialized countries was also important but far less significant as a percentage of the total, and also more temporary, since these countries could more easily take steps to restructure their energy consumption.

What happened to the world surplus funneled through the oil-producing countries? Some of it of course went into the "national development" programs of oil-producing states such as Nigeria, Algeria, Iraq, Iran, Mexico, Venezuela, and the U.S.S.R. Some of it went into heavy luxury consumption in oil-producing states, which meant it was transferred to the OECD states—as the purchasing of commodities, as investment, or as individual capital flight. And the remaining money was placed in U.S. and European banks. This money that was placed in the banks was then refunneled out to Third World and socialist states (including even the oil-producing states) as state loans. These state loans solved the immediate problems of the balance of payments of these states, which were in particularly bad shape precisely because of the oil price rise. With the state loans, the governments were able to stave off for a time political opposition by using the money to maintain imports (even while exports were falling). This in turn sustained world demand for the manufactured goods of the OECD countries and thus minimized the effects on them of the world economic stagnation.

Even during the 1970s a number of Third World states began nonetheless to feel the effects of a decline in the growth rate combined with an exhaustion of monetary and social reserves. By the 1980s the effects were to be felt everywhere (with the exception of East Asia). The first great public expression of the debt crisis was Poland in 1980. The Gierek government had played the 1970s like everyone else, borrowing and spending. But the bill was coming due, and the Polish government sought to reduce it by increasing internal prices, thereby making the Polish working class assume the burden. The result was Gdańsk and Solidarność.

The 1980s saw a cascade of economic difficulties for peripheral and semiperipheral countries. In virtually all, two elements were the same. The first common element was popular discontent with the regime in power, followed by political disillusionment. Even when regimes were overthrown—whether by violence or by collapse of a rotting regime, whether they were military dictatorships or Communist parties or one-party African regimes—the pressure for political transformation was more negative than affirmative. The changes occurred less out of hope than despair. The second was the hard financial face of the OECD countries. Faced with their own economic difficulties, they exhibited little patience for the financial dilemmas of Third World and socialist governments. The latter were handed harsh IMF conditions to fulfill, given risible assistance, and subjected to sermonizing about the virtues of the market and privatization. Gone were the Keynesian indulgences of the 1950s and 1960s.

In the early 1980s the Latin American countries saw a wave of developmentalist military dictatorships being dismantled; and they discovered "democracy." In the Arab world, developmentalist secular regimes were under sharp attack from Islamists. In Black Africa, where one-partyism was once the sustaining structure of developmentalist hopes, the myth had become ashes in the mouth. And the dramatic transformations of 1989 in east and central Europe came as a great surprise to the world, although they were clearly inscribed in the events of 1980 in Poland.

In the Soviet Union, where in some senses the developmentalist trek began, we have witnessed the disintegration of the CPSU and of the U.S.S.R. itself. When developmentalism failed in Brazil or Algeria, one could argue that it was because they had not followed the political path of the U.S.S.R. But when it failed in the U.S.S.R.?

IV

The story of 1917–1989 deserves both elegy and requiem. The elegy is for the triumph of the Wilsonian-Leninist ideal of the self-determination of nations. In these seventy years, the world has been largely decolonized. The world outside Europe has been integrated into the formal political institutions of the interstate system.

This decolonization was partly *octroyée*, partially *arrachée*. In the process, an incredible political mobilization was required across the world, which has awakened consciousnesses everywhere. It will be very difficult ever to put the genie back into the box. Indeed, the main problem is how to contain the spreading virus of micronationalism as ever smaller entities seek to claim peoplehood and therefore the right to self-determination.

From the beginning, however, it was clear that everyone wanted self-determination primarily in order to make their way to prosperity. And from the beginning the road to prosperity was recognized as a difficult one. As we have argued, this has taken the form of the search for national development. And this search for a long time found itself relatively more comfortable with Leninist than with Wilsonian rhetoric, just as the struggle for decolonization had found itself relatively more comfortable with Wilsonian rhetoric.

Since the process was in two steps—first the decolonization (or comparable political change), then the economic development—it meant that the Wilsonian half of the package was always waiting for its Leninist fulfillment. The prospect of national development served as the legitimization of the world-system's overall structure. In this sense, the fate of Wilsonian ideology was dependent on the fate of Leninist ideology. To put it more crudely and less kindly, Leninist ideology was the fig leaf of Wilsonian ideology.

Today the fig leaf has fallen, and the emperor is naked. All the shouting about the triumph of democracy in 1989 around the world will not long hide the absence of any serious prospect for the economic transformation of the periphery within the framework of the capitalist world-economy. Thus, it will not be the

Leninists who sing the requiem for Leninism but the Wilsonians. It is they who are in a quandary and who have no plausible political alternatives. This was captured in the no-win dilemmas of President Bush in the Persian Gulf crisis. But the Persian Gulf crisis was only the beginning of the story.

As the North-South confrontations take ever more dramatic (and violent) forms in the decades to come, we shall begin to see just how much the world will miss the ideological cement of the Wilsonian-Leninist ideological antinomy. It represented a glorious but historically passing panoply of ideas, hopes, and human energy. It will not be easy to replace. And yet it is only by finding a new and far more solid utopian vision that we shall be able to transcend the imminent time of troubles.

PART III

THE HISTORICAL DILEMMAS
OF LIBERALS

CHAPTER SEVEN

THE END OF WHAT MODERNITY?

When I went to college in the late 1940s, we learned about the virtues and the realities of being modern. Today, almost a half-century later, we are being told of the virtues and the realities of being postmodern. What happened to modernity that it is no longer our salvation, but has become instead our demon? Is the modernity we were speaking of then the one we are speaking of now? Of which modernity are we at an end?

The Oxford English Dictionary, always a first place to look, tells us that one meaning of *modern* is historiographical: "commonly applied (in contradistinction to ancient and medieval) to the time subsequent to the Middle Ages." The OED cites an author using modern in this sense as early as 1585. Furthermore, the OED informs us that modern also means "pertaining to or originating in the current age or period," in which case *postmodern* is an oxymoron, which one should, I think, deconstruct.

Some fifty years ago, modern had two clear connotations. One was positive and forward-looking. Modern signified the most advanced technology. The term was situated in a conceptual framework of the presumed endlessness of technological progress, and, therefore, of constant innovation. This modernity was in consequence a fleeting modernity—what is modern today will be outdated tomorrow. This modernity was quite material in form: airplanes, air-conditioning, television, computers. The appeal of this kind of modernity has still not exhausted itself. There may no doubt be millions of children of the new age who assert that they reject this eternal quest for speed and for control of the environment as something that is unhealthy, indeed nefarious. But there are billions—billions, not millions—of persons in Asia and Africa, in Eastern Europe and Latin America, in the slums and ghettos of Western Europe and North America, who yearn to enjoy fully this kind of modernity.

There was in addition, however, a second major connotation to the concept of modern, one that was more oppositional than affirmative. One could characterize this other connotation less as forward-looking than as militant (and also self-satisfied), less material than ideological. To be modern signified being antimedieval, in an antinomy in which the concept *medieval* incarnated narrow-mindedness, dogmatism, and above all the constraints of authority. It was Voltaire shouting "Ecrasez l'infâme." It was Milton in *Paradise Lost* virtually celebrating Lucifer. It was all the classical "Revolutions"—the English, the American, the French to be sure, but also the Russian and the Chinese. In the United States, it was the doctrine of the separation of church and state, the first ten amendments to the U.S. Constitution, the Emancipation Proclamation, Clarence Darrow at the Scopes trial, *Brown v. the Board of Education,* and *Roe v. Wade.*

It was in short the presumptive triumph of human freedom against the forces of evil and ignorance. It was a trajectory as inevitably progressive as that of technological advance. But it was not a triumph of humanity over nature; it was rather a triumph of humanity over itself, or over those with privilege. Its path was not one of intellectual discovery but of social conflict. This modernity was not the modernity of technology, of Prometheus unbound, of boundless wealth; it was rather the modernity of liberation, of substantive democracy (the rule of the people as opposed to that of the aristocracy, or the rule of the best), of human fulfillment, and, yes, of moderation. This modernity of liberation was not a fleeting modernity, but an eternal modernity. Once achieved, it was never to be yielded.

The two stories, the two discourses, the two quests, the two modernities were quite different, even contrary to each other. They were also, however, historically deeply intertwined one with the other, such that there has resulted deep confusion, uncertain results, and much disappointment and disillusionment. This symbiotic pair has formed the central cultural contradiction of our modern world-system, the system of historical capitalism. And this contradiction has never been as acute as it is today, leading to moral, as well as institutional, crisis.

Let us trace the history of this confusing symbiosis between the two modernities—the modernity of technology and the modernity of liberation—over the history of our modern world-system. I will divide my story into three parts: the 300 to 350 years that run between the origins of our modern world-system in the middle of the fifteenth century to the end of the eighteenth century; the nineteenth and most of the twentieth centuries, or to use two symbolic dates for this second period, the era from 1789 to 1968; the post-1968 period.

The modern world-system has never been fully comfortable with the idea of modernity, but for different reasons in each of the three periods. During the first period, only part of the globe (primarily most of Europe and the Americas) constituted this historical system, which we may call a capitalist world-economy. This is a designation we may indeed use for the system for that era, primarily because the system already had in place the three defining features of a capitalist world-economy: a single axial division of labor existed within its boundaries, with a polarization between core-like and peripheral economic activities; the principal political structures, the states, were linked together within, and constrained by, an interstate system whose boundaries matched those of the axial division of labor; those who pursued the ceaseless accumulation of capital prevailed in the middle run over those who did not.

Nonetheless, the geoculture of this capitalist world-economy was not yet firmly in place in this first period. Indeed, this was a period in which, for the parts of the world located within the capitalist world-economy, there were no clear geocultural norms. There existed no social consensus, even a minimal one, about such fundamental issues as whether the states should be secular; in whom the moral location of sovereignty was invested; the legitimacy of partial corporate autonomy for intellectuals; or the social permissibility of multiple religions. These are all familiar stories. They seem to be stories of those with power and privilege seeking to contain the forces of progress, in a situation in which the former still controlled the principal political and social institutions.

The crucial thing to note is that, during this long period, those who defended the modernity of technology and those who defended the modernity of liberation tended to have the same powerful political enemies. The two modernities seemed to be in tandem, and few would have used a language that made a distinction between the two. Galileo, forced to submit to the church, but muttering (probably apocryphally), "Eppur si muove," was seen as fighting both for technological progress and for human liberation. One way of resuming Enlightenment thought might be to say that it constituted a belief in the identity of the modernity of technology and the modernity of liberation.

If there was cultural contradiction, it was that the capitalist world-economy was functioning economically and politically within a framework that lacked the necessary geoculture to sustain it and reinforce it. The overall system was thus maladapted to its own dynamic thrusts. It may be thought of as uncoordinated, or as struggling against itself. The continuing dilemma of the system was geocultural. It required a major adjustment if the capitalist world-economy was to thrive and expand in the way its internal logic required.

IT WAS THE FRENCH REVOLUTION THAT FORCED THE ISSUE, NOT merely for France but for the modern world-system as a whole. The French Revolution was not an isolated event. It might rather be thought of as the eye of a hurricane. It was bounded (preceded and succeeded) by the decolonization of the Americas—the settler decolonizations of British North America, Hispanic America, and Brazil; the slave revolution of Haiti; and the abortive Native American uprisings such as Túpac Amaru in Peru. The French Revolution connected with, and stimulated struggles for, liberation of various kinds as well as nascent nationalisms throughout Europe and around its edges—from Ireland to Russia, from Spain to Egypt. It did this not only by evoking in these countries resonances of sympathy for French revolutionary doctrines but also by provoking reactions against French (that is, Napoleonic) imperialism, couched in the name of these very same French revolutionary doctrines.

Above all, the French Revolution made it apparent, in some ways for the first time, that the modernity of technology and the modernity of liberation were not at all identical. Indeed, it might be said that those who wanted primarily the modernity of technology suddenly took fright at the strength of the advocates of the modernity of liberation.

In 1815, Napoleon was defeated. There was a "Restoration" in France. The European powers established a Concert of Nations, which, at least for some, was supposed to guarantee a reactionary status quo. But this was in fact to prove impossible. And in the years between 1815 and 1848, a geoculture was elaborated that was designed instead to promote the modernity of technology while simultaneously containing the modernity of liberation.

Given the symbiotic relationship between the two modernities, it was not an easy task to obtain this partial unyoking of the two. Yet it was accomplished, and it thereby created a lasting geocultural basis for legitimating the operations of the capitalist world-economy. At least it succeeded for 150 years or so. The key to the operation was the elaboration of the ideology of liberalism, and its acceptance as the emblematic ideology of the capitalist world-economy.

Ideologies themselves were an innovation emerging out of the new cultural situation created by the French Revolution.[31] Those who thought, in 1815, that they were reestablishing order and tradition discovered that in fact it was too late: a sea change in mentalities had occurred, and it was historically irreversible. Two radically new ideas had become very widely accepted as almost self-evident. The first was that political change was a normal, rather than an exceptional, occurrence. The second was that sovereignty lay in an entity called the "people."

Both concepts were explosive. To be sure, the Holy Alliance rejected both these ideas totally. However, the British Tory government, the government of the new hegemonic power in the world-system, was far more equivocal, as was the Restoration monarchy of Louis XVIII in France. Conservative in instinct, but intelligent in the exercise of power, these two governments were equivocal because they were aware of the strength of the typhoon in public opinion, and they decided to bend with it rather than risk a break.

Thus emerged the ideologies, which were quite simply the long-run political strategies designed to cope with the new beliefs in the normality of political change and the moral sovereignty of the people. Three principal ideologies emerged. The first was conservatism, the ideology of those who were most dismayed by the new ideas and thought them morally wrong, that is, those who rejected modernity as nefarious.

Liberalism arose in response to conservatism as the doctrine of those who sought to achieve a full flourishing of modernity in a methodical fashion, with a minimum of sharp disruption, and with a maximum of controlled manipulation. As the U.S. Supreme Court said in 1954 when it outlawed segregation, liberals believed that the changes should proceed "with all deliberate speed," which as we know really means "not too fast, but then again not too slow." The liberals were totally committed to the modernity of technology, but they were rather queasy about the modernity of liberation. Liberation for the technicians, they thought, was a splendid idea; liberation for ordinary people, however, presented dangers.

The third great ideology of the nineteenth century, socialism, emerged last. Like the liberals, socialists accepted the inevitability and desirability of progress. Unlike the liberals, they were suspicious of top-down reform. They were impatient for the full benefits of modernity—the modernity of technology to be sure, but even more the modernity of liberation. They suspected, quite correctly, that the liberals intended "liberalism" to be limited in both its scope of application and the persons to whom it was intended to apply.

In the emerging triad of ideologies, the liberals situated themselves in the political center. While liberals sought to remove the state, particularly the monarchical state, from many arenas of decision making, they were always equally insistent on putting the state into the center of rational reformism. In Great Britain, for example, the repeal of the Corn Laws was no doubt the culmination of a long effort to remove the state from the business of protecting internal markets against foreign competition. But in the very same decade the very same parliament passed the Factory Acts, the beginning (not the end) of a long effort to get the state *into* the business of regulating conditions of work and employment.

Liberalism, far from being a doctrine that was antistate in essence, became the central justification for the strengthening of the efficacy of the state machinery.[32] This was because liberals saw the state as essential to achieving their central objective— furthering the modernity of technology while simultaneously judiciously appeasing the "dangerous classes." They hoped thereby to check the precipitate implications of the concept of the sovereignty of the "people" that were derived from a modernity of liberation.

In the nineteenth-century core zones of the capitalist world-economy, liberal ideology translated itself into three principal political objectives—suffrage, the welfare state, and national identity. Liberals hoped the combination of these three would appease the "dangerous classes" while nonetheless ensuring the modernity of technology.

The debate over suffrage was a continuous one throughout the century and beyond. In practice, there was a steady upward curve of expansion of voting elegibility, in most places in this order: first to smaller property holders, then to propertyless males, then to younger persons, then to women. The liberal gamble was that previously excluded persons, once they received the vote, would accept the idea that the periodic vote represented their full claim to political rights, and that therefore they would then drop more radical ideas about effective participation in collective decision making.

The debate over the welfare state, really a debate about the redistribution of surplus value, was also a continuous one and also showed a steady upward curve of concessions—at least until the 1980s, when it started to recede for the first time. What the welfare state essentially involved was a social wage, where a portion (a growing portion) of the income of wageworkers came not directly from employers' wage packets but indirectly via governmental agencies. This system partially detached income from employment; it enabled some slight equalization of wages across skill levels and wage-rents; and it shifted part of the negotiations between capital and labor to the political arena, where, with suffrage, workers had somewhat more leverage. The welfare state did, however, less for workers at the bottom end of the wage scale than it did for a middle stratum, whose size was growing and whose political centrality was becoming the strong underpinning of centrist governments committed to the active reinforcement of liberal ideology.

Neither suffrage nor the welfare state (and not even the two together) would have been enough to tame the dangerous classes without the addition of a third crucial variable, which ensured that these dangerous classes would not inspect too closely how great the concessions of the suffrage and the welfare state were. This third variable was the creation of national identity. In 1845, Benjamin Disraeli, first Earl of Beaconsfield, future "enlightened Conservative" prime minister of Great Britain, published a novel entitled *Sybil, or the Two Nations.* In his "Advertisement," Disraeli tells us that the subject is "the Condition of the People," something apparently so terrible in that year that, in order not to be accused by readers of exaggeration, he "found the absolute necessity of suppressing much that is genuine." It is a novel that incorporated in the plot the then powerful Chartist movement. The novel is about the "Two Nations of England, the Rich and the Poor" who, it is suggested, derive from two ethnic groups, the Normans and the Saxons.[33]

Disraeli, in the concluding pages, is quite harsh about the limited relevance to the "people" of formal political reform, that is, of classical liberalism. His text reads:

> **The written history of our country for the last ten reigns has been a mere phantasma, giving the origin and consequence of public transactions a character and colour in every respect dissimilar to their natural form and hue. In this mighty mystery all thoughts and things have assumed an aspect and title contrary to their real quality and style:**

Oligarchy has been called Liberty; an exclusive Priesthood has been christened a National church; Sovereignty has been the title of something that has had no dominion, while absolute power has been wielded by those who profess themselves the servants of the People. In the selfish strife of factions, two great existences have been blotted out of the history of England, the Monarch and the Multitude; as the power of the Crown has diminished, the privileges of the People have disappeared; till at length the sceptre has become a pageant, and its subject has degenerated again into a serf.

But Time, that brings all things, has brought also to the mind of England some suspicion that the idols they have so long worshipped, and the oracles that have so long deluded them, are not the true ones. There is a whisper rising in this country that Loyalty is not a phrase, Faith not a delusion, and Popular Liberty something more diffusive and substantial than the profane exercise of the sacred rights of sovereignty by political classes.[34]

If Great Britain (and France, and indeed all countries) were "two nations," the Rich and the Poor, Disraeli's solution clearly was to make them into one—one in sentiment, one in loyalty, one in self-abnegation. This "oneness" we call national identity. The great program of liberalism was not to make states out of nations, but to create nations out of states. That is to say, the strategy was to take those who were located within the boundaries of the state—formerly the "subjects" of the king-sovereign, now the sovereign "people"—and make them into "citizens," all identifying with their state.

In practice this was accomplished by various institutional requirements. The first consisted of establishing clear legal defin-itions of membership in the polity. The rules varied, but always tended to exclude (with lesser or greater rigor) new arrivals in the state ("migrants") while usually including all those who were con-sidered "normally" resident. The unity of this latter group was then usually reinforced by moving toward linguistic uniformity: a single language within the state, and, quite often just as important, a language different from that of neighboring states. This was accomplished by requiring all state activities to be conducted in a single language, by sustaining the activity of scholarly unification of the language (e.g., national academies controlling dictionaries), and by forcing the acquisition of this language on linguistic minorities.

The great unifying institutions of the people were the educational system and the armed forces. In at least all the core countries, elementary education became compulsory; in many, military training did too. The schools and the armies taught languages, civic duties, and nationalist loyalty. Within a century, states that had been two "nations"—the Rich and the Poor, the Normans and the Saxons—became one nation in self-regard, in this particular case, the "English."

One should not miss one final crucial element in the task of creating national identity—racism. Racism unites the race deemed superior. It unites it within the state at the expense of minorities to be excluded from full or partial citizenship rights. But it unites the "nation" of the nation-state vis-à-vis the rest of the world; not only vis-à-vis neighbors, but even more vis-à-vis the peripheral zones. In the nineteenth century, the states of the core became nation-states concomitant with becoming imperial states, who established colonies in the name of a "civilizing mission."

What this liberal package of suffrage, the welfare state, and national identity offered above all to the dangerous classes of the core states was hope—hope that the gradual but steady reforms promised by liberal politicians and technocrats would *eventually* mean betterment for the dangerous classes, an equalization of recompense, a disappearance of Disraeli's "two nations." The hope was offered directly to be sure, but it was also offered in more subtle ways. It was offered in the form of a theory of history that posited as inevitable this amelioration of conditions, under the heading of the irresistible drive to human liberty. This was the so-called Whig interpretation of history. However the politico-cultural struggle had been seen in the sixteenth to eighteenth centuries, the two struggles—for the modernity of technology and the modernity of liberation—were definitively defined in the nineteenth century retrospectively as a single struggle centered around the social hero of the individual. This was the heart of the Whig interpretation of history. This retrospective interpretation was itself part, indeed a major part, of the process of imposing a dominant geoculture in the nineteenth century on the capitalist world-economy.

Hence, precisely at the moment in historical time when, in the eyes of the dominant strata, the two modernities seemed more than ever to be divergent and even in conflict with each other, the official ideology (the dominant geoculture) proclaimed the two to be identical. The dominant strata undertook a major educational campaign (via the school system and the armed forces) to persuade their internal dangerous classes of this identity of object. The intent was to convince the dangerous classes to mute their claims to the modernity of liberation, and to invest their energies instead in the modernity of technology.

At an ideological level, this was what the class struggles of the nineteenth century were about. And to the degree that workers' and socialist movements came to accept the centrality and even the primacy of the modernity of technology, they lost the class struggle. They exchanged their loyalty to the states for very modest (albeit real) concessions in the achievement of the modernity of liberation. And by the time the First World War had arrived, all sense of the primacy of the struggle for the modernity of liberation had indeed been muted, as the workers of each European country rallied round the sacred flag and national honor.

The First World War marked the triumph of liberal ideology in the European-North American core of the world-system. But it also marked the point at which the core-periphery political cleavage in the world-system came to the fore. The European powers had barely realized their final world conquests of the last third of the nineteenth century when the rollback of the West began.

Throughout East Asia, southern Asia, and the Middle East (with later prolongations in Africa, and resonances in nominally independent Latin America), national liberation movements began to emerge—in multiple guises, and with varying degrees of success. In the period from 1900 to 1917, various forms of nationalist uprising and revolution occurred in Mexico and China; in Ireland and India; in the Balkans and Turkey; in Afghanistan, Persia, and the Arab world. New "dangerous classes" had now raised their heads, waving the banner of the modernity of liberation. It was not that they were opposed to the modernity of technology. It was that they thought that their own hope for technological modernity would be a function of first achieving liberation.

The years from 1914 to 1945 were marked by one long struggle in the core, primarily between Germany and the United States, for hegemony in the world-system, a struggle in which, as we know, the United States triumphed. But the same years, and beyond, were a period of far more fundamental North-South struggle. Once again, the dominant strata (located in the North) tried to persuade the new dangerous classes of the identity of the two modernities. Woodrow Wilson offered the self-determination of nations and Presidents Roosevelt, Truman, and Kennedy offered the economic development of the underdeveloped nations, the structural equivalents on a world scale of universal suffrage and the welfare state at the national level within the core zone.

The concessions were indeed modest. The dominant strata also offered "identity" in the form of the unity of the free world against the Communist world. But this form of identity was greeted with enormous suspicion by the so-called Third World (that is, the peripheral and semiperipheral zones *minus* those in the so-called Soviet bloc). The Third World considered the so-called Second World as in fact part of their zone and therefore objectively in the same camp. Faced however with the realities of U.S. power combined with the symbolic (but for the most part only symbolic) oppositional role of the U.S.S.R., the Third World by and large opted for nonalignment, which meant that they never came to "identify" with the core zone in the way that the working classes in the core had come to identify with the dominant strata in a shared nationalism and racism. The liberal geoculture was working less well on a world scale in the twentieth century than it had on a national scale in the core zones in the nineteenth.

Still, liberalism was not yet at bay. Wilsonian liberalism was able to seduce and to tame Leninist socialism in ways parallel to

those in which European liberalism had seduced and tamed social
democracy in the nineteenth century.[35] The Leninist program
became not world revolution but anti-imperialism plus socialist
construction, which on inspection turned out to be mere rhetorical variants on the Wilsonian/Rooseveltian concepts of the self-
determination of nations and the economic development of
underdeveloped countries. In Leninist reality, the modernity
of technology had once again taken priority over the modernity of
liberation. And just like the dominant liberals, the supposedly
oppositional Leninists argued that the two modernities were in
fact identical. And, with the aid of the Leninists, the liberals of
the North began to make headway in persuading the national
liberation movements of the South of this identity of the two
modernities.

IN 1968, THIS CONVENIENT CONCEPTUAL BLURRING OF THE TWO
modernities was loudly and vigorously challenged by a worldwide
revolution that took the form primarily, but not at all exclusively,
of student uprisings. In the United States and in France, in
Czechoslovakia and in China, in Mexico and in Tunisia, in
Germany and in Japan, there were insurrections (and sometimes
deaths), which, however different locally, all essentially shared the
same fundamental themes: The modernity of liberation is all,
and has not been achieved. The modernity of technology is a deceptive trap. Liberals of all varieties—liberal liberals, conservative
liberals, and above all socialist liberals (that is, the Old Left)—
are not to be trusted, are indeed the prime obstacle to liberation.[36]

   I myself was caught up in the centerpiece of the U.S. struggles
—Columbia University[37]—and I have two overwhelming memories of that "revolution." One is the students' genuine elation;
they were discovering through the practice of collective liberation
what they were experiencing as a process of personal liberation.
The second was the deep fear this release of liberatory sentiment
evoked among most of the professorate and the administration,
and most especially among those who considered themselves apos-
tles of liberalism and modernity, who saw in this upsurge an
irrational rejection of the obvious benefits of the modernity of

technology.

The world revolution of 1968 flamed up and then subsided, or rather was suppressed. By 1970 it was more or less over everywhere. Yet it had a profound impact on the geoculture. For 1968 shook the dominance of the liberal ideology in the geoculture of the world-system. It thereby reopened the questions that the triumph of liberalism in the nineteenth century had closed or relegated to the margins of public debate. Both the world Right and the world Left moved away once again from the liberal center. The so-called new conservatism was in many ways the old conservatism of the first half of the nineteenth century resurrected. And the New Left was in many ways similarly the resurrection of the radicalism of the early nineteenth century, which I remind you was at that time still symbolized by the term "democracy," a term later to be appropriated by centrist ideologues.

Liberalism did not disappear in 1968; it did, however, lose its role as the defining ideology of the geoculture. The 1970s saw the ideological spectrum return to that of a real triad, undoing the blurring of the three ideologies that had occurred when they had become simply three de facto variants of liberalism between about 1850 and the 1960s. The debate seemed to turn back 150 years or so. Except that the world had moved on, in two senses: The modernity of technology had transformed the world social structure in ways that threatened to destabilize the social and economic underpinnings of the capitalist world-economy. And the ideological history of the world-system was now a memory that affected the current ability of the dominant strata to maintain political stability in the world-system.

Let us look at the second change first. Some of you may be surprised that I place so much emphasis on 1968 as a turning point. You may think: Is not 1989, the symbolic year of the collapse of the Communisms, a more significant date in the history of the modern world-system? Did 1989 not in fact represent the collapse of the socialist challenge to capitalism, and therefore the final achievement of the objective of liberal ideology, the taming of the dangerous classes, the universal acceptance of the virtues of the modernity of technology? Well, no, precisely not! I come to tell you that 1989 was the continuation of 1968, and that 1989 marked not the triumph of liberalism and therefore the permanence of capitalism but quite the opposite, the collapse of liberalism and an enormous political defeat for those who would sustain the capitalist world-economy.

What happened economically in the 1970s and 1980s was that, as a result of a Kondratieff-B downturn or stagnation in the world-economy, state budgets almost everywhere were severely squeezed, and the negative effects on welfare were particularly painful in the peripheral and semiperipheral zones of the world-economy. This was not true of an extended East Asian zone in the 1980s, but in such downturns there is always one relatively small zone that does well precisely because of the overall downturn, and the East Asian growth of the 1980s in no way refutes the general pattern.

Such downturns have of course happened repeatedly in the history of the modern world-system. However, the political consequences of this particular Kondratieff-B phase were more severe than those of any previous one, just because the previous A-phase, 1945–1970, seemingly marked the worldwide political triumph of the movements of national liberation and other antisystemic movements. In other words, just because liberalism had seemed to pay off so well worldwide in 1945–1970 (self-determination plus economic development), the letdown of the 1970s and 1980s was all the more severe. It was hope betrayed and illusions shattered, particularly but not only, in the peripheral and semiperipheral zones. The slogans of 1968 came to seem all the more plausible. Rational reformism (*a fortiori* when it had been clothed in "revolutionary" rhetoric) seemed a bitter deception.

In country after country of the so-called Third World, the populaces turned against the movements of the Old Left and charged fraud. The populaces may not have known what to substitute—a riot here, religious fundamentalism there, antipolitics in a third place—but they were sure that the pseudoradicalism of the Old Left was in fact a phony liberalism that paid off only for a small elite. In one way or another the populaces of those countries sought to oust these elites. They had lost faith in their states as the agents of a modernity of liberation. Let us be clear: they had not lost their desire for liberation, merely their faith in the old strategy of achieving it.

The collapse of the Communisms in 1989–91 then was merely the last in a long series, the discovery that even the most radical rhetoric was no guarantor of the modernity of liberation, and probably a poor guarantor of the modernity of technology.[38] Of course, in desperation and momentarily, these populaces accepted the slogans of the revitalized world Right, the mythology of the "free market" (of a kind, be it said, not to be found even in the United States or Western Europe), but this was a passing mirage. We are already seeing the political rebound in Lithuania, in Poland, in Hungary, and elsewhere.

It is, however, also true that neither in Eastern Europe nor anywhere else in the world is it likely that people will ever again believe in the Leninist version of the promises of rational reformism (under the appelation of socialist revolution). This is of course a disaster for world capitalism, for the belief in Leninism served for fifty years at least as the major *constraining* force on the dangerous classes in the world-system. Leninism in practice was a very conservative influence, preaching the inevitable triumph of the people (hence implicitly preaching patience). The protective cloak of Leninism has now been lost to the dominant strata in the modern world-system.[39] The dangerous classes may now become truly dangerous once again. Politically, the world-system has become unstable.

At the very same time, the socioeconomic underpinnings of the world-system have been seriously weakening. Let me just mention four such trends, which do not exhaust the list of structural transformations. First, there is a serious depletion of the world pool of available cheap labor. For four centuries now, urban wage laborers have been able repeatedly to use their bargaining power to raise the portion of surplus value they can obtain for their labor. Capitalists have nonetheless been able to counter the negative effect this has had on the rate of profit by expanding, just as repeatedly, the labor pool, thereby bringing into the wage labor market new groups of previously nonwaged laborers who were initially ready to accept very low wages. The final geographical expansion of the capitalist world-economy in the late nineteenth century to include the entire globe forced an acceleration of the process of deruralization of the world labor force, a process which is far advanced and may be substantially completed in the near future.[40] This inevitably means a sharp increase in worldwide labor costs as a percentage of the total cost of worldwide production.

A second structural problem is the squeeze on the middle strata. They have been correctly perceived as a political pillar of the existing world-system. But their demands, on both employers and the states, have been expanding steadily, and the worldwide cost of sustaining a vastly expanded middle stratum at ever higher *per personam* levels is becoming too much to bear for both enterprises and state treasuries. This is what is behind the multiple attempts of the last decade to roll back the welfare state. But of two things one. Either these costs are not rolled back, in which case both states and enterprises will be in grave trouble and frequent bankruptcy. Or they will be rolled back, in which case there will be significant political disaffection among precisely the strata that have provided the strongest support for the present world-system.

A third structural problem is the ecological crunch, which poses for the world-system an acute economic problem. The accumulation of capital has for five centuries now been based on the ability of enterprises to externalize costs. This has essentially meant the overutilization of world resources at great collective cost but at virtually no cost to the enterprises. But at a certain point the resources are used up, and the negative toxicity reaches a level that is impossible to maintain. Today we find we are required to invest heavily in cleanup, and we shall have to cut back in usage to keep from repeating the problem. But it is equally true, as enterprises have been shouting, that such actions will lower the global rate of profit.

Finally, the demographic gap doubling the economic gap between North and South is accelerating rather than diminishing. This is creating an incredibly strong pressure for South-to-North migratory movement, which in turn is generating an equally strong antiliberal political reaction in the North. It is easy to predict what will happen. Despite increased barriers, illegal immigration will rise everywhere in the North, as will know-nothing movements. The internal demographic balances of states in the North will change radically, and acute social conflict can be expected.

Thus it is that today, and for the next forty to fifty years, the world-system is finding itself in acute moral and institutional crisis. To return to our opening discourse on the two modernities, what is happening is that there is at last a clear and overt tension between the modernity of technology and the modernity of liberation. Between 1500 and 1800, the two modernities seemed to be in tandem. Between 1789 and 1968, their latent conflict was kept in check by the successful attempt of liberal ideology to pretend that the two modernities were identical. But since 1968, the mask is off. They are in open struggle with each other.

THERE ARE TWO PRINCIPAL CULTURAL SIGNS OF THIS RECOGNI-tion of the conflict of the two modernities. One is the "new science," the science of complexity. Suddenly, in the last ten years, a very large number of physical scientists and mathematicians have turned against the Newtonian-Baconian-Cartesian ideology, which has claimed for five hundred years at least to be the only possible expression of science. With the triumph of liberal ideology in the nineteenth century, Newtonian science became enshrined as universal truth.

The new scientists challenge not the validity of Newtonian science but its universality. Essentially they argue that the laws of Newtonian science are those of a limited special case of reality, and that in order to understand reality scientifically, one must greatly expand our framework of reference and our tools of analysis. Hence, today, we hear the new buzzwords of chaos, bifur-cations, fuzzy logic, fractals, and most fundamentally the arrow of time. The natural world and all its phenomena have become historicized.[41] The new science is distinctly *not* linear. But the modernity of technology was erected on the pillar of linearity. Hence the new science raises the most fundamental questions about the modernity of technology, at least the form in which it has been expounded classically.

The other cultural sign that recognizes the conflict of the two modernities is the movement, primarily in the humanities and the social sciences, of postmodernism. Postmodernism, I hope I have made clear, is not *post*-modern at all. It is a mode of rejecting the modernity of technology on behalf of the modernity of liberation. If it has been cast in this bizarre linguistic form, it is because the postmodernists have been seeking a way to break out of the linguistic hold that liberal ideology has had on our discourse. Postmodernism as an explanatory concept is confusing. Postmodernism as an annunciatory doctrine is no doubt prescient. For we are indeed moving in the direction of another historical system. The modern world-system is coming to an end. It will, however, require at least another fifty years of terminal crisis, that is, of "chaos," before we can hope to emerge into a new social order.

Our task today, and for the next fifty years, is the task of utopistics. It is the task of imagining, and struggling to create, this new social order. For it is by no means assured that the end of one inegalitarian historical system will result in a better one. The struggle is quite open. We need today to define the concrete institutions through which human liberation can finally be expressed. We have lived through its pretended expression in our existing world-system, in which liberal ideology tried to persuade us of a reality that the liberals were in fact struggling against—the reality of increasing equality and democracy. And we have lived through the disillusionment of failed antisystemic movements, movements that were themselves part of the problem as much as they were a part of the solution.

We must engage in an enormous worldwide multilogue, for the solutions are by no means evident. And those who wish to continue the present under other guises are very powerful. The end of what modernity? Let it be the end of false modernity, and the onset, for the first time, of a true modernity of liberation.

CHAPTER EIGHT

THE INSURMOUNTABLE CONTRADICTIONS OF LIBERALISM:

HUMAN RIGHTS AND THE RIGHTS OF PEOPLES IN THE GEOCULTURE OF THE MODERN WORLD-SYSTEM

The French National Assembly adopted on August 26, 1789 the Declaration of the Rights of Man and the Citizen.[42] It has remained ever since the symbolic assertion of what we today call human rights. It was in effect reaffirmed and updated in the Universal Declaration of Human Rights, adopted with few abstentions and no negative votes by the United Nations on December 10, 1948.[43] There was never, however, a parallel emblematic assertion of the rights of "peoples," at least until the United Nations on December 14, 1960 adopted the Declaration on the Granting of Independence to Colonial Countries and Peoples.[44]

The preamble to the 1789 declaration offers as its opening consideration "that ignorance, neglect, and scorn of the rights of man are the sole causes of public misfortune and of the corruption of governments. . . ." We begin thus with the problem of ignorance, as befits a document of the Enlightenment, and the immediate implication is that, when ignorance is overcome, there will no longer be public misfortune.

Why didn't the French Revolution draw up a similar declaration on the rights of peoples? In fact, Abbé Grégoire did suggest in 1793 to the Convention that it seek to codify the laws relating to "the rights and reciprocal duties of nations, the rights of peoples (*gens*)." But Merlin de Douai argued that "this was a proposal that should not be addressed to the Convention of the French people but rather to a general congress of the peoples of Europe,"[45] and this suggestion was put aside.

The observation was pertinent, but there was of course no such general congress at that time. And when it did eventually come into existence (more or less), in the form first of the League of Nations and then the United Nations, such a declaration was not immediately forthcoming. In 1945 the colonial powers, victorious

in the fight for their own freedom, had still not admitted the il-
legitimacy of colonialism. It was only in the 1960 declaration, after
a large part of the colonial world had already won its independence, that the UN reaffirmed its "faith in fundamental human
rights, in the dignity and worth of the human person, in the equal
rights of men and women and of nations large and small," and
therefore "solemnly proclaim(ed) the necessity of bringing to a
speedy and unconditional end colonialism in all its forms and
manifestations."

I do not wish to discuss whether human rights or the rights
of peoples are inscribed or not in natural law, nor do I wish to
review the history of these ideas as intellectual constructs. Rather,
I wish to analyze their role as key elements in liberal ideology,
insofar as it became the geoculture of the modern world-system in
the nineteenth and twentieth centuries. I also wish to argue the case
that the geocultural construct is not only self-contradictory in
terms of its logic but that the insurmountable contradiction it
presents is itself an essential part of the geoculture.

World-systems all have geocultures, although it may take
some time for one to settle into place in a given historical system.
I use the word "culture" here in the sense traditionally used by
anthropologists, as the set of values and basic rules that, both
consciously and subconsciously, govern reward within the system
and create a set of illusions that tend to persuade members to
accept the legitimacy of the system. There are always persons and
groups within any world-system who reject the geocultural values
in whole or in part, and who even struggle against them. But as long
as the majority of the cadres of the system accept these values
actively, and the majority of the ordinary people are not in active
skepticism, we can say that the geoculture exists and its values are
prevailing.

Furthermore, it is important to distinguish between fundamental values, cosmology, and teleology on the one hand and the politics of implementing them on the other. The fact that groups are
in active political revolt does not necessarily mean that they do
not subscribe, perhaps subconsciously, to the fundamental values,
cosmology, and teleology of the system. It may simply mean that

they feel these values are not being implemented fairly. And finally, we must keep in mind historical process. Geocultures come into existence at one moment, and at a later moment they may cease to hold sway. Specifically, in the case of the modern world-system, I am going to argue that its geoculture came into existence with the French Revolution and began to lose its widespread acceptability with the world revolution of 1968.

The modern world-system—the capitalist world-economy—has been in existence since the long sixteenth century. It functioned for three centuries, however, without any geoculture firmly in place. That is to say, there existed between the sixteenth and eighteenth centuries no set of values and basic rules within the capitalist world-economy about which it could be said that the majority of the cadres accepted them actively and the majority of the ordinary people accepted them at least passively. The French Revolution, *latō sensū* changed that. It established two new principles: the normality of political change and the sovereignty of the people.[46] These principles were so quickly and so deeply rooted in popular consciousness that neither Thermidor nor Waterloo could dislodge them. As a result, the so-called Restoration in France (and indeed throughout the world-system) was at no point and in no sense a true restoration of the Ancien Régime.

The key point to note about these two principles is that they were, in and by themselves, quite revolutionary in their implications for the world-system. Far from ensuring the legitimacy of the capitalist world-economy, they threatened to delegitimate it in the long run. It is in this sense that I have previously argued that "the French Revolution represented the first of the antisystemic revolutions of the capitalist world-economy—in small part a success, in larger part a failure."[47] It was therefore in order to contain these ideas by drowning them in a larger whole that the cadres of the world-system felt it urgent to elaborate and impose a larger geoculture.

The elaboration of this larger geoculture took the form of the debate about ideologies. I am using the term *ideology* here in a quite specific sense. I believe that the trinity of ideologies that were developed in the nineteenth century—conservatism, liberalism, and socialism—were in fact the responses to a single question: Given the widespread acceptance of the two concepts of the normality of change and the sovereignty of the people, what political program would be most likely to ensure the good society?

The answers were extraordinarily simple. Conservatives, horrified by these concepts and basically abhorring them, advocated the utmost caution in public action. Political changes, they said, should be enacted only when the claims in their favor were overwhelming, and even then the changes should be undertaken with the minimum of disruption possible. As for popular sovereignty, they argued that it was most wisely utilized when effective power is de facto turned over to the hands of those who traditionally exercise it and who represent the wisdom of continuous tradition.

The opposite view was that of the socialists (or radicals). They welcomed change and called upon the people to exercise fully and directly their sovereignty in the interests of maximizing the speed with which changes in the direction of a more egalitarian society could be effectuated.

The conservative and socialist positions were clear-cut and easy to understand: as slow versus as quickly as possible! As much resistance to equalizing tendencies as possible versus as much dismantling of inegalitarian structures as possible! The belief that very little real change is possible versus the belief that anything can be done if only one overcomes the deliberate social obstacles that exist! These are the familiar contours of Right versus Left, a pair of terms that were themselves directly derived from the French Revolution.

But what then is liberalism, which claimed to stand opposed to conservatism on the one side and to socialism on the other? The answer was formally clear but substantively ambiguous. In formal terms, liberalism was the *via media*, the "vital center" (to use a self-description of the twentieth century).[48] Neither too fast nor too slow, but change at just the right speed! But in substantive terms, what did this mean? Here liberals could in fact seldom agree among themselves, not even within the confines of a specific place at a specific time, and certainly not among liberals located in different places and different time periods.

Consequently, what has defined liberalism as an ideology has been not the clarity of its program but rather its emphasis on process. To be sure, liberals believed political change was inevitable, but they also believed that it would lead to the good society only insofar as the process was rational, that is, that social decisions were the product of careful intellectual analysis. It was therefore crucial that the actual policies be conceived and implemented by those who had the greatest capacity for making such rational decisions, that is, by the technicians or specialists. It was they who could best elaborate the necessary reforms that could, and would, perfect the system in which they lived. For liberals were by definition not at all radical. They sought to perfect the system, not to transform it, because in their view the world of the nineteenth century was already the culmination of human progress, or in a phrase recently revived, "the end of history." If we are living in the last epoch of human history, then naturally our prime (indeed our only possible) task is to perfect the system, that is, to engage in rational reformism.

The three ideologies of modern times have been, then, three political strategies to cope with the popular beliefs that have dominated our modern world since 1789. Two things are most interesting about this trinity of ideologies. The first is that although all three ideologies were formally antistate, in practice they all worked to reinforce the state structures. The second is that, among the three, liberalism emerged swiftly and clearly triumphant, which can be seen by a pair of political developments: over time, both conservatives and socialists moved their actual programs toward the liberal center, rather than away from it: and it was the conservatives and the socialists, acting separately but in complementary ways, who were in fact largely responsible for implementing the liberal political program, far more than the capital "L" Liberals themselves were. This is why, as liberal ideology triumphed, Liberal political parties tended to disappear.[49]

Within the framework of triumphant liberal ideology, what are human rights and from where are they supposed to come? To be sure, there have been diverse answers to this question. But in general, for liberals the answer has been that human rights inhere in natural law. Such an answer gives human rights a powerful base with which to resist opposing claims. However, once this is asserted, and once a specific list of human rights is enumerated, most questions still remain open: Who has the moral (and legal) right to enumerate these rights? If one set of rights conflicts with another set, which set prevails and who decides this? Are rights absolute, or are they limited by some rational appreciation of the consequences of their utilization? (This last dilemma is reflected in the famous declaration of Justice Oliver Wendell Holmes, that freedom of speech does not include the right to shout "Fire!" in a crowded theater.) And above all, who has the right to exercise human rights?

The last question may seem surprising. Is it not obvious that the correct answer is "everyone"? Not at all! In fact, absolutely no one has ever said this. For example, it is almost universally agreed that an infant does not have these rights, or at least not all of them, on the obvious grounds that an infant does not have the mental capacity to exercise them wisely or safely for himself and others. But if not infants, then what about successively the senile aged, small children, sociopaths, felons? And thereupon the list may be extended ad infinitum: what about the young, the neurotic, the soldiers, the aliens, the uneducated, the poor, women? Where is the self-evident line distinguishing capacity from incapacity? There is of course no such self-evident line, and surely not one deducible from natural law. Thus it is that the definition of the persons to whom these human rights apply is inescapably a constantly recurring, current political question.

The definition of who has human rights is in turn closely connected with who may claim to exercise the rights of the people. And here enters another concept deriving from the French Revolution, that of the citizen. For the people who were most clearly authorized to exercise the sovereignty of the people were the "citizens." But who are the citizens? This is meant to be no doubt a group larger than the "king" or the "nobility" or even "persons of property," but it is also a group far smaller than "everyone," even smaller than "everyone resident within the geographic bounds of a given sovereign state."

And therein lies a tale. Over whom does a sovereign's authority lie? Within the feudal system, authority was parcellized. One person could be subject to several overlords and indeed often was. The overlord therefore could not count on undisputed authority over his subjects. The modern world-system created a legal and moral structure that was radically different, one in which the sovereign states, located within and constrained by an interstate system, asserted *exclusive* jurisdiction over all persons falling within their territory. Furthermore, all these territories were bounded geographically, that is, bounded by surveyors' measurements and thus distinct from other territories. In addition, no area within the interstate system was unassigned.

Thus, when "subjects" were transformed into "citizens," the current inhabitants were then immediately divided between "citizens" and "noncitizens" (or aliens). Aliens came in manifold guises; they ranged from long-term (even lifetime) migrants at one extreme to passing visitors at the other. But in no case were such aliens citizens. On the other hand, since the states were congeries of "regions" and "localities," in the early nineteenth century the actual citizens, however defined, were normally persons themselves of quite varied backgrounds—speaking different languages, having different customs, and being bearers of different historical memories. Once subjects became citizens, citizens had therefore to be actively transformed into nationals, that is, persons who would give loyalty to their state priority over other social loyalties. This was not easy, but it was essential if the exercise of popular sovereignty was not to result in presumably irrational intergroup conflict.

Hence while such states as Great Britain, France, and the United States were fostering a sense of nationalism among their citizens,[50] in other places like Germany and Italy, prestate nationalists were struggling to create states that would in turn foster such nationalism. Two institutions were given the primary responsibility in most nineteenth-century states to promote such a sense of national identity: the primary schools and the army. Those countries who did best in this task were those who flourished most. As William McNeill notes:

Under these circumstances, the fiction of ethnic uniformity within separate national jurisdictions took root in recent centuries, as some of the leading nations of Europe harked back to suitably idealized and arbitrarily selected barbarian predecessors. (It is surely amusing to note that the French and British chose Gauls and Britons as their putative national ancestors, in cheerful disregard of subsequent conquerors and invaders from whom they inherited their respective national languages.) The fiction of ethnic uniformity flourished, especially after 1789, when the practical advantages of a neo-barbarian polity in which all adult males, trained to the use of arms, united by a sense of national solidarity, and willingly obedient to chosen leaders, demonstrated its power against governments that limited their mobilization for war to smaller segments of the population.[51]

If you reflect upon it, neither primary schools nor armies have been notorious in their practice of human rights. They are both top-down, quite authoritarian, structures. Transforming ordinary people into citizen-voters and citizen-soldiers may be very useful if one wants to ensure state cohesion, both vis-à-vis other states and in terms of minimizing intrastate civil violence or class struggle, but what does it really do for the promotion and realization of human rights?

The political project of nineteenth-century liberalism for the core countries of the capitalist world-economy was to tame the dangerous classes by offering a triple program of rational reform: suffrage, the welfare state, and national identity. The hope and assumption was that ordinary people would be contented by this limited devolution of reward and therefore would not in fact press for the fullness of their "human rights." The propagation of the slogans—human rights, or freedom, or democracy—was itself part of the process of taming the dangerous classes. The thinness of the social concessions bestowed upon the dangerous classes might have become more salient except for two facts. One, the overall living standards of the core countries were benefiting from the effective transfer of surplus from the peripheral zones. And the local nationalisms of each of these states was complemented by a collective nationalism of the "civilized" nations vis-à-vis the "barbarians." Today, we call this racism, a doctrine explicitly codified in just this period in just these states, and which came to permeate profoundly all the social institutions and all public discourse. At least, this was true until the Nazis brought racism to its logical conclusion, its ne plus ultra version, and thereby shamed the Western world into a formal, but only partial, theoretical repudiation of racism.

Who were the "barbarians"? The colonial peoples, to be sure. Blacks and Yellows to Whites. The "East" to the "West." The "nonhistoric" nations of Eastern Europe to the "historic nations" of Western Europe. The Jews to the Christians. From the beginning, the human rights of "civilized" nations were predicated on the assumption that they were "civilized." The discourse of imperialism was the obverse of the coin. The duty of the countries who asserted that they respected human rights was, therefore, to "civilize" those who did not respect them, who had "barbarous" customs, and who consequently had to be taken in tow and taught, as children might be taught.

It followed that any "rights of peoples" were reserved for a very few specific peoples, and were not at all the rights of all the other peoples. Indeed, to grant "barbarians" their rights as peoples was thought to result, in practice, in the denial of the individual "human rights" of these peoples. The two sets of rights were therefore placed in the nineteenth century in direct conflict one with the other. There was no way the world could have both.

LIBERALISM IN THE NINETEENTH CENTURY SOLVED THE PROBLEM it had set out to solve. Given a world-system in which the doctrines of the normality of change and the sovereignty of the people had come to prevail, how could an upper stratum of men of reason, goodwill, competence, and property keep the "dangerous classes" from upsetting the applecart? The answer had been that it could be achieved by implementing the proper dose of rational reforms. This answer meant in practice limiting the group who could exercise their human rights to *some* of the people as

well as limiting the peoples who could exercise sovereignty at all
even more strictly. Since, however, in the logic of liberalism, the
rights were theoretically universal, the restrictions had to be
justified on convoluted grounds and speciously. In theory, then, the
rights were asserted as universal, but the last thing liberals wanted
was for these liberal principles to be taken literally, that is, to be
truly applied universally. In order for these principles not to be
taken literally, liberalism needed a constraining force. The
constraining force was racism combined with sexism. But of course
this could never be avowed by liberals, since both racism and
sexism were by definition antiuniversal and antiliberal. Edward
Said caught very well the spirit of this second face of liberalism
and its consequences:

> Along with other peoples variously designated as backward,
> degenerate, uncivilized, and retarded, the Orientals were
> viewed in a framework constructed out of biological deter-
> minism and moral-political admonishment. The Oriental
> was linked thus to elements in Western society (delinquents,
> the insane, women, the poor) having in common an iden-
> tity best described as lamentably alien. Orientals were rarely
> seen or looked at; they were seen through, analyzed not as
> citizens, or even people, but as problems to be solved or
> confined or—as the colonial powers openly coveted their
> territory—taken over. . . .

> My point is that the metamorphosis of a relatively inno-
> cuous philological subspecialty [Orientalism] into a ca-
> pacity for managing political movements, administering
> colonies, making nearly apocalyptic statements represent-
> ing the White Man's difficult civilizing mission—all
> this is something at work within a purportedly liberal
> culture, one full of concern for its vaunted norms of
> catholicity, plurality, and open-mindedness. In fact, what
> took place was the very opposite of liberal: the hardening
> of doctrine and meaning, imparted by "science," into
> "truth." For if such truth reserved for itself the right to

> judge the Orient as immutably Oriental in the ways I have
> indicated, then liberality was no more than a form of oppres-
> sion and mentalistic prejudice.[52]

What happened in the twentieth century was that those oppressed by racism and sexism insisted on claiming the rights that
liberals said they theoretically had, in the form both of human
rights and the rights of peoples. The First World War marked a
political caesura. The breakdown of order among the core states,
the "thirty years' war" that went from 1914 to 1945, opened the
space for the new movements.

Since the most immediate problem on the world scene was colo-
nialism/imperialism, that is, the juridical control of large parts of
Asia, Africa, and the Caribbean by European states (but also by
the United States and Japan), the most immediate claim was the
rights of peoples rather than human rights. The legitimacy of this
demand was recognized most spectacularly by Woodrow Wilson
when he made as the centerpiece of global liberalism the theme of
the "self-determination of nations." Of course, Wilson intended
self-determination to be doled out judiciously, methodically,
rationally, when nations were ready. Until then, these nations could
be held "in trust" (to use the language of the UN Charter of 1945).

Conservatives tended to be even more cautious, as might be
expected, and to consider that any "readiness" was likely to occur
only at an indefinitely long time in the future, if ever. Often
conservatives fell back on the theme of human rights during the
first half of the twentieth century to argue against the rights of
peoples. They argued that these colonized populations were not
true "peoples," but simply congeries of individuals whose individual human rights might be recognized when an individual had
sufficient education and had adopted a sufficiently Western life-
style to have shown himself—it was rarely herself—to have reached
the status of a "civilized person." This was the logic of the formal
assimilationist doctrines of a number of colonial powers (e.g.,
France, Belgium, and Portugal), but the other colonial powers
practiced a similar, though informal, mode of categorization and
of doling out human rights.

These socialists who were radically antisystemic and antiliberal at the time of the First World War, that is to say, the Bolsheviks (or Leninists) and the Third International, were initially quite suspicious of all talk of the rights of peoples, which they associated with European middle-class nationalist movements. For a long time, they had been openly hostile to the concept. Then, rather suddenly, in 1920, they shifted course quite radically. At the Baku Congress of the Peoples of the East,[53] the tactical priority of the class struggle within Europe/North America was quietly shelved in favor of a tactical priority for anti-imperialism, a theme around which the Third International hoped to build a political alliance between largely European Communist parties and at least those national liberation movements of Asia (and other parts of the peripheral zones) that were more radical. But, by doing this, the Leninists were in fact joining the liberals in the pursuit of the Wilsonian agenda of the self-determination of nations. And when, after the Second World War, the U.S.S.R. pursued an active policy of fostering "socialist construction" in a series of countries politically linked to it more or less closely, the U.S.S.R. was de facto joining in the pursuit of the world liberal agenda of the economic development of underdeveloped countries.

Hence, we can say that in the years 1945–1970, liberalism had a second apotheosis. If, in the several decades prior to 1914, it had seemed to triumph in Europe, in 1945–1970 it seemed to triumph throughout the world. The United States, world spokesman for liberalism, was the hegemonic power. Its only theoretical opponent, the U.S.S.R., was pursuing a tactical agenda that was not substantively different in terms of the rights of peoples. Hence it was thereby in fact assisting the United States in taming the dangerous classes of the world-system. Furthermore, this liberal policy seemed to be actually paying off for these dangerous classes. The national liberation movements had come or were coming to power throughout the Third World. And they seemed as well to have achieved power (at least partial power) elsewhere, not only via Communist regimes in the Soviet bloc but in the strong role of social-democratic parties in Western Europe and the White Commonwealth nations. And, as part of the incredible global economic expansion of 1945–1970, the economic growth rates in virtually all peripheral countries were reasonably high. These were years of optimism, even where (as in Vietnam) the struggle seemed quite ferocious and destructive.

On looking back on what seems in retrospect almost a golden era, it is striking how missing any concern for human rights was. Human rights were conspicuous by their absence or diminished role everywhere. From the purge trials in Eastern Europe to various forms of dictatorship in Third World countries (but also let us not forget McCarthyism in the United States and the *Berufsverbot* in the Federal Republic of Germany), it was scarcely an era of the triumph of human rights. But even more significantly, it was not a period in which there was very much rhetorical concern with human rights by the world's political movements. Advocates of human rights causes everywhere were seen as threatening national unity in the cold war struggle. And there was no greater degree of complying with human rights among those Third World states most closely linked to the West than among those most closely linked to the Soviet bloc. Furthermore, U.S./Soviet expressed concern with human rights in each other's sphere was limited to propaganda broadcasts, and it had no serious impact on actual policy.

What has happened since then? Two things, principally: the annunciatory and denunciatory world revolution of 1968, which challenged the liberal geoculture; and the subsequent evidence beginning in the 1970s that the liberal package of concessions was barren. In 1968, what the students and their allies were saying everywhere—in the Western countries, the Communist bloc, and the peripheral zones—was that liberal ideology (including the verbally distinct but substantively similar Soviet variant) consisted of a set of fraudulent promises whose reality was in fact largely negative for the large majority of the world's population. Of course, the revolutionaries tended to talk everywhere in terms of the specifics of their countries—which were different in the United States and Germany, Czechoslovakia and China, Mexico and Portugal, India and Japan—but the same themes recurred.[54]

The world revolution of 1968 did not dismantle the world-system. Far from it. But it did dislodge liberalism from its place as the defining ideology of the world-system. Both conservatism and radicalism moved away from the liberal center, more or less back to their topographical location of the first half of the nineteenth century. And this thereby upset the delicate balance that liberalism had sought to establish in limiting the revolutionary implications of both human rights and the rights of peoples.

How this balance was upset can be seen by looking at the impact of the second major change, that of the socioeconomic structuring of the world-system. Since circa 1967/73, the world-economy has been in a Kondratieff B-phase, a period of stagnation. This stagnation has effectively nullified the economic gains of most peripheral zones, with the exception of an East Asian corner, which has been the locus for the kind of production relocation to a limited segment of the world-economy that is a normal feature of Kondratieff B-phases. It has also resulted (at varying paces) in a decline in the real income of the working classes of the North. The bloom is off the rose. And the deception has become enormous. The hope for steady, orderly improvement of life prospects held out by world liberal forces (and their de facto allies, the world Communist movement) has collapsed. And, as it collapsed, the degree to which the rights of peoples was in fact meaningfully achieved has come into question by the presumed beneficiaries themselves.

This questioning of the meaningfulness of what had previously been considered the successful achievement of the rights of the peoples in the post-1945 era had two political consequences. On the one hand, many persons turned to pursuing the rights of new "peoples." Perhaps, they thought, it was that the rights of their "people" had not been recognized. Hence new and more militant ethnicities, secessionism, claims of "minority" peoples within existing states which went along with claims for other groups or quasi peoples such as women, gays and lesbians, the disabled, the aged. And, on the other hand, if the rights of the peoples had not paid off, then why suppress concern with human rights in order to achieve the rights of the peoples? Hence, within the Soviet bloc and within Third World one-party states or military dictatorships, there was a sudden upsurge in claims for the immediate implementation of human rights. This was the movement for so-called democratization. But also within the Western world this was a time of the dismantling of structures that had previously seriously limited the expression of human rights, as well as a time of the creation of new rights, such as the "right to privacy" in the United States.

Furthermore, not only did everyone seem to start talking about human rights in their own countries, but they started talking about it for other countries: Carter's proclamation of human rights as a concern of U.S. foreign policy, the Helsinki accords, the spread of movements like Amnesty International and Médecins du Monde, and the willingness of intellectuals in the Third World to discuss human rights as a general issue and indeed as a priority issue.

The two movements of the last ten to twenty years—the search for new "peoples" whose rights needed to be affirmed, and the more intense claims concerning "human rights"—were both reactions to the deceptions concerning the era 1945–1970, which resulted in the world revolution of 1968—a revolution that centered precisely around the theme of the falsity of the hopes of global liberalism and the nefarious intents of world liberalism in having offered its program of rational reformism. The two responses seemed at first to be a single one. The same people who were asserting the rights of the "new" peoples were also demanding greater human rights.

However, by the late 1980s, and particularly with the geopolitical upheaval of the erstwhile U.S. hegemonic system, marked by the collapse of the Communisms, the two movements began to move in separate, and even opposite, ways. By the 1990s there were whole movements using (once again) the theme of human rights precisely to counter the rights of the "new" peoples. This may be seen in the neoconservative anti–political correctness campaign in the United States. But it may be seen just as much in the proclamation by Médecins du Monde and allied French intellectuals of the *droit d'ingérance*[55] (the right to interfere)—to interfere, that is, in Bosnia and Somalia today; in China and Iran tomorrow; and (why not?) in Black-dominated municipal governments in the United States the day after tomorrow.

Liberalism is today cornered by its own logic. It continues to assert the legitimacy of human rights and, a bit less loudly, the rights of peoples. It still doesn't mean it. It asserts the rights in order that they *not* be fully implemented. But this is getting more difficult. And liberals, caught, as they say, between a rock and a hard place, are showing their true colors by transforming themselves for the most part into conservatives and only occasionally into radicals.

Let us take a simple, very important, and very immediately relevant issue: migration. The political economy of the migration issue is extremely simple. The world-economy is more polarized than ever in two ways: socioeconomically and demographically. The gap is yawning between North and South and shows every sign of widening still further in the next several decades. The consequence is obvious. There is an enormous South-North migratory pressure.

Look at this from the perspective of liberal ideology. The concept of human rights obviously includes the right to move about. In the logic of liberalism, there should be no passports and no visas. Everyone should be allowed to work and to settle everywhere, as is, for example, true within the United States and within most sovereign states today—certainly within any state that pretends to be a liberal state.

In practice, of course, most people in the North are literally aghast at the idea of open frontiers. The politics of the last twenty-five years have moved in exactly the opposite direction. The U.K. was an early erector of new barriers against their erstwhile colonial subjects. In 1993 alone, three major moves have occurred. The German parliament has severely curtailed the welcome for "refugees," now that the peoples of Eastern Europe can actually come. (It was a good show to denounce evil Communists for not letting their peoples go, but we see today what happens when there are no longer evil Communists in power and in a position to restrain emigration.) In France, the government has passed laws that not only limit migrants from their erstwhile colonies but even make it more difficult for migrants' children, themselves born in France, to become citizens. And in the United States in 1993, the governor of our largest state, California—and, a fact that is not without relevance, a state that looks forward shortly to having a non-White majority—calls for amending the U.S. Constitution to end one of our most revered traditions, the jus soli that makes of anyone born on U.S. soil a U.S. citizen by birth.

What is the argument put forward in Great Britain, Germany, France, the United States? That we (the North) cannot assume the burdens (that is, the economic burdens) of the whole world. Well, why not? Merely a century ago, the same North was assuming the "White man's burden" of a "civilizing mission" among the barbarians. Now the barbarians, the dangerous classes, are saying Thank you very much. Forget about civilizing us; just let us have some human rights, like, say, the right to move about freely and take jobs where we can find them.

The self-contradiction of liberal ideology is total. If all humans have equal rights, and all peoples have equal rights, we cannot maintain the kind of inegalitarian system that the capitalist world-economy has always been and always will be. But if this is openly admitted, then the capitalist world-economy will have no legitimation in the eyes of the dangerous (that is, the dispossessed) classes. And if a system has no legitimation, it will not survive.

The crisis is total; the dilemma is total. We shall live out its consequences in the next half-century. However we collectively resolve this crisis, whatever kind of new historical system we build and whether it is better or it is worse, whether we have more or fewer human rights and rights of peoples, one thing is sure: It will not be a system based on liberal ideology as we have known that ideology for two centuries now.

CHAPTER NINE

THE GEOCULTURE OF DEVELOPMENT,
OR THE TRANSFORMATION OF OUR GEOCULTURE?

Development is a term that has gained wide currency in the domains of social science and public policy since the 1950s. *Culture* is a term reintroduced into these domains with much éclat and new emphasis in the 1970s.

The explanation of this terminological history is not very difficult to discern. The emergence of the term development was one immediate consequence of the political emergence of the so-called Third World in the post-1945 era. The peoples of the peripheral zones of the world-system were organizing efficaciously to achieve two principal objectives: greater political autonomy within the world-system, and greater wealth. Greater autonomy meant political independence for peoples that had been colonized, and more strongly nationalist governments for states that were already sovereign. Generally speaking, this goal was achieved in one form or another in almost all peripheral zones in the period 1945–1970. Its legitimacy was endorsed not only in the structure of the United Nations but also in the widespread acceptance of the concept of the "self-determination of nations," and the parallel delegitimization of imperialism.

The objective of greater wealth was equally legitimated. It was, however, far harder to implement, even at a surface level, than the objective of greater political autonomy. However, here too, the years 1945–1970 seemed to be good years. There was a remarkable expansion of the world-economy, and almost all parts of the world seemed to be better off in that period than they had been in the period 1920–1945. There was a widespread optimism about the prospects for further increases in wealth. While it was recognized that there was a serious gap between "industrial" and "agricultural" countries (or between "developed" and "underdeveloped" countries, or in later language, between the "North" and the

"South")—and some persons were already noting as early as the 1950s that the gap was a growing gap—still it was believed that, one way or another, the absolute (and relative) poverty of the peripheral zones could be overcome. This process of overcoming the gap is what came to be called development.

The possibility of the (economic) development of all countries came to be a universal faith, shared alike by conservatives, liberals, and Marxists. The formulas each put forward to achieve such development were fiercely debated, but the possibility itself was not. In this sense, the concept of development became a basic element of the geocultural underpinning of the world-system. It was incarnated in the unanimous decision of the United Nations to designate the 1970s "The Decade of Development."

The timing could not have been worse. The expansion of the world-economy, the Kondratieff A-phase, had peaked. The world-economy was entering into a Kondratieff B-phase of economic stagnation. Stagnation does not imply that everyone's absolute wealth necessarily declines; B-phases are rather times in which this is true of *most* people, but definitely not *all* people. Some people, some geographic locales, find B-phases in fact to be moments of great personal or local advantage.

For the vast majority, however, that have suffered economically in the period 1970–1990 (and continuing on), this B-phase has been an era of great disenchantment, in particular because the vast majority had come to invest so much in the geocultural faith in the possibility of development. Development had been a lodestar; it now seemed an illusion.[56]

This is where the concept of "culture" entered the picture. To be sure, culture had previously been discussed during the development debates of the period 1945–1970. But it had been discussed primarily as an "obstacle." In the view of many theorists, especially, but not only, liberal ideologists, culture represented the "traditional," a concept that was counterposed to the "modern." The peoples of the peripheral zones were said to continue to believe in many so-called traditional values, which were said to keep them from engaging in the practices that would enable them to develop most rapidly. They therefore needed to "modernize" themselves. This was thought not to be an easy task. Nonetheless, enlightened local governments, with the aid of international agencies and the governments of already "developed" states, might undertake "reforms" that would in fact speed up this process of modernization. The primary form of outside support for this work of local reform was called "technical assistance." The word *technical* was supposed to underline two essential features: the assistance was said to be scientifically self-evident; and it was said to be disinterested. "Technical" implied "merely technical," which therefore implicitly meant "apolitical."

As of the 1970s, neither technical assistance nor national reform seemed to be paying off. The economic situation in most countries was visibly deteriorating. The concept that "aid" was a mere matter of transmitting scientific wisdom turned sour. The idea that aid was disinterested seemed to bear bitter fruit, as many countries entered into cycles of very high external debt, capital flight, and negative investment.

One result was that many of those who were among the most "faithful" to the concept of development began to turn on their ideologists. They said in effect the following: You (you the politicians, you the social scientists) told us that economic development is universally possible, and that the path to it is deliberate political change (either liberal reformism or revolutionary transformation). But this has proven manifestly false. For these erstwhile believers, there was a sense of being bereft, of hope denied. Enter a new candidate for hope! If changing the political economy was no longer considered to be a promising, or even a plausible, path to follow; if, in other words, development as it had been preached in the period 1945–1970 was indeed a deception; then perhaps salvation might be found in cultural reassertion. "Culture," which in the years 1945–1970 had been discussed as an "obstacle" that was to be removed as rapidly as possible, was now reclad as a rampart of resistance to the degeneration, disintegration, and worsening of one's economic and political position, which was the consequence of the widening commodification of everything. Culture had ceased being the villain; it had become the hero.

And so it is that we are at a conference cosponsored by UNESCO entitled "Culture and Development," and not merely "development" but "sustainable development." This same UNESCO in 1953 had published a study Margaret Mead did for the World Federation of Mental Health, which took a quite different approach to this topic. That study was undertaken in pursuance of two UNESCO resolutions,[57] and these resolutions are worth citing. The first, No. 3.231 of 1951, requested UNESCO "to study possible methods of relieving tensions caused by the introduction of modern techniques in non-industrialized countries and those in process of industrialization." The second, Resolution 3.24 of 1952, called upon UNESCO "to encourage studies of the methods of harmonizing the introduction of modern technology in countries in process of industrialization, with respect for their cultural values so as to ensure the social progress of the peoples."

These resolutions are telling. UNESCO was saying then in effect: Modern techniques are being introduced in the periphery. This is, of course, good; but it creates tensions, both cultural and personal (the study focused on individual mental health). Someone needs to "harmonize" this. The grammar of the resolutions is awful because of the absence of "with" after the "harmonize"; one is unsure with what precisely modern technology is to be harmonized. One may presume, however, that the intent was simply to calm people down. "Cultural values" were suspect, although they merited "respect." UNESCO wanted most of all to ensure "the social progress of the peoples," whatever that piety may mean.

Today, however, "culture" is no longer merely a piety to invoke and then ignore. It has become a battle cry to invoke in order to denounce. What is this "culture" that is a battle cry? And why have we added the adjective "sustainable" to "development"? Can one possibly develop in an unsustainable manner? The answers to these queries are not scientifically self-evident. They are surely not today a matter of universal consensus. The current answers in fact vary enormously, depending on where you're coming from.

The first problem is, Whose "culture" or "cultures" are we speaking about? *Culture* is a word that has two diametrically opposite usages. It indicates things that are common to two or more individuals; but it also indicates things that are *not* common to two or more specific individuals. That is to say, culture is what unites people, but it is also that which divides them.[58] When we raise the issue today of "culture" in relation to "development," we are using culture in the sense of that which divides peoples. We are talking of the fact that Korean "culture" is different from Chinese "culture" and from British "culture."

The problem is, what is Korean or Chinese or British culture? Is it the set of values and customs preached and somewhat observed by the majority of persons in Korea or China or Great Britain in 1993? Or is it that subset of values and customs preached and somewhat observed by the majority of persons in Korea or China or Great Britain both in 1993 and in 1793? or both in 1993 and 993? It is not in the least self-evident what we intend by the locution "Korean" or "Chinese" or "British" culture. Furthermore, it is not at all self-evident that there is a single culture referred to by these adjectives. Culture varies over time, over regional space within the boundaries indicated by these names, and of course by class. So when we say, as did Margaret Mead, that we must respect cultural values, we need to know whose cultural values or which cultural values we are talking about. Otherwise, the reference is far too vague.

Likewise, when we say "sustainable development," the referent is not clear. If Korea or China or Great Britain is said to "develop," is it in fact South Korea, southern China, the southern counties of Great Britain that we really mean, or truly the entire county? For in each of these specific cases, in the year 1993, the southern zone is doing better economically than the northern zone; and for reasons that are different in each of these cases, the difference between the southern and northern zones not only has been widening in the past twenty-five years, but seems likely to continue to widen further for the next twenty-five at least.

THE GEOCULTURE OF DEVELOPMENT IS CONSTITUTED OF THREE beliefs: (a) that the states that are presently or prospectively members of the United Nations are politically sovereign and, at least potentially, economically autonomous; (b) that each of these states has a national "culture," and in fact only one, or only one that is primary and primordial; (c) that these states may each over time separately "develop" (which in practice seems to mean approach the living standards of the current members of the OECD).

I believe that the first two statements are not quite true, or only true if one qualifies them considerably, and I believe that the third is flat-out false. The political sovereignty of independent states, the first asserted verity, is for the most part a fiction, even for those that are quite strong militarily; furthermore, the concept of economic autonomy is totally mystifying. As for the second verity—the existence of national "cultures," one per country—no doubt there is something that we may designate in this way. But such national "cultures" are not at all coherent, well-defined, relatively unchanging modes of behavior; rather they are constructed and regularly reconstructed mythologies. There are, to be sure, great differences between what people believe in and how they behave among Korea, China, and Great Britain. But it is far harder to argue that in each state there is a single national culture with relatively unbroken historical pedigree, and that intrastate cultural discrepancies can be safely ignored.

As for the possibility of national development within the framework of the capitalist world-economy, it is simply impossible for *all* states to do it. The process of capital accumulation requires a hierarchical system in which surplus value is unequally distributed, both spatially and in class terms. Furthermore, the development of capitalist production over historical time has in fact led to, indeed required, an ever-increasing socioeconomic polarization of the world's population, doubled by a demographic polarization. Thus, it is true on the one hand that some so-called national development is always possible, indeed is a recurrent process of the system. But it is equally true that, since the overall maldistribution of reward is a constant, both historically and theoretically, any "development" in one part of the world-economy is in fact the obverse face of some "decline" or "de-development" or "underdevelopment" somewhere else in the world-economy. And this was no less true in 1893 than it was in 1993; indeed it was no less true in 1593. So I am not saying that it would be impossible for x-country to "develop" (today, yesterday, or tomorrow). What I am saying is that there is no way, within the framework of our current system, for all (or even many) countries simultaneously to "develop."

This does not mean that all countries cannot introduce new forms of mechanized production or advanced information technologies or high-rise buildings or any of the other outward symbols of modernization. They can, to some degree. But this does not mean necessarily that the country, or at least the majority of its population, will in fact be better off. Both the country and the people may in fact be worse off, despite the apparent "development." This is why we are now talking of "sustainable development," that is, something real and lasting, and not a statistical mirage. And this is, of course, why we are talking about culture. For it suggests that not all "development" is good—only a "development" that somehow maintains, perhaps even reinforces, certain local cultural values that we believe are positive, and whose preservation is a great plus not only for the local group but also for the world as a whole.

This is why I have posed my title in the form of a question: The geoculture of development, or the transformation of the geoculture? The geoculture of development—the historical construction of a cultural pressure for all states to pursue a program of "modernization" or "development," a program which for most countries must necessarily be futile—has led us to the cul-de-sac in which we find ourselves today. We are disenchanted with "development" as it was preached in the period 1945–1970. We are aware that it may lead nowhere.

We look, therefore, for alternatives, often still formulated, however, as alternative roads to "national development." Yesterday it was state planning and import substitution; today it is structural adjustment (or shock therapy) and export-led market specialization. And in a few places, it is some unclear third path. We run from shibboleth to shibboleth, frenetically, despairingly, sometimes cynically. In the process, a few do well and better, but most do not. Shall we spend the next thirty years in this revolving cage?

I hope not, for surely we would go mad and throw tantrums. Indeed, to some extent, throwing tantrums is what we are already doing—from Sarajevo to Mogadishu, from Los Angeles to Rostock, from Algiers to Pyongyang.

Instead of the unfruitful search for unlikely alternative solutions to the impossible dilemmas posed by the geoculture of development, we should turn our attention to the transformation of the geoculture that is going on before our very eyes, and pose the questions, Where are we heading? and Where do we want to head?

THE DISILLUSIONMENT WITH THE GEOCULTURE OF DEVELOP-ment has produced a loss of faith in the state as a channel of reform and a bulwark of personal security. This has launched a self-reinforcing cycle. The less legitimacy that states are accorded, the more difficult it is for states to impose order or guarantee minimal levels of social well-being. And the more difficult it is for states to perform these functions, which for most people are their raison d'être, the less legitimacy is accorded to the states.

The prospects frighten people. After five hundred years of the steadily increasing power and legitimacy of state structures (to the point where most people have renounced alternative guarantors of security and well-being), the states suddenly are beginning to lose their aura. (Of course, it has not been five hundred years in all parts of the world, since many zones were incorporated into the modern world-system more recently; but for such areas the statement is true for as long as they have been included within the modern world-system.) Frightened people seek protection. They have turned for protection to "groups"—to ethnic groups, to religious groups, to racial groups, to groups that incarnate "traditional" values.

At the same time, and as part of the very same process of disillusionment with reformism via state-led or state-endorsed or state-supported action, there has been a surge of "democratization," that is, of claims for political equality that go far beyond the mere right to suffrage. This demand for "democratization" is posed not merely vis-à-vis authoritarian states, but vis-à-vis the liberal states as well, since the liberal state as a concept was invented not to further democratization but in fact to prevent it.

In the last twenty-five years the demand for "democratization" has taken the form of claiming more rights for "groups"—for the "majority" within any state that is not a liberal state, but even more ferociously for the "minorities" within any states that claim to be liberal states. Of course, "minority" is a relative concept. "Minorities" may be numerically over fifty percent of the population. Blacks in South Africa, Indians in Guatemala, women in every state in the world are such "minorities" because, whatever the statistics, they are politically and socially oppressed groups. But, of course, Blacks in the United States, Turks in Germany, Kurds in Turkey, and Koreans in Japan are examples of such minorities as well (both socially and statistically).

Thus the new turn to "groups" has two quite different, almost contradictory, sources. On the one hand, it is fueled by fear, by disintegration, and, above all, by fear of further disintegration. And on the other hand it is fueled by the self-assertion of the oppressed, by their positive demands for a truly egalitarian world. This double source of the new reliance on groups can lead to an enormous tangle. Nothing illustrates this better than what has been occurring with the collapse of the erstwhile Yugoslav state. Let us not forget that not so many years ago, Yugoslavia was considered to be a model of how sensibly to avoid intergroup strife. Today it seems the world and all the peoples of erstwhile Yugoslavia stand fatalistically before a steadily spreading and worsening carnage.

Are not these "groups" in which people put their faith the same entities we are talking about when we speak of "cultures"? We are liberated by asserting our distinctive culture. We use it to defend ourselves, to secure our rights, to demand equal treatment. But at the same time, each time we assert our distinctiveness we begin to impinge on the assertions of others. In erstwhile Yugoslavia, to return to our example, the political disintegration of the state began a few years ago when Serbia revoked the autonomous status of Kosovo. There are two clear facts about Kosovo. Fact one: Most of the population today is Moslem in religion and speaks primarily

Albanian. Fact two: Most Serbians consider Kosovo the historical hearth of Serbian culture. Serbia without Kosovo is Serbia deprived of its cultural history. It is not easy to satisfy simultaneously the claims deriving from these two facts.

To the Serbs, Serbia without Kosovo is like Israel without Jerusalem. Ah, that is another good example! And are these "cultural" claims really different from the claims of Iraq to Kuwait? And if so, how? How might it be possible to extract ourselves from what threatens to be a morass of claims and counterclaims that translates into endless violence? Certainly it would be futile, and furthermore hypocritical, to preach a pacifism based on a specious universalism that in fact masks a call to live with a status quo itself sustained by the momentary immediate distribution of firepower in the world.

The fact is that we live in a deeply inegalitarian world, and we have no moral right to ask anyone to desist from seeking to make it less so. Hence we must want a "sustainable development" for all, and we must recognize each group's, each country's, claim to its "cultural" integrity. If these claims are causing us problems today, it is not because the claims are being made but because the repressive mechanisms of the world-system are weakening. The great world disorder into which we have entered is caused not by the struggles of the oppressed but by the crisis of the structure that oppresses them.

In this period of great world disorder, of crisis in our modern world-system of historical capitalism, we shall come out ahead only if we are able to envisage clearly the whole picture. For this period will be one of double struggle—a struggle for immediate survival, and one of shaping the coming historical system that eventually will emerge out of the current systemic chaos. Those who are seeking to create a new structure in such a way as to replicate the key feature of the existing structure—hierarchical inequality—will do everything to keep our attention focused on immediate survival, in order to prevent the emergence of historical alternatives to their project of factitious transformation, of a surface transformation that leaves intact the inequalities.

The fact that an historical system is in crisis does not mean that people do not continue day by day to do, or try to do, the same kinds of things (or at least many of the same kinds of things) that they have been doing. World production of commodities for the market will continue. States will continue to have armies and wage wars. Governments will still use police forces to uphold their policies. The accumulation of capital will proceed, albeit with increasing difficulty, and the socioeconomic polarization of the world-system will deepen. And both states and individuals will still seek to promote their upward mobility in the ranking of the system, or at least to prevent their downward mobility.

With one great difference from the last 500 years, however! The fluctuations within the system will be ever wilder and sharper. When the historical system was relatively stable, large actions (e.g., so-called revolutions) had a relatively small impact on the operations of the system, whereas now even small actions may have a relatively large impact—less in reforming the current system than in determining the contours of the eventual replacement system or systems. Therefore, the reward for human action is potentially very great, and the penalty for inaction or misguided action equally great.

LET US THEREFORE LOOK AT THE ANTISYSTEMIC CULTURAL critique of our existing system and its geoculture over five hundred years. With great loudness over the past twenty-five years, the critique has focused on four central issues: materialism, individualism, ethnocentrism, and the destructiveness of the Promethean drive. Each of these critiques has been very strong, but each has found it difficult effectively to persuade.

1) The critique of materialism has been very obvious: The pursuit of wealth, comfort, and material advantage generally has led to, indeed forced, the neglect of other values, sometimes referred to as spiritual values. This has been the consequence of the relentless trend toward the secularization of the states and of all major social institutions. This secularization has been an essential pillar of the states system, which has provided the framework within which an endless accumulation of capital could take place. Indeed the endless accumulation of capital, the defining feature of our historical system, is the quintessential materialist value.

There have been two problems with this critique historically. First, it has tended to be made in the interests of old privileged strata who were being displaced by new privileged strata. Hence it was often less than an honest critique. It was not truly antimaterialist but primarily a question of whose ox was being gored. Or it was being used not as a critique of the powerful but as a critique of the weak, whose protests were taking somewhat anarchic forms. And it was therefore a form of blaming the victim.

Secondly, an antimaterialist critique only makes sense if one argues that the materialism is exaggerated. Fulfilling what have come to be called "basic needs" (and then some) is not materialist but a matter of survival and human dignity. Antimaterialism has never been very persuasive to the have-nots. And in a hierarchical system based on invidious distinctions of access to capital, antimaterialism has also not been very persuasive to middle cadres who have a proximate view of what goes on at the very top.

2) The critique of individualism derives from the critique of materialism. A system giving pride of place to materialist values endorses the rat race of all against all. In the end, this leads to a totally egocentric view of the world, at most modified by some loyalty to the nuclear family (the result in this situation of human mortality). The critics have vaunted in individualism's place the "society," the "group," the "community," often the "family." And some critics have talked of the primacy of all humanity.

Here the critics have been somewhat more successful, in terms of being able to convince large groups of people to submit their individual aspirations to some group objectives. But this devotion to collectivities has proven fragile. Whenever achieved, these collectivities have sought to institutionalize their ability to pursue their collective interests by obtaining some kind of political power. Thereby, they reenter the operative processes of the modern world-system, which has proved too powerful for individual resolve, particularly that of group leaders: Power "corrupts," as Lord Acton said. But it was not just any power; it was power within this particular historical system, with its enormous opportunities for channeling capital accumulation.

Corruption has had the inevitable effect of disillusioning the collectivity. Those who sacrificed their individualist objectives found both that others had simply profited in their place, and that in the long run they were not significantly better off (indeed, often worse off).

3) The third critique has been of ethnocentrism, and most particularly of its dominant and most virulent form within historical capitalism, Eurocentrism, whose obverse side has been racism. The critics have pointed out that the crude version of Eurocentrism appears as racism, which leads to social discrimination against, and segregation of, groups labeled "inferior." But the critics have gone further. Eurocentrism, they say, has a sophisticated face, one that is more "liberal": It is the face of universalism.

Europeans have imposed their particular values on the rest of the world in the guise of defining their values as universal values. And they have done so in ways that have furthered their own domination and material interests. Indeed, the final, most sophisticated, form of ethnocentric universalism has been the concept of meritocracy, which has ordained that the "rat race" be fairly run but has ignored the fact that the runners begin the race from varying starting points, which are socially, and not genetically, determined.

This critique has been very powerful, but it has been vitiated by the consequences of a very elementary *divide et impera* tactic on the part of the powerful. As attacks on ethnocentrism have built up steam, the dividing line between who is considered superior and who inferior has constantly shifted, including inside the top stratum some of the most vigorous protestors, who thereupon have changed their line. Since there is constant demographic polarization in the world-system, shifting the dividing line has been easy, serving merely to keep the percentage of persons on top roughly stable. But politically it has meant that each generation of protestors had virtually to start anew.

4) Finally, the critique of the Promethean drive has been the most recent, but in many ways the most telling. The pressures for capital accumulation have led not merely to technological advance (presumably neutral at worst, virtuous at best) but also to enormous destructiveness. The concern about the sociopsychological corrosiveness of historical capitalism, put forward in terms of

"alienation" and "anomie," have been joined with a concern about the geophysical corrosiveness of historical capitalism in terms of ecology.

Today it is admitted that the self-destructiveness of historical capitalism has been enormous and is growing at a rapid pace. But this critique too has had its limits, in terms of the recuperability of the complaints. Alienation and anomie have been turned into the commodity of therapy. Ecology is being turned into the commodities of cleanup and reuse. Instead of rooting out the causes of destruction, we are seeking to mend the torn fabric.

THE CHALLENGE BEFORE US TODAY, IN THIS EPOCH OF TRANSITION to a new historical system, is to take the four critiques of historical capitalism—profound critiques that have, however, been formulated in ways that have been insufficiently persuasive—and transform them into a positive model of an alternative social order that does not fall into the traps into which past (partial) critics have fallen. We must be radical—that is, we must go to the roots of the issue. And we must offer truly fundamental reconstruction. This is a project of fifty years at least. It is a worldwide project and cannot be done locally or partially, although local action must be a major part of the construction. And it requires the full use of the human imagination. But it is possible.

It is possible, but by no means certain. Triumphalism will undo our efforts. It is rather the proper combination of sobriety and fantasy that we must look for. And we may find it in the strangest places, in every corner of the world.

CHAPTER TEN

AMERICA AND THE WORLD:
TODAY, YESTERDAY, AND TOMORROW

God, it seems, has distributed his blessing to the United States thrice: in the present, in the past, and in the future. I say it seems so, because the ways of God are mysterious, and we cannot pretend to be sure we understand them. The blessings of which I speak are these: in the present, prosperity; in the past, liberty; in the future, equality.

Each of these blessings has always involved measuring the United States of America by the yardstick of the world. Despite the United States's long history of seeing itself as remote from the world, and removed especially from Europe, its self-definition has always in fact been in terms of the world. And the rest of the world has in turn always kept the United States in the forefront of its attention for some two hundred years now.

The problem with God's blessings is that they have a price. And the price we are willing to pay is always a call upon our righteousness. Each blessing has been accompanied by its contradictions. And it is not always obvious that those who received the blessings were those who paid its price. As we move from today into tomorrow, it is time once again to count our blessings, assess our sins, and behold our reckoning sheet.

TODAY

The today of which I speak began in 1945 and came to an end in 1990. In this period, in precisely this period and no longer, the United States was the hegemonic power of our world-system. The origin of this hegemony was our prosperity; the consequence of this hegemony was our prosperity; the sign of this hegemony was our prosperity. What did we do to merit this singular and rare privilege? Were we born great? Did we achieve greatness? Was greatness thrust upon us?

The present began in 1945. The world had just emerged from a long and terrible world war. Its battlefield was the whole Eurasian landmass, reaching from the island in the west (Great Britain) to the islands in the east (Japan, the Philippines, and the Pacific islands) and from the northern zones of Eurasia to northern Africa, Southeast Asia, and Melanesia in the south. Throughout this vast zone there was immense devastation of human life and the physical stock that was the basis of world production. Some areas were more devastated than others, but almost no part of this vast zone escaped free and clear. Indeed, the only major industrial zone whose equipment and national infrastructure remained intact was North America. The factories of the United States were not only unbombed but also had been brought to new levels of efficiency by wartime planning and mobilization.

Since the United States entered the war with productive machinery that was already a match (at least) for that of all others in the world, the wartime destruction of everyone else's machinery created a gap in productive capacity and efficiency that was enormous. It was this gap that created the possibility for U.S. enterprises to flourish in the twenty-five years to come as they had never done before. And it was this gap that ensured that the only way these enterprises could flourish was by permitting a significant increase in the real wages of the workers at these enterprises. And it was this rise in real wages—translated into the ownership of homes, automobiles, and household durables, along with a vast expansion of educational opportunity (college education in particular)—that constituted the prosperity that Americans knew and that amazed the world.

Prosperity is above all things an opportunity, an opportunity to enjoy, an opportunity to create, an opportunity to share. But prosperity is also a burden. And the first burden that prosperity imposes is the pressure to maintain it. Who wishes to give up the good things of life? There has always existed a minority of ascetics and another minority of those willing to divest themselves of privilege out of shame or guilt. But for most people, renouncing the good life is a mark of sainthood or madness and, however admirable, is not for them. The United States as a country in the period 1945–1990 acted normally. The country was prosperous and sought to maintain that prosperity.

Our country—its leaders, but also its citizens—pursued as an obvious national goal not happiness (the perhaps utopian and romantic image that Thomas Jefferson inscribed in our Declaration of Independence) but prosperity. What did it take for the United States to maintain the prosperity it had in hand? Seen from the perspective of the immediate post-1945 years, the United States needed three things: customers for its immense industrial park; world order such that commerce could be pursued at lowest cost; and assurances that the production processes would not be interrupted.

None of the three seemed too easy to achieve in 1945. The very destructiveness of the world war that gave the United States its incredible edge had simultaneously impoverished many of the wealthier areas of the world. There was hunger in Europe and Asia, and its peoples could scarcely afford Detroit's automobiles. The ending of the war left unresolved large numbers of "national" issues, not only in Europe and northern Asia but also in many countries outside the war zones, in countries we came later to call the Third World. Social peace seemed remote. And, in the United States, Americans were poised to resume their own disruptive social conflicts of the 1930s, which had been adjourned but scarcely resolved by wartime political unity.

The United States moved, with less hesitancy than it had anticipated, to do what was necessary to eliminate these threats to its prosperity and its hopes for still greater prosperity. The United States invoked its idealism in the service of its national interests. The United States believed in itself and in its goodness and sought to serve and lead the world in a manner it thought just and wise. In the process, the United States obtained the applause of many and incurred the wrath of others. It felt hurt by the wrath and warmed by the applause, but above all it felt impelled to pursue the path it had designed for itself and that it considered to be the path of righteousness.

The United States tends to look back upon the postwar world and celebrate four great achievements, for which it gives itself a large part of the credit. The first is the reconstruction of the devastated Eurasian landmass and its reinsertion into the ongoing productive activity of the world-economy. The second is the maintenance of peace in the world-system, the simultaneous prevention of nuclear war and military aggression. The third is the largely peaceful decolonization of the ex-colonial world, accompanied by significant aid for economic development. The fourth is the integration of the American working class into economic well-being and full political participation, along with the ending of racial segregation and discrimination in the United States.

When, just after the Second World War, Henry Luce proclaimed that this was "the American century," it was to the expectation of just such accomplishments that he was pointing. This has indeed been the American century. These achievements were real. But each has had its price and each has had unanticipated consequences. The correct balance sheet is far more complex morally and analytically than we are wont to admit.

It is of course true that the United States sought to aid in the reconstruction of the Eurasian landmass. It offered immediate relief in 1945, collectively through UNRRA and individually through CARE packages. It moved soon thereafter to more substantial, long-term measures, most notably through the Marshall Plan. A great deal of money and political energy was invested in the years between 1945 and 1960 in this reconstruction of Western Europe and Japan. The objects of these initiatives were clear: to rebuild the destroyed factories and infrastructure; to re-create functioning market systems with stable currencies well integrated into the international division of labor; and to ensure sufficient employment opportunities. Nor did the United States limit itself to direct economic assistance. It also sought to encourage the creation of inter-European structures that would prevent the revival of the protectionist barriers that were associated with the tensions of the interwar period.

To be sure, this was not simply altruistic. The United States needed a significant sector of foreign customers for its productive enterprises if they were to produce efficiently and profitably. A rebuilt Western Europe and Japan would provide exactly the necessary base. Furthermore, the United States needed reliable allies who would take their political cues from the United States in the world arena; the Western European states plus Japan were the most likely countries to play this role. This alliance was institutionalized not only in the form of NATO and the U.S.-Japan Defense Treaty but even more in the close continuing political coordination of these countries under U.S. "leadership." The net result was that, at least at the beginning, all the major decisions of international life were being taken in Washington, with the largely unquestioning acquiescence and support of a set of powerful client-states.

The only serious obstacle the United States perceived in the world political arena was the U.S.S.R., which seemed to be pursuing political objectives quite disparate from, even opposite to, those of the United States. The U.S.S.R. was at one and the same time the only other signficant military power in the post-1945 world and the political center of the world Communist movement, ostensibly dedicated to world revolution.

When we discuss relations between the United States and the U.S.S.R. in the postwar period, we tend to use two code words to express U.S. policy: *Yalta* and *containment*. They seem to be rather different. Yalta has acquired the flavor of a cynical deal, if not that of a Western "sellout." Containment symbolizes, by contrast, U.S. determination to stop Soviet expansion. In reality, however, Yalta and containment were not two separate, let alone opposing, policies. They were one and the same thing. The deal was containment. Like most deals, it was basically offered by the stronger (the United States) to the weaker (the U.S.S.R.) and accepted by both because it served their mutual interests.

The war ended with Soviet troops occupying the eastern half of Europe and U.S. troops occupying the western half. The boundary was the river Elbe, or the line from Stettin to Trieste, which Churchill was to describe in 1946 as the "Iron Curtain." On the surface, the deal merely provided for the military status quo and peace in Europe, with the United States and the U.S.S.R. free to make what political arrangements they preferred within their respective zones. This military status quo—call it Yalta or call it containment—was scrupulously respected by both sides from 1945 to 1990. It will one day be called the "Great American Peace" and looked back upon nostalgically as a golden era.

The deal had, however, three codicils, which are less often discussed. The first codicil had to do with the functioning of the world-economy. The Soviet zone was neither to ask for, nor to receive, U.S. assistance in reconstruction. They were permitted to, indeed required to, withdraw into a quasi-autarkic shell. The advantages to the United States were several. The costs of reconstruction of the Soviet zone threatened to be enormous, and the United States already had more than enough on its plate in assisting Western Europe and Japan. Furthermore, it was not at all clear that even a reconstructed U.S.S.R. (and China) could provide a rapidly available significant market for U.S. exports—certainly nothing like what Western Europe and Japan might offer. The investment in reconstruction would have therefore been insufficiently remunerative. Yalta represented a net economic gain for the United States in the short run.

The second codicil was in the ideological arena. Each side was allowed, indeed encouraged, to raise the decibels of mutual condemnation. John Foster Dulles intoned, and Stalin agreed, that neutralism was to be considered "immoral." The struggle between the so-called Communist and Free Worlds permitted a tight internal control within each camp: anti-Communist McCarthyism in the West, and spy trials and purges in the East. What was really being controlled—both in the West and in the East—was the "Left," in the sense of all those elements who wished to question radically the existing world order, the capitalist world-economy that was reviving and flourishing under U.S. hegemony with the collusion of what may be called its subimperialist agent, the U.S.S.R.

The third codicil was that nothing in the extra-European world —what we later came to call the Third World, and more recently the South—was to be allowed to call into question the Great American Peace in Europe, and its institutional underpinning, the Yalta-containment doctrine. Both sides were pledged to this and ultimately respected it. But it was a difficult codicil to interpret, and turned out to be even more difficult to enforce.

In 1945, the United States did not anticipate that the Third World would be as tempestuous as it in fact became. The United States approached the problems of the Third World with a Wilsonian worldview, but languidly. It was in favor of the self-determination of nations; it was in favor of improvement in their economic well-being. But it did not consider the matter to be urgent. (Nor, despite the rhetoric, did the Soviet Union.) In general, the United States gave priority to its relations with the U.S.S.R. and with Western Europe. In 1945 the European states were still the colonial powers in Africa, a good part of Asia, and the Caribbean, and they were determined to pursue any changes at their own pace and in their own style. They were therefore far less acquiescent to U.S. interference in their colonial realm than they were to U.S. interference in other arenas, even in their domestic affairs. (The U.S.S.R., be it noted, had similar problems with Western European Communist parties.)

European foot-dragging and Soviet hesitancy meant that the initial U.S. position was one of minimal involvement in the ongoing political struggles of the Third World. But in fact, Western Europe turned out to be politically far weaker in the colonial world than they had anticipated, and the U.S.S.R. was forced to be more activist than it had hoped because of pressures on it to be consistent with its Leninist ideological rhetoric. Therefore, the United States was forced as well into a somewhat more activist role. President Truman proclaimed "Point Four"—the doctrine of aid for economic development. It was only the last of the points in his speech, but it is the one we remember. The United States began to put quite gentle pressure on Western European countries to speed up the process of decolonization and to accept full political independence as a legitimate outcome of the process. In addition, the United States began to cultivate "moderate" nationalist leaders. The definition of "moderate" seems very clear in retrospect. A "moderate" nationalist movement was one that, while seeking political independence, was ready to accept (even expand) the integration of the country into the production processes of the world-economy, including the possibility of transnational investment. In any case, the United States perceived its policy as one of maintaining and fulfilling its historic commitment to anticolonialism, a commitment deriving from its own origins as a nation.

Finally, there was no neglect of the home front. We often forget today how conflict ridden the United States was in the 1930s. At that time, we were engaged in a full-fledged and vituperative debate about our role in world affairs: isolationism vs. interventionism. There was also an acute class struggle between capital and labor. One of the folk heroes of the postwar period, Walter Reuther, was having his head bashed in on a Detroit bridge during the sit-down strikes of 1937. In the South, the Ku Klux Klan was very strong, and Negroes were still being lynched. The wartime years were years of social truce, but many feared the resumption of the social conflict within the United States with the ending of the war. It would be difficult to be a hegemonic power, however, if the country were to remain as disunited as it had been in the 1930s. And it would be hard to take full profit from U.S. economic advantage if production were to be constantly disrupted by strikes and labor conflict.

Within a very short time the United States seemed to put its house in order. Isolationism was buried with the symbolic but very significant conversion of Senator Vandenberg, who launched the idea of a "bipartisan foreign policy" for a United States that was now ready "to assume its responsibilities" in the world arena. The great General Motors strike of 1945, led by the same Walter Reuther, came to a happy ending with a compromise that was to set the pattern for all the unionized major industries for twenty-five years to come: significant wage increases, combined with a no-strike pledge, a rise in productivity, and price rises for the final product. Two fundamental steps were taken to end the post-Reconstruction patterns of legalized segregation of Blacks and Whites: President Truman's integration of the armed forces in 1948 and the Supreme Court's 1954 unanimous ruling in *Brown v. the Board of Education* (reversing *Plessy v. Ferguson*) that segregation was unconstitutional. The United States was very proud of itself, and the Voice of America was not reluctant to boast of our practical commitment to freedom.

By 1960, it seemed that the United States was achieving its objectives admirably. The new prosperity was visible. Suburbia was flourishing. Facilities for higher education and health care had expanded enormously. A truly national air-and-road network had been constructed. Western Europe and Japan were back on their feet. The U.S.S.R. was well contained. The U.S. labor movement, purged of its left wing, was a recognized component of the Washington establishment. And 1960 was the Year of Africa, the year in which sixteen African states, formerly colonies of four different European states, proclaimed their independence and joined the United Nations. The election of John F. Kennedy that year seemed the apotheosis of the new American reality. Power had passed, he said, to a new generation, born in this century, and therefore, he implied, fully rid of old hesitations and inadequacies, fully committed to a world of permanent prosperity and, presumably, of expanding freedom.

It was precisely at this point, however, that the price of prosperity began to become clear, its unanticipated consequences began to be felt, and its institutional structures began, if not to crumble, at least to shake, even to tremble. Along with U.S. prosperity and even world prosperity came the realization of the growing gap, internationally and within the United States, between rich and poor, core and periphery, the included and the excluded. In the 1960s the gap was only relative; in the 1970s, and even more in the 1980s, it became absolute. But even a relative gap, perhaps especially a relative gap, spelled trouble. The trouble was worldwide.

The trouble in Western Europe and Japan seemed relatively innocent at first. By the 1960s, these countries were "catching up" with the United States—first of all in productivity; then, with some lag, in standard of living. By the 1980s, they exceeded the United States in productivity and had come to equal the United States in standard of living. This might be called an "innocent" form of trouble since it bred a quiet form of rejection of U.S. hegemony, a form of rejection that was all the more efficacious precisely because it was quiet and self-confident about the future. To be sure, our allies were restrained by their gratitude; nonetheless, bit by bit, they tried to emerge from their political tutelage to assert their separate roles in the world-system. The United States had to utilize all its institutional and ideological strength to hold its allies in check, and this succeeded in part up to the end of the 1980s.

Elsewhere, however, the rebellions were less "innocent." Most persons in the Eastern European countries, both on the Left and on the Right, refused to accept the legitimacy of the Yalta arrangements. The initial cold war ideological tightness could not hold, either in the United States or in the U.S.S.R. The U.S. Senate censured McCarthy in 1954, and Khrushchev at the XXth Party Congress of the CPSU revealed and denounced Stalin's crimes. The peoples of Eastern Europe took advantage of every loosening of the ideological cement to try to regain a freedom of action they were denied. This occurred most notably in 1956 in Poland and Hungary, in 1968 in Czechoslovakia, and in 1980 again in Poland. Since all these political uprisings were directed not against the United States but, in the immediate sense, against the U.S.S.R., the United States felt free not to intervene in any way. Thus it remained faithful to its arrangement with the Soviet Union, while the latter was free to take the measures necessary to repress the uprisings.

It is in the Third World that events came to be most out of control, and right from the beginning. Stalin pressed the Chinese Communists to come to an arrangement with the Kuomintang. They ignored him and marched into Shanghai in 1949. The real worry for the United States was not that China would now be a Soviet puppet but that it would not be. The fear turned out to be justified. Within a year, U.S. troops would find themselves involved in a long, costly military operation in Korea merely to preserve the status quo. Nor was peaceful moderate decolonization to occur in Indochina. First the French, then the United States were drawn into an even longer, even more costly war, which the United States would eventually lose at the military level. The languid scenario for the Middle East—conservative Arab states plus Israel, all safely pro-Western—was upset by the rise of Nasser and Nasserism, which would be echoed in various forms from North Africa to Iraq. Algeria's war of independence would topple the Fourth

French Republic and bring to power in France the figure least sympathetic to U.S. tutelage, Charles de Gaulle. And in Latin America, the long-standing political turmoil took a new more radical form with the arrival of Castro to power in Cuba.

Since these uprisings of the Third World were in fact directed primarily not against the U.S.S.R. but against the United States (unlike those in Eastern Europe), the United States felt free to intervene. And intervene it did, with some vigor. If one looks at the balance sheet over forty-five years, one can say that at the military level the United States won some and lost some, and that at the political level the United States seemed to win some and lose some. The United States's main strength was at the economic level, in its ability to punish states it deemed hostile (Vietnam, Cuba, Nicaragua). What is, I think, crucial to note is that globally, in all these affairs, the U.S.S.R. played a minor role. On the one hand, the movements in the Third World were engaged in defiance to the U.S. world order, and the U.S.S.R. was part of that world order. The impetus was local. The Great American Peace did not serve, in their views, the interests of the peoples of the Third World. On the other hand, while these uprisings forced the United States to pay much more military and political attention to the Third World than anyone ever conceived of in 1945, the fact is that none of the movements singly, nor even all of them collectively, was able to dismantle the Great American Peace or immediately threaten American prosperity. The price for the United States nonetheless became higher and higher.

There was a price to pay at home as well. There was the cost of maintaining order in the Third World, the most spectacular instance of which was the Vietnam War. The cost in lives and the cost to the government's financial stability were both high. But ultimately the highest cost was the cost to the state's legitimacy. Watergate would never have forced a president to resign had not the presidency itself already been undermined by Vietnam.

There was also the cost of relative deprivation. It was precisely the integration of trade unions into the political establishment, the ending of legal segregation, and the real increase in the incomes of skilled workers and the middle classes that brought to the fore the degree to which there were exclusions. The United States had moved from its pre-1945 situation, when only a minority of the population was prosperous, to its post-1945 situation, when the majority felt prosperous, or at least moderately so. This was a trigger to action for the excluded, action that took the form of new consciousnesses—most notably Black consciousness, womens' consciousness, and later that of other minority groups.

In 1968, all these challenges were brought together into one big melting pot—resentment of U.S. imperialism; resentment of Soviet subimperialism and collusion with the United States; resentment of the integration of Old Left movements into the system, reducing their presumed opposition to complicity; resentment of the exclusion of oppressed minority strata and of women (extended subsequently to all sorts of other groups—the handicapped, gays, indigenous populations, etc.). The worldwide explosion of 1968—in the United States and Western Europe, in Czechoslovakia and China, in Mexico and India—went on for three years, more or less, until the raging fires were brought under control by the forces sustaining the world-system. The fire was reduced to embers, but in the process it gravely damaged the ideological supports of the Great American Peace. It would now be only a matter of time until this peace came to an end.

The Great American Peace found its origin in American economic strength. It found its reward in American prosperity. It would now find its undoing in American success. Starting from about 1967, the reconstruction of Western Europe and Japan reached the point where these countries were competitive with the United States. Even more, the total of world production thereby achieved brought on a long downturn in the world-economy—one in which we have been living ever since and one that began to erode American prosperity. From 1967 to 1990 the United States sought to stem the tide of decline, but after twenty-odd years the effort required became too great. There were two modes of stemming the tide. One was the "low posture" of Nixon, Ford, and Carter. It stumbled on Iran. The second was the fake machismo of Reagan and Bush. It stumbled on Iraq.

The "low posture" solution to the threatened loss of U.S.

hegemony had three main pillars: Trilateralism, the OPEC oil rise, and the post-Vietnam syndrome. Trilateralism was an attempt to keep Western Europe and Japan from achieving political autonomy by offering them a junior partnership in decision making. Trilateralism succeeded to the degree that it forestalled any significant falling-out of the OECD countries on military policies, political strategies, and world financial arrangements. The Western Europeans and the Japanese continued to respect U.S. leadership in form. But in reality, and without rhetoric, they pursued unremittingly the improvement of their relative positions in world productive processes, knowing that eventually the U.S. hegemonic position would inevitably crumble for lack of an economic base.

The OPEC oil price rise, under the leadership of the United States's chief agents in the affair (Saudi Arabia and the Shah of Iran), was designed primarily to pump world surplus capital into a central fund that would then be recycled to Third World and socialist countries largely in the form of loans to states, providing short-run stability in these states and artificially sustaining the world market for industrial production. A secondary advantage of the OPEC oil price rise was supposed to be that it created greater difficulties for Western Europe and Japan than it did for the United States and hence slowed them down competitively. A tertiary consequence was that, by stimulating inflation in the OECD countries, but especially in the United States, it reduced real wages. During the 1970s the OPEC oil price rise had the desired effect on the world-economy: It did indeed work to slow down the decline of U.S. economic advantage.

The third aspect of the "low posture" response was the post-Vietnam syndrome, which was not a reaction against Nixon but a fulfillment of his strategy: the opening to China and the withdrawal from Indochina, both of which were inevitably followed by such developments as the Clark Amendment on Angola and the belated withdrawal of support to Somoza in Nicaragua and to the Shah in Iran. Even the Soviet invasion of Afghanistan furthered this development, since it mired down Soviet political energies in an impossible situation, disabled them from gaining advantage in the Islamic world, and gave the United States an excuse to fan the ideological fires once again in a flagging Western Europe.

What the United States obviously did not count on was that the movement led by Ayatollah Khomeini was of an entirely different stripe from the movements of national liberation the Third World had known in the postwar period. The Chinese Communist Party and the Vietminh, the Nasserists and the Algerian FLN, Cuba's 26th of July Movement and Angola's MPLA—all were opposed to U.S. hegemony and the existing world-system, but they operated nonetheless within the basic framework of its eighteenth-century Enlightenment Weltanschauung. They were against the system but also of the system. That is why in the end they could all, once in power, be incorporated into the system's ongoing structures without too much difficulty.

Khomeini would have none of that. He knew Satan when he saw him. The number one Satan was the United States, the number two, the U.S.S.R. Khomeini would play by no rules of the game that served either of their interests. The United States did not know how to handle such fundamental otherness, which is why Khomeini could so profoundly humiliate the United States and thereby undermine its hegemony even more effectively than had the 1968 world revolution of the New Lefts and the excluded. Khomeini brought down Carter and the "low posture."

The United States then played its last card—Reagan's fake machismo. The enemy, said Reagan, is less Khomeini than Carter (and implicitly, Nixon and Ford). The solution was to puff power. To our allies, no more trilateral fluff, but reideologizing. The allies responded by continuing their own "low posture" vis-à-vis the United States. To the Third World, invade Grenada, bomb Libya (once), and eventually depose our renegade agent in Panama, Noriega. The Third World responded by suicide-bombing two hundred Marines, forcing the United States out of Lebanon. To the folks at home, cut real wages not by inflation but by union busting (starting with the air traffic controllers); by reallocation of national income to the wealthy; and by an acute recession that would transfer many middle-income earners to low-income jobs. Faced with the debt crisis in the world-economy (the direct consequence of the OPEC oil price rise scam), engage in military Keynesianism in the United States by selling off the U.S. patrimony to our allies via a monumental U.S. debt burden, which could not but deflate U.S. currency in the long run. And, of course, denounce the Evil Empire.

Ronald Reagan may believe he intimidated the U.S.S.R. into producing Gorbachev. But Gorbachev emerged in the U.S.S.R. because Ronald Reagan demonstrated that the United States was no longer strong enough to sustain the special arrangement with the U.S.S.R. The U.S.S.R. was now forced to be on its own, and on its own, without a cold war deal, it was in desperately bad shape. Its economy, which could keep its head above water and even show significant growth during the great expansion of the world-economy in the 1950s and 1960s, was too inflexibly structured to cope with the great stagnation of the world-economy in the 1970s and 1980s. Its ideological steam had totally evaporated. Leninist developmentalism proved as inefficacious as all the other varieties of developmentalism—socialist or free-market—have in the last fifty years.

Gorbachev pursued the only policy that was available to the U.S.S.R. (or perhaps one should better say Russia), if it were to maintain significant power in the twenty-first century: He needed to terminate the drain on Soviet resources of its pseudoempire. He thus sought to force the pace of liquidating the cold war's military facade (now that the cold war's political utility was over) by engaging in a quasi-unilateral disarmament (withdrawing from Afghanistan, dismantling missiles, etc.), thereby forcing the United States to follow suit. He needed as well to divest himself of an ever more restive imperial burden in Eastern Europe. The Eastern Europeans were of course happy to oblige. They had wanted nothing more for at least twenty-five years. But the miracle of 1989 was made possible not because the United States changed its traditional position but because the U.S.S.R. did. And the U.S.S.R. changed its position not because of U.S. strength but because of U.S. weakness. Gorbachev's third task was to restore the U.S.S.R. to a viable internal structure, including dealing with the now-released nationalisms. Here he failed.

The miracle of 1989 (continued by the unsuccessful coup in the U.S.S.R. in 1991) was no doubt a blessing for the peoples of Eastern and Central Europe, including the peoples of the U.S.S.R. It will not be an unmixed blessing, but at the very least it opens up the possibility of renewal. Nonetheless, it was not a blessing for the United States. The United States has not won the cold war but lost the cold war, because the cold war was not a game to be won but rather a minuet to be danced. By transforming it at last into a game, there was a victory, but the victory was Pyrrhic. The end of the cold war in effect eliminated the last major prop of U.S. hegemony and U.S. prosperity—the Soviet shield.

The result was Iraq and the Persian Gulf crisis. Iraq did not suddenly discover its claims upon Kuwait. It had been making these claims for thirty years at least. Why did it choose this moment in time to invade? The immediate motivation seems quite clear. Iraq, like one hundred other countries, was suffering from the catastrophic consequences of the OPEC oil scam and the subsequent debt crisis. This was particularly aggravated in Iraq's case by the costly and futile Iran-Iraq war, in which Iraq was strongly abetted by a coalition, less strange than it appears, of the United States, France, Saudi Arabia, and the U.S.S.R., which was intended to sap the strength of Khomeini's Iran. In 1990, Iraq was determined not to sink, and seizing Kuwaiti oil revenue (and incidentally liquidating a goodly part of its world debt) seemed to be a solution.

But how did Saddam Hussein dare? I do not believe he miscalculated. I think he calculated very well. He was playing "va banque." He had two strong cards. Card number one was the knowledge that the U.S.S.R. would *not* be on his side. Had he invaded Kuwait five years earlier, the invasion would have rapidly provoked a U.S.-U.S.S.R. confrontation involving the likelihood of nuclear destruction, and hence it would have just as rapidly followed the usual path of a U.S.-U.S.S.R. arrangement. Iraq would have had no choice but to back down, as Cuba did in 1962. Iraq could invade because it had been liberated from Soviet constraint.

Hussein's second strong card was regional. In the wake of the new Gorbachev diplomacy, the United States and the U.S.S.R.

entered into a process of resolving so-called regional conflicts, that is, no longer sustaining confrontational conflicts in the four regions where they had been most vigorously sustained in the 1970s and 1980s: Indochina, southern Africa, Central America, and the Middle East. In the first three areas, negotiations were ongoing. Only in the Middle East had these negotiations broken down. When it was clear that Israeli-PLO negotiations were blocked and that the United States did not have the political power to force Israel to continue them, Iraq moved from the wings to center stage. As long as negotiations had been ongoing, Saddam Hussein could do nothing, since he couldn't risk being blamed by the Palestinians and the Arab world for scuttling the negotiations. But once the Israelis scuttled them, Saddam Hussein could pose as the liberator of the Palestinians.

There was one final element in Iraq's calculations. The United States would lose no matter what. If the United States did nothing, Saddam Hussein was on his way to becoming the Bismarck of the Arab world. And if the United States reacted as it did in fact react, and built a military coalition against Iraq centered on the direct use of U.S. troops, Saddam Hussein might fall (this is why the game was "va banque"), but the United States could not win. The war was unavoidable from Day One because neither Hussein nor Bush could accept any outcome other than military combat. Iraq of course lost disastrously in military terms, and it lost immensely in the destruction of lives and infrastructure. But it is still too early to argue that it lost in fact politically.

The United States proved to the world that it was indeed the strongest military power in the world. But, for the first time since 1945, be it noted, it was called upon to demonstrate that fact, by an act of deliberate military provocation. To win in such circumstances is already to lose in part. For if one challenger can dare, a second more careful challenger may start to prepare himself. Even Joe Louis grew tired.

The demonstration of U.S. military strength has underlined its economic weakness. It has been widely noticed that the U.S. war effort was financed by others because the United States could not finance it. The United States has loudly shouted that it is now the world's diplomatic broker. However, it plays this role not as a respected elder but rather as a power that wields a big stick but that also has economic feet of clay.

Being a broker is an advantage only if one can produce lasting results. The United States was thus forced to begin on its own, in the Middle East, a second game of "va banque." If the United States can bring about significant accord between Israel and the PLO, everyone will applaud. But this is a result that seems unlikely. If, in the coming two to three years, we collapse into more wars in the Middle East, possibly now with nuclear weapons, the United States will bear the brunt of the blame, its conservative Arab allies will collapse, and Europe will be called in to salvage a possibly unsalvageable situation. If all of this happens, may not Saddam Hussein still be around to crow? Nothing positive for U.S. power in the world has emerged from the Persian Gulf War.

The Iran crisis of 1980 and the Iraq crisis of 1990 were quite different from each other. They were two alternative models of Third World reaction to the Great American Peace. The Iran reaction used the way of fundamental rejection of Western values. The Iraq reaction was quite different. The regime in Iraq was Baathist, and the Baath is the most secularized movement in the Arab world. The Iraq reaction was in the end a military reaction, the attempt to construct large Third World states based on enough modern military strength to impose a new *rapport de forces* between North and South. These are the two faces of the future. The "low posture" of the United States was laid low by Khomeini. The "fake machismo" of the United States has been laid low by Saddam Hussein.

The heyday of U.S. prosperity is now over. The scaffolding is being dismantled. The bases are crumbling. How shall we assess the era of U.S. hegemony, 1945 to 1990? On the one hand, it was the Great American Peace and an era of great material prosperity. It was also, by comparative historical standards, an era of tolerance, at least for the most part, despite the many conflicts, or perhaps because of the form the conflicts took. But it was built on too many exclusions to survive. And it is now over.

We are now entering into America's future, about which we have cause to be both despairing and very hopeful. But we cannot know which ways the winds will blow until we look at America's past.

When shall we begin our story of America's past? I shall start the story somewhat unconventionally in 1791 on the basis of two important events—the adoption of the Bill of Rights and the admission of the Republic of Vermont to the Union.

There is no greater symbol and concrete foundation to American liberty than the Bill of Rights. We hail it rightfully. We tend to forget that it was adopted only in 1791, as the first ten amendments to the Constitution. That is, one should note that these clauses were not in the original Constitution, as written in 1787. This is because there was strong opposition to them. Happily, in the end, those who opposed these provisions lost the battle. But it is salutary to remember that the U.S. commitment to basic human rights was far from self-evident to the Founding Fathers. We know of course that the Constitution sanctioned slavery and excluded Native Americans from the polity. It was a Constitution that was the product of White settlers, many of whom, but not all of whom, wanted to ensconce basic human rights in their political structure, at least for themselves.

The admission of Vermont points to further ambivalences. Vermont, as we know, was not one of the thirteen colonies that proclaimed the Declaration of Independence, for Vermont proclaimed itself an autonomous entity only in 1777, was not recommended for recognition as such by the Continental Congress until 1784, and was not in fact admitted to the Union until 1791, when New York withdrew its objections. This struggle for recognition illustrates the many ambiguities of the American War of Independence. While the thirteen colonies were struggling for their independence from Great Britain, Vermont was struggling for its independence against New York (and, to a lesser extent, New Hampshire). Vermont's attitude to the British was complex. Although it was most often on the side of the Continental Congress, various of its leaders were at various moments of time from 1776 up to 1791 in quasi-negotiations with Great Britain.

What was the quarrel about? On the one hand, human rights. When Vermont adopted its state constitution in 1777, it was the first state to abolish slavery and provide for universal manhood suffrage at age twenty-one. Vermont was in the avant-garde then, and seems to have tried ever since to remain there. Vermont's constitution was indeed in sharp contrast to the oligarchic constitution New York had adopted the year before, with its severely restricted franchise in a state where slavery was still important and would not be abolished until 1827.

But on the other hand, it was merely a quarrel between multiple groups of land speculators in which no particular moral virtue attached to any. If New York State blocked Vermont's admission to the American structures from 1777 to 1791, it was in order to defend the interests of its land speculators. And if New York State was to withdraw its objections in 1791, it was because Kentucky had posed its application for admission to the Union, and New York, counting votes in the Senate, wanted Vermont there as a "northern" state to counterbalance another "southern" state. In this way, 1791 prefigured 1861.

In what sense, and for whom, was America the "land of liberty"? It is normal that there was a multitude of motives impelling different groups to participate in the war of independence. Plantation owners, large merchants, urban wageworkers, and small farmers had disparate interests. Only some of their motivations had to do with human rights or greater equality. Many were far more interested in safeguarding their property rights, against both British taxation and American radicalism. For example, the right to expropriate Native American lands was one of the rights the White settlers were afraid the British were too reluctant to sustain.

Nonetheless, the American Revolution was a revolution in the name of liberty. And the authors of the Declaration of Independence proclaimed it to the world. It was after all a revolution; that is, it did reaffirm in a most vigorous fashion not only that "all men are created equal" but also that governments were instituted among men to secure "life, liberty, and the pursuit of happiness," and that, should any government ever become "destructive of these ends," it became "the right of the people to alter or abolish it." Revolution therefore was not only legitimate but obligatory, even if "prudence . . . will dictate that governments long established should not be changed for light and transient causes. . . ."

The new United States of America, born out of revolt against the mother country, legitimated by a written constitution which laid claim to being a consciously constructed social compact that created a government which had "the consent of the governed," fortified by a Bill of Rights that spelled out protections against this very government, seemed to itself and to the European world to be a beacon of hope, rationalism, and human possibility. The liberty it preached seemed to be triple: the freedom of the individual vis-à-vis the state and any and all social institutions (most notably the freedom of speech); the freedom of the group against other more powerful groups (most notably, the freedom of religion); and the freedom of the people as a whole against outside control (independence).

These rights were not unknown elsewhere at the time, but they seemed more secure and more extensive in the United States than anywhere else, especially once the French Revolution seemed to go awry, ending by 1815 in a Restoration. Furthermore, to Europeans who felt oppressed in their own countries, the United States beckoned as the land of individual opportunity, actually carrying out the French Revolution's motto of *"la carrière ouverte aux talents."* An open land, a vastly underpopulated land, the United States wanted immigrants and offered its children instant citizenship (jus soli). It was vast, fresh, and above all, new (not weighed down by feudal history).

Or so we said, then and ever since. And so it has been believed, here and elsewhere, then and ever since. And in fact it was largely true, provided we remember it was true for Whites only, primarily for White males, and for a long time only for Western European Protestant White males. This political primacy of European Whites was not peculiar to the United States. The point is that, despite its proclamations of universalist freedoms, the United States was no different from other countries in this regard. For this privileged group, the United States throughout its history had very much to offer. The boundaries expanded; the so-called frontier was settled; the migrants were assimilated; and the country kept itself, as George Washington adjured it, free from "the insidious wiles of foreign influence. . . ." The United States was thus not only a land of opportunity but also a land of refuge.

In a very famous phrase, Abraham Lincoln in 1858 said, "I believe this government cannot endure permanently half slave and half free." In retrospect, was he right? Despite the Emancipation Proclamation, despite the Thirteenth, Fourteenth, and Fifteenth Amendments to the Constitution, despite even *Brown v. the Board of Education,* have we not long endured being half slave and half free? Has there been any moment in our history when it was not possible to say that some, even many, suffered or were deprived merely because of the color of their skin or other irrelevancies?

We must take a cold, hard look at our history and ask whether the very real liberty of half the population was not at the price of the very real lack of liberty of the other half. Was slavery (defined loosely) merely an anachronism, which it was our historical destiny to overcome, or was it a structural foundation and integral concomitant of the American Dream? Was the American dilemma an inconsistency to be surmounted by wisdom and rationality, or was it a building block of our system?

The fact is that, at the moment we moved from our past to our present (as of 1945, that is), our record was glorious in some regards but utterly dismal in others. There was petty apartheid not merely in the South but in most of the great cities and great universities of the North. It was not until the 1970s that we were ready even to admit and discuss widely this dismal side of the record. And even today, much of the discussion is obscurantist.

The ancient Greeks developed a system comprising liberty and equal political participation for the citizens, and slavery for the (foreign) Helots. We have developed our own political imagery based on a contrast between, on the one hand, tyranny, despotism, or an absolutist monarchy and, on the other hand, a republican democracy or a democratic republic. We forget that one of the historic founts of our political tradition, the Magna Carta of 1215, was a document that was imposed on the king of England by his lords and barons to guarantee their rights vis-à-vis him, not the rights of the serfs.

We think of a despotic system as one in which one man, or a very few at the top, can rule over and exploit all the others. But in fact, a very few at the top are limited in their political capacity to extract too much from the bottom; nor do they need all that much to sustain themselves very comfortably indeed. But, as we expand the size of this group at the top, as we make this group at the top more equal in their political rights vis-à-vis each other, it becomes possible to extract more from the bottom; indeed more is required to feed the needs of those at the top. A political structure with complete liberty for the top half can be the most oppressive form conceivable for the bottom half. And in many ways, it can be the most stable. Perhaps a country half free, half slave can long endure.

The very possibility of individual upward mobility, which the United States as a country has pioneered and institutionalized, and which the rest of the world has been borrowing, is one of the most efficacious instruments in maintaining the society as half slave, half free. Upward mobility justifies the reality of social polarization. It minimizes the unrest by removing many potential leaders of protest from the bottom half while holding out the mirage of potential promotion to those left behind. It transforms the search for betterment into competition with others. And whenever one stratum has more or less moved up, there is always another to enter at the bottom.

It does, however, have one downside. The ideology of liberty and of potential betterment is a universalist doctrine. And while it may require that half be slave for the other half to be free, it promotes unease. Hence Myrdal could speak of an American dilemma, and our history would bear him out. For we have struggled mightily with the devil, and, having sinned, must always fear God's wrath. This combination of *hybris* and profound Calvinist guilt has been the daily bread of Americans of all origins and faiths for all our history.

In a sense, then, our past, from 1791 (or 1776 or 1607) to 1945, was one long prelude to our present. We proclaimed liberty throughout the land. We worked hard to transform nature and to become the economic giant of 1945. We used our liberty to achieve our prosperity. And in so doing, we set an example for the world. Of course, it was an impossible example. If our country was half slave, half free, so was the world. If the price of freedom was slavery, if the price of prosperity was misery, if the price of inclusion was exclusion, how could everyone achieve what America stood for? How even could all Americans achieve it? That was our historical dilemma, our historical fate, our historical prison.

It is said that the earliest formal protest against slavery was made by the Germantown Mennonites in 1688 who asked: "Have these poor negers not as much right to fight for their freedom, as you have to keep them slaves?" Of course, all those who did not have their full share of liberty in these United States have always answered yes to the Mennonites. They had the right, and fought for it as best they could. Whenever they fought especially hard, they received some concession. But the concessions have never ante-dated the demands, and have never been more generous than politically required.

The blessing of liberty has been a true blessing; but it has also been a moral burden because it has always been, and up to now has always had to be, a blessing only for some, even if the some were many, or (once again I repeat) probably *especially* when the some were many.

So thus we crossed the Sinai from 1791 to 1945 without "entangling alliances" and secure in the path of the Lord, to arrive in the land of milk and honey from 1945 to 1990. Will we now be expelled from the promised land?

TOMORROW

Is decline so terrible? Perhaps it is the greatest blessing of all. Once again, it was Abraham Lincoln who sounded the moral note: "As I would not be a slave, so I would not be a master." We have been masters of the world, perhaps benign and beneficent masters (or so say some of us), but masters nonetheless. That day is over. Is it so bad? As masters, we have been loved but also hated. We have loved ourselves but also hated ourselves. Can we now arrive at a more equilibrated vision? Perhaps, but not yet, I fear. I believe we are coming to the third part of our historical trajectory, possibly the bumpiest, most exhilarating, and most terrible of all.

We are not the first hegemonic power to have declined. Great Britain did. The United Provinces did. And Venice did, at least within the context of the Mediterranean world-economy. All these declines were slow and materially relatively comfortable. There is a lot of fat in a hegemonic power, and one can live off that fat for fifty to one hundred years. No doubt one cannot be too extravagant, but we are not, as a nation, going to be consigned to some dustbin.

For one thing, we shall remain for quite some time the strongest military power in the world, despite the fact that we have become too weak to prevent upstarts like Iraq from forcing us to do battle, or at least we have become too weak to do battle at anything but a very high political cost. And although our economy is faltering, and the dollar is crumbling, no doubt we shall do quite well in the next major expansion of the world-economy, which will probably occur within five to ten years. Even though we would be the junior partner of an eventual Japanese-American economic cartel, the returns in global revenue would be high. And politically the United States will remain a heavyweight power, even if it becomes only one among several.

But psychologically the decline will be terrible. The nation has been on a high, and we must come down from it. It took us thirty years to learn how to perform gracefully and effectively the responsibilities of world leadership. It will no doubt take at least thirty years to learn to accept gracefully and effectively the lesser roles to which we shall now be consigned.

Since there will be less global income, the question will immediately and urgently arise as to who will bear the burden of the decline, even a small decline, in our standard of living. We are seeing the difficulties already in our current debates over who is to pay for the enormous waste and rip-off of the savings and loan disaster, and who is to pay for reducing the debt burden. As our ecological sensitivities grow apace—and they will no doubt continue to do so—who will pay to repair Exxon spills in Alaska, Love Canals, and the far greater dangerous rubbish piles we shall doubtless be uncovering in the decades to come? It has indeed been voodoo economics, and not just in Reagan's time. There is nothing more sobering than having a big fat bill, no funds to pay it off with, and credit that has been exhausted. For credit is creditability, and U.S. economic creditability is slipping away fast. No doubt we shall live off our fat, and even off some Euro-Japanese charity given in fond memory of the Great American Peace and all our past marvels, but in the long run this will be even more humiliating than Khomeini imprisoning a whole American embassy.

What will we do then, we as a nation? There are fundamentally two paths open to us. There is the uptight path of violent social conflict, in which the restive underclasses are held down forcefully with brutality and prejudice—a sort of neofascist path. And there is the path of national solidarity, a communal reaction to a shared social stress, in which we shall move beyond the blessings of liberty and prosperity to the blessing of equality, perhaps a less than perfect equality but a real one nonetheless, one with no major exclusions.

I shall take the optimistic road of relegating the neofascist path to the box of low likelihood. I do not believe that neofascism is impossible, but there is quite a lot in our national tradition that militates against the success of neofascist movements. Furthermore, I do not think we will be quite desperate enough to take the leap, for it would be a leap, down this road. I think rather we are going to see a realization of more equality than we have ever dreamed possible, and more equality than any other country knows. This will be the third of God's blessings. And like the other two, it will have its price and its unanticipated consequences.

The reason why we shall move remarkably forward in the next thirty years in the domain of equality of life chances and life rewards is very straightforward. It will be the direct consequence of our two previous blessings: liberty and prosperity. Because of our long-standing ideological and institutional commitment to liberty, however imperfect in execution, we have developed political structures that are remarkably susceptible to truly democratic decision making provided there is the will and the capacity to organize politically. If one takes the four major arenas of unequal distribution—

gender, race and ethnicity, age, and class—it is clear that those who receive less than their fair share add up to a majority of the voters, provided they define matters in this way.

That is where the era of prosperity comes in. It was precisely the realization of a prosperous America that underlined the gaps and the exclusions and, in the language that was developed in that era, created "consciousness." The first explosion of that consciousness was in 1968. It was but a rehearsal for the second explosion of consciousness that may be expected in the coming decade. This consciousness will provide the will. And the prosperity has provided the capacity. In no country in the world today are the disadvantaged strata so materially strong, strong enough in any case to finance their political struggle. And finally the inevitable cutbacks will provide the incentive. The fuse will be ignited.

Congress will not know what hits it. The demands will come from all sides and simultaneously. And very quickly, in my view, the United States may move from being the world leader of conservative, status quo, free market economics to being perhaps the most social-welfare-oriented state in the world, the one with the most advanced redistributive structures. If it were not for the fact that everyone is telling us these days that socialism is a dead idea, it might even be thought—let us whisper the unspeakable—that the United States will become a quasi-socialist state. Who knows? Maybe the Republican Party might even take the lead, as Disraeli and Bismarck did in the nineteenth century. Some may be horrified by this prospect, and some may be elated, but let us hesitate a moment before expressing our emotions.

I shall make two further presumptions. One is that our traditions of liberty will not be in any way hurt by this new egalitarianism—the Supreme Court will further extend the definition of our civil liberties; state police power will not grow at the expense of individual rights; and cultural and political diversity will prosper. The second presumption is that this new egalitarianism will not have a negative impact on our productive efficiencies. We will, for reasons discussed previously, probably have a lower GNP per capita, but the new egalitarianism will be the response, not the cause. And in any case the GNP per capita will still be high.

Will we then have arrived at Utopia? Surely not. For the price of Utopia would be very high, and the unanticipated consequences frightening. The fundamental cost will be exclusion. As we eliminate exclusions within the state, we will accentuate them on the world level. Perhaps the United States will for the first time cease to be half slave, half free. But thereby the world will become even more sharply half slave, half free. If, from 1945 to 1990, we asked half our population to sustain the other half at a high income level, imagine what it will require to sustain 90 percent of our population at reasonably high income levels. It will require even more exploitation, and essentially this will have to be exploitation of peoples of the Third World.

It is not hard to guess what would happen twenty years down the road. In the first place, the pressure to come to America will be greater than it has ever been in all our history. If the United States looked attractive in the nineteenth century, and even more in the post-1945 period, imagine how it would look in the twenty-first century if my double prediction—a fairly well-off, highly egalitarian country and a very economically polarized world-system—proves correct. Both the push and pull of migration would reach a maximum point. How could the United States stop unauthorized migration in the millions, even tens of millions? The answer is, it could not.

Meanwhile, those who do not emigrate but remain at home in the South, excluded ever more effectively from the prosperity of the North—not only North America but also Europe and northern Asia—will surely begin, in one area after another, to follow the example of either Iran or Iraq. The United States will want to do something about it (as indeed will Europe and Japan) because of the plausible fear of a global fireball. Remember, nuclear weapons are being secretly developed—may already be fully developed—in Brazil and Argentina, Israel and Iraq, South Africa and Pakistan, and soon many others. During the Great American Peace, we feared a nuclear holocaust when in fact the likelihood was very low because of the U.S.-Soviet deal. The chances of nuclear wars, perhaps only regional (but that is terrible enough), are far more real in the next fifty years.

Faced with the threat of massive unauthorized immigration and regional nuclear wars in the South, what will the United States do? Chances are that a quasi-socialist America would become a fortress America. Trying to isolate itself from the hopelessness and costs of Third World wars, it might turn to protecting its wealth and its patrimony. Failing to stem the tide of migration, it might turn toward creating a dike between the entitlements of citizens and those of noncitizens. Within no time, the United States could find itself in a position where the bottom thirty percent, even fifty percent, of its wage-labor force was noncitizens, with no suffrage and limited access to social welfare. Were that to happen, we would have reversed the clock by 150 to 200 years. The whole story of the United States and the Western world from, say, 1800 to 1950 was the extension of political, economic, and social rights to the working classes. But if that gets defined as citizens only, then we are back at the starting point with a large part of the resident population excluded from political, economic, and social rights.

Nor will our problems stop there. We will discover, as we are discovering, that the fastest, least expensive route to an ecologically clean United States is to dump the garbage elsewhere—in the Third World, in the high seas, even in space. Of course this only postpones our own problems for fifty years, and at the price of increasing the problems of others during those fifty years as well as later. But, with one's back against the wall, is it not extremely tempting to postpone problems for fifty years? In fifty years, most of today's adult voters will be dead.

Thus, America's third blessing, equality, will at best have bought America time for twenty-five to fifty years. Somewhere down the line, in 2025 or 2050, the day of reckoning will arrive. And the world will face the same kind of choice then that the United States has today. Either the world-system will move toward a repressive restructuring or it will move toward an egalitarian restructuring. But an egalitarian restructuring on a world scale will require a far greater reallocation of goods and services than would an egalitarian redistribution merely within the United States of today.

Of course, at this point, we are talking of the demise of our existing world-system and its replacement by something fundamentally different. And it is intrinsically impossible to predict what will be the outcome. We will be at a bifurcation point, and the random fluctuations will be immense in effect. All that we can do is be lucid and active, for our own activity will be part of those fluctuations and will have a profound effect on the outcome.

I have tried to make clear my vision of the coming fifty years: on one side, an increasingly wealthy North, a relatively internally egalitarian North (for its citizens), and a United States no longer in the lead economically or even geopolitically but in the lead in terms of social equality; on the other side, an increasingly disadvantaged South, ready to use its military power, which shall increase to disrupt the world-system, often turning against all the values the West has cherished, with a large part of its population trying the route of individual migration to the North, and creating thereby the South within the North.

Some will say this is a pessimistic vision. I respond that it is not only realistic but it is also optimistic. For it leaves wide open the door of will. In the demise of our current world-system we can indeed create a far better one. It is simply in no way historically inevitable that we do so. We must seize the chance and struggle for salvation. Part of my realism is to assert that the United States cannot achieve salvation alone. It tried this from 1791 to 1945. It tried this in other ways from 1945 to 1990. I am predicting that it will try this again in still other ways from 1990 to, say, 2025. But unless it realizes that there is no salvation that is not the salvation of all humankind, neither it nor the rest of the world will surmount the structural crisis of our world-system.

CODA ON AMERICAN EXCEPTIONALISM

America has always believed that it is exceptional. And I may have played into this belief by focusing my analysis around God's three successive blessings to America. However, not only is America not exceptional but even American exceptionalism is not exceptional. We are not the only country in modern history whose thinkers have sought to prove that their country is historically unique, different from the mass of other countries in the world. I have met French exceptionalists and I have met Russian exceptionalists. There are Indian and Japanese, Italian and Portuguese, Jewish and Greek, English and Hungarian exceptionalists. Chinese and Egyptian exceptionalism is a veritable mark of national character. And Polish exceptionalism is the match of any other. Exceptionalism is the marrow in the bones of almost all the civilizations our world has produced.

I asserted that the American spirit has long been a combination of *hybris* and Calvinist guilt. Perhaps we might remember that what the Greeks meant by *hybris* is the pretention of humans to be gods; and that the strong point of Calvinist theology has always been that, if we believe God to be omnipotent, it follows logically that we cannot pretend that anything is predestined, since if it were it would thereby limit the power of God.

Perhaps the new Jerusalem is neither here nor in Jerusalem nor anywhere else. Perhaps the promised land is simply our earth, our home, our world. Perhaps the only people God chose is humankind. Perhaps we can redeem ourselves if we try.

PART IV

THE DEATH OF SOCIALISM, OR CAPITALISM IN MORTAL DANGER?

REVOLUTION AS STRATEGY
AND TACTICS OF TRANSFORMATION

Did the French Revolution fail? Did the Russian Revolution fail? These are two questions that at one time might have seemed absurd. They no longer seem absurd. But how does one answer such questions?

Revolution is a strange word. Originally it was used in its etymological sense to mean a circular movement that returns to the point of origin. It can still be used to mean this. But it soon became extended to mean simply a turning and then an over-turning. The OED records its usage as early as 1600 in the sense of the overthrow of a government by persons subject to it. But of course the overthrow of a government is not necessarily inconsistent with the concept of a return to a point of origin. Many a political event called a "revolution" by its protagonists has been asserted by them to be the restoration of rights infringed, and hence a return to an earlier, better system.

In the Marxist tradition, however, revolution has been firmly ensconced within a linear theory of progress. Victor Kiernan captures it best, I believe, when he asserts that it means a "cataclysmic leap" from one mode of production to another.[59] Still, like most concepts, merely defining it is insufficient; it must be placed in opposition to some alternative. And, as we know, again in the Marxist tradition (but not only), the alternative to "revolution" is "reform."

Reform versus revolution came to mean, in the debates of the late nineteenth and twentieth centuries, slow aggregative change versus swift change, small-scale changes versus large-scale change, reversible change versus irreversible change, improving change (which is therefore prosystemic) versus transforming change (which is therefore antisystemic), and inefficacious change versus efficacious change. Of course, in each of these antinomies

I have loaded the dice, giving each the characterization that revolutionary discourse utilized.

There is, in addition, an ambiguity within the Marxist tradition itself. Marxists often made a distinction between a political revolution (which could be a surface phenomenon) and a social revolution (the real thing). In addition, Marx and Engels themselves were not averse to using the word *revolution* for such concepts as *industrial revolution,* and even to suggest that the "industrial revolution" was more important or more fundamental than the "French Revolution." This suggestion was of course quite consonant with the basic philosophical bias of historical materialism, but it was not necessarily a great succor to voluntarist political action. Hence it was that revolution came to symbolize more and more in the tradition of the Marxism of the parties, and especially in the Bolshevik tradition, the violent overthrow of a bourgeois government by the proletariat, or at the very least the violent overthrow of a reactionary government by popular, progressive forces.

We are not at an end of the ambiguities. The concept of "violent overthrow" is not self-evident. Does a so-called spontaneous uprising, or a disintegration of the existing power structure, constitute a revolution, or is it only one if such an uprising is then canalized by a revolutionary party? When did the French Revolution occur—with the attack on the Bastille, or with the effective coming to power of the Jacobins? The Russian (October) Revolution was traditionally thought to have begun with the storming of the Winter Palace. Later, however, "revolutions" were thought to start before the actual seizure of state power. That is, it was thought essential to lead up to such a seizure with long guerilla campaigns, the whole being characterized by Mao Zedong as "protracted struggle." The protracted struggle was thereupon put forward as the essential element of the revolutionary process, and not only before the seizure of the state organs but also afterwards (the "cultural revolution").

And one last ambiguity remains to be noted. After the Baku Congress, anti-imperialist struggle was given the label of "revolutionary" activity, but the theoretical relationship of such anti-imperialist revolution to socialist revolution has never been entirely clear. This is because there has been no consensus whatsoever. Was the Algerian revolution in a category with, or quite different from, the Vietnamese revolution? There have been many actual trajectories. In Cuba, the "revolution" was not Marxist or even socialist before the seizure of power, but Marxist and socialist afterwards. In Zimbabwe, the rhetorical road traveled was the inverse.

In any case, as we now see clearly, the results have been extraordinarily mixed. The Mexican Revolution does not seem today to have had very revolutionary results. And the Chinese? The Russian revolutionaries are now an historical memory, and, at the moment, not one very honored in Russia. The first question that it seems reasonable to ask, therefore, is whether the so-called revolutionary trajectory has indeed been more or less efficacious than the reform trajectory has been. Of course, we can do the same skeptical review of the accomplishments of social-democratic reform. How fundamentally was the Labour Party able to transform Great Britain? Or even the Swedish Social-Democratic Party? In the 1990s when almost everyone from China to Sweden to Mexico is talking the language of the "market," one may wonder legitimately whether 150 to 200 years of revolutionary tradition have paid off.

One may wonder even more how great has been the distinction between revolutionary and reformist activity. Particular parties, particular social movements, and particular complexes of social activity perceived as a long and large "revolutionary" event can all be described (probably without exception) as the locus of shifting tactics, such that they looked revolutionary (or insurrectionary, or radical, or transformatory) at some points in time and distinctly less so at others.

Real-existing revolutionary leaders have always tried to steer a middle course, often in zigzag form, between "selling out" at one end and "adventurism" on the other. Of course, one person's "adventurism" has been another's "true revolutionary commitment." One person's "sellout" has been another's "one step backward, two steps forward."

It is perhaps time to stop throwing stones at one another and take a sober look at the objective constraints on left political activity over the past two centuries throughout the world, and the degree of strength of the underground pressure for transformation. Let us start with the givens. We live in a capitalist world-system that is deeply inegalitarian and oppressive. It has also been successful in expanding world production, which has therefore placed considerable economic strength in the hands of those who are the chief beneficiaries of the world-system. We may assume that those who benefit wish to maintain the system more or less as it is, and will invest considerable political energy in maintaining the status quo. Can we assume that those who do not benefit wish with equal fervor to transform it? No we cannot, for several reasons: ignorance, fear, and apathy. Furthermore, individual upward mobility provides an outlet for a clever minority of the oppressed. In addition, the nonbeneficiaries are weaker—economically and militarily —than the beneficiaries.

This asymmetry of political strength and sociopsychological stance is the basic dilemma that has faced the world Left since it began to organize itself consciously in the nineteenth century. It was the debate about what we should do about this asymmetry that the reform versus revolution debate was about. It is remarkable in retrospect to see how similar to each other were the answers each side gave. Collective self-education will overcome ignorance; collective self-organization will overcome fear and apathy. An organized class culture will restrain potential deserters who are tempted by individual social mobility by offering them leadership roles in the present movements and future governments. And the imbalance of social strength between the beneficiaries and the nonbeneficiaries can be overcome by taking away from the beneficiaries the control of the state machineries.

This is what major movements have been doing for 150-odd years now. The strategy and the tactics of the Chinese Communist Party, the African National Congress of South Africa, and the Austrian Social-Democratic Party—to take three well-known examples—have been remarkably similar, given how different their historical circumstances have been. One can label all three movements either magnificent successes or miserable failures. What I find difficult to accept is any analysis that gives a different success rating to each of the three. They have been magnificent successes in their ability at mass mobilization, in achieving some significant reforms in their respective countries such that the situation today is radically different from the situation in, say, 1900 and, for some persons and in some respects, radically better. They have been miserable failures in that we are still living in a capitalist world-economy that is, if anything, more inegalitarian than it was in 1900. There are still multiple forms of oppression in each of these countries, and these movements have in various ways constrained, rather than facilitated, current protests against some of these forms of oppression.

Cup half full or cup half empty? Perhaps we are asking the wrong question. The question is whether, in the nineteenth and twentieth centuries, there were historical alternative strategies for each of these movements that in retrospect seem plausible and could have achieved more. I doubt it. It is in many ways a silly exercise to rewrite history on the basis of a simulation. But it does seem to me that the alternative movements that actually presented themselves in each of these cases lost out because they were obviously less efficacious from the point of view of the nonbeneficiaries of the system, and that the sum of the reforms achieved by the dominant movements have been worth something, even if there is no post-capitalist utopia in any of the three countries. Quite the contrary.

Having said this, the sum total is very disappointing, given the incredible social energy that was put into revolutionary activity in the twentieth (and nineteenth) centuries. I share the sense of the revolutionaries of 1968 that the Old Left in all its versions had become by that point in time "part of the problem." Since then, however, the world Left has moved on. The worldwide revolution of 1968 has had an immense impact on forces everywhere that think of themselves as antisystemic. Our mode of analysis reveals six major consequences, each of which I wish to state in a restrained way.

1. The two-step strategy—first take state power, then transform society—has moved from the status of self-evident truth (for most persons) to the status of doubtful proposition.

2. The organizational assumption that political activity in each

state would be most efficacious if channeled through a single cohesive party is no longer widely accepted.

3. The concept that the only conflict within capitalism that is fundamental is the conflict between capital and labor—and that other conflicts based on gender, race, ethnicity, sexuality, etc. are all secondary, derived, or atavistic—no longer has wide credence.

4. The idea that democracy is a bourgeois concept that blocks revolutionary activity has been giving way to an idea that democracy may be a profoundly anticapitalist and revolutionary idea.

5. The idea that an increase in productivity is the essential prerequisite of socialist construction has been replaced by a concern with the consequences of productivism in terms of ecology, the quality of life, and the consequent commodification of everything.

6. The faith in science as the foundation stone of the construction of utopia has given way to a skepticism about classical science and popular scientism, in favor of a willingness to think in terms of a more complex relationship between determinism and free will, order and chaos. Progress is no longer self-evident.

None of these six revisions of our premises is totally new. But the revolution of 1968, by shaking the legitimacy of the Old Left, has transformed the doubts held by a small handful of persons into a far more widespread revisionism, a veritable "cultural revolution." Each of these six revisions of premises is complex and could be elaborated at length. I cannot do that here. I can only address the implications of these revisions for antisystemic political activity, particularly for the strategy and tactics of "revolution."

The first and most fundamental implication is that "revolution" —as the word was used in Marxist-Leninist movements—is no longer a viable concept. It has no meaning, at least no meaning now. "Revolution" was supposed to describe an activity by a party, its struggle to achieve state power, its role as the standard-bearer of labor in the capital-labor struggle, its scorn for democracy as mere "bourgeois rights," its dedication to increased productivity, its self-description as scientific. Do parties meeting this description and attracting significant support still exist? I don't see very many, if any.

What we see in their place are two things. The first are Old Left parties, often with changed names, struggling to survive electorally on the basis of eclectic centrist programs about which they don't seem to feel very strongly, heirs of a vague sentiment for social justice (in the manner in which the Radical Socialists in the France of the Third Republic incarnated the tradition of laicity). The second is the ever-evolving panoply of parties and movements who are the diluted heirs of the revolution of 1968: Green parties, feminist movements, movements of oppressed ethnic and racial so-called minorities, gay and lesbian movements, and what might be called base community movements.

In the United States, in the 1980s, there was talk of creating a Rainbow Coalition of such movements. But in the end nothing much came of this idea. Indeed, as we come into the 1990s, we observe two enormous political dilemmas for the world's antisystemic movements.

First, the new antisystemic movements that emerged out of the revolution of 1968 were quite successful in their attack on the premises that undergirded the Old Left, but they have floundered ever since in their quest for an alternative strategy. Is state power still relevant, or not? What could be the basis of any lasting alliance between movements? As time goes on, the answers seem increasingly similar to those of the now highly eclectic Old Left movements.

Secondly, the 1990s are seeing the spread of movements, launched in the 1980s, which are racist and populist. But quite often they use themes and assume tonalities that overlap partially with what the new antisystemic movements do. There is enormous risk of political confusion of multiple types.

So here we are: tired and eclectic shells of Old Left parties; no viable concept of "*a* revolution;" new antisystemic movements that are vigorous but with no clear strategic vision; and new racist-populist movements of growing strength. Amidst all this, the besieged defenders of the existing capitalist world-system are by no means disarmed and are pursuing a policy of the flexible postponement of contradictions, waiting as they are for the moment when they can pursue a radical transformation of their own, away from a capitalist mode of production to some new but equally inegalitarian, undemocratic world-system.

It is time long past when we need to define with some clarity an alternative strategy to the defunct one of "revolution." I think that such redefinition is a collective worldwide task. I can only suggest here a few lines of action that might be elements of such a strategy, but which do not add up to a total strategy.

1. The first is a return to a traditional tactic. Everywhere, in every workplace, we should push for more, that is—that more of the surplus value be retained by the working class. This once seemed so obvious, but it came to be neglected for a variety of reasons: the parties' fear of trade unionism and economism; protectionist tactics of workers in high-wage areas; movement-dominated state structures acting with the logic of employers. Simultaneously, we must press for the full internalization of costs by every enterprise. Local-level constant pressure for such internalization and for more—more in Detroit, more in Gdańsk, more in São Paulo, more in Fiji—can deeply shake the patterns of accumulation of capital.

2. Second, everywhere in every political structure at every level, more democracy, that is, more popular participation and more open decision making. Again, once thought obvious, this has been restrained by Left movements' deep distrust of mass psychology, the origin of their vanguardism. Perhaps this was legitimate in the nineteenth century, but a transformation to a better world-system will not be possible without genuine, deeply motivated popular support, which has to be created and developed through more democracy now.

3. Third, the world Left has to come to terms with its dilemma concerning universalism versus particularism. The Napoleonic imperial universalism affected by the Old Left has no merit. But an endless glorification of smaller and smaller particularisms has none either. We need to search for a way of constructing a new universalism that is based on a foundation of countless groups and not on the mythical atomic individual. But this requires a kind of global social liberalism that we are reluctant to accept. We need thus to give operational meaning (and not mere puffery) to

Senghor's "rendez-vous de donner et de recevoir." It should be tried at countless local levels.

4. Fourth, we need to think of state power as a tactic, utilizing it whenever we can and for whatever immediate needs, without investing in it or strengthening it. Above all, we must shun managing the system, at any level. We must cease to be terrified of the political breakdown of the system.

Will this transform the system? I do not know. I see it as a strategy of "overloading" the system by taking the ideological slogans of liberalism seriously, something never intended by the liberals. What could overload the system more than the free movement of people, for example? And, along with overloading the system, it is a strategy of "preserving our options," of moving toward better things immediately, of leaving the total responsibility of managing the existing world-system to its beneficiaries, of concentrating on creating a new sociality at the local and world levels.

We must, in short, become practical, consequential, constant workers in the vineyard, discussing our utopias, and pushing forward. As the present world-system crashes down upon us in the next fifty years, we must have a substantive alternative to offer that is a collective creation. Only then will we have a chance of obtaining a Gramscian hegemony in world civil society, and thereby a chance of winning the struggle against those who are seeking to change everything in order that nothing change.

CHAPTER TWELVE

MARXISM AFTER THE COLLAPSE
OF THE COMMUNISMS

MARXISM . . . IS INEVITABLY BOUND TO PERISH, SOONER OR
LATER, AND THIS APPLIES, TOO, TO ITS FORM AS *THEORY*. . . .
IN RETROSPECT (AND ONLY IN RETROSPECT),
IT WILL BE POSSIBLE TO SAY,
FROM THE MANNER OF ITS PERISHING,
WHAT KIND OF STUFF MARXISM WAS MADE OF.
Balibar, 1991, 154

Marx has been pronounced dead regularly and he has been resuscitated just as often. As with any thinker of his stature, he is worth rereading primarily in the light of current realities. Today it is not only Marx who is once more dying but also a whole series of states that have labeled themselves Marxist-Leninist and that are, by and large, collapsing. Some are happy about this, some sad, but few are trying to draw up a careful and judicious balance sheet of the experience.

Let us remember at the outset that Marxism is not the summa of the ideas and writings of Marx but rather a set of theories, analyses, and recipes for political action, no doubt inspired by Marx's reasoning, that were made into a sort of dogma. This version of Marxism, the dominant one, was the product of two historical parties that constructed it, in tandem and successively, jointly but not in collaboration with each other: the German Social-Democratic Party (especially before 1914) and the Bolshevik Party, later to become the Communist Party of the Soviet Union.

Although this dominant version of "Marxism" was never the only one, other versions have had a very limited audience, at least until rather recently. The true origins of the "explosion" of Marxism, of which Lefebvre (1980) wrote, is to be found in the world revolution of 1968. This event coincides more or less with the onset of the Brezhnevian stagnation in the U.S.S.R. and the subsequent growing turmoil and disintegration within the so-called socialist bloc.

This coincidence confuses the analysis somewhat, for it makes it incumbent on us to attempt the difficult exercise of distinguishing between the arguments of the "Marxism of the parties" (the dominant version of Marxism)—which have been strongly compromised, if not totally refuted, by the collapse of "really-existing socialism"—and the arguments of Marx himself (or at least those aspects of his thought and of Marxist praxis), which were not, or at least not essentially, involved in this historical experience. My argument will be quite simple. What has died is Marxism as a theory of modernity, a theory that was elaborated alongside the theory of modernity of liberalism, indeed largely inspired by it. What has not yet died is Marxism as a critique of modernity and of its historical manifestation, the capitalist world-economy. What has died is Marxism-Leninism as a reformist strategy. What has not yet died is the antisystemic thrust— popular and "Marxian" in language—which inspires real social forces.

I believe that dominant Marxism, which became Marxism-Leninism, was based on five principal propositions, made not by Marx-scholars but by Marxist militants, as spelled out over the years in the praxis of the parties.

* *In order to achieve a communist society, humanity's ultimate goal, the necessary first step was to take state power as fast as possible. This was possible only by making a revolution.*

This thesis is less self-evident than it seems. What does it mean to "take state power"? And even harder, what is a "revolution"? The internal party debates about these tactical questions were always heated and never reached definitive conclusions. This is why the actual political decisions were quite diverse and always seemed somewhat opportunistic.

However, two images predominated: either a popular insurrection or an overwhelming victory in elections, either of which was seen as launching a fundamental, lasting change in the structures of power from which no turning back was presumed to be possible.

Parties out of power sought to reach such a turning point by whatever means they could. Those who had achieved power (even if by a route not envisaged in theory) sought to remain in power by whatever means they could, thereby to prove that the "revolution" was indeed such an irreversible turning point. The coming to power of the party was in that sense seen as analogous to Christ's coming to earth. It did not represent the end of time—far from it —but it was a moment in which history was transformed. If the events of 1989–91 were so earthshaking, especially for Marxist-Leninists, it was because the concept of an irreversible historical transformation was therein given the lie. More than a deep disappointment, the events meant the collapse of the basic premises of political action.

* *In order to obtain and retain state power, it was essential that so-called progressive forces and/or the working class create an organized, universal party.*

Whether it was the mass party advocated by the German Social-Democrats or the avant-garde party advocated by the Bolsheviks, the party was supposed to act as the spiritual home of its leaders and its members, who were called upon to devote their whole lives to the attainment and retention of state power.

The party was thus seen as being the central (even the only) focus of the lives of its members. Any link with other organizations, or even any interest outside the party's program, was thought to be a serious threat to its efficacy. This, far more than doctrinal atheism, is the genesis of the great suspicion of religions. This is the same reason why the party was hostile to nationalist, ethnic, feminist, and other such movements.

In short, the party asserted that class conflicts were primordial and all other conflicts were epiphenomenal. Therefore the party repeatedly argued that these other struggles constituted a diversion from the central task, unless they were integrated into its current program for momentary, secondary, tactical reasons. What the party feared above all was that its members were not unremittingly loyal to it. While one may doubt that the parties in power ever created truly totalitarian states, there seems little doubt they created totalitarian parties.

There was a fundamental contradiction between these two theses. While the second thesis on the structure of the party was conceived for, and seemed well adapted to, the mobilization necessary to achieve power, it did not at all serve well as a principle once the party was in power. The role of the party in power was deeply ambiguous. In reality, to the extent that it functioned at all, the party in power was simply a decision-making body in which a tiny group settled all current issues. The power of the leadership was quite personal and surrounded by a sort of complicit opaqueness. For most members, the party became nothing but an instrument of individual upward mobility in daily life.

At that point, the party had become anything but a spiritual home. To those outside it, it seemed to be a quite illegitimate structure, and those within it tended to be cynical about it. The party was a reality that had to be taken into account, but no one was devoted to it. If the "revolution" did not turn out to be irreversible, it was precisely because of the nature of the party once it had taken power. The main objective of those seeking to destroy Communist regimes was to throw out this kind of party, as soon as the changed world context made this possible.

* *In order to go from capitalism to communism, it was necessary to pass through a phase called the dictatorship of the proletariat, that is, to turn over power entirely and exclusively to the working class.*

The two key words, *dictatorship* and *proletariat,* both raised questions. Regardless of what meaning attached to "dictatorship" originally, its actual historical meaning was the denial in these regimes of all so-called bourgeois civil rights, which had been created (at least partially) in the parliamentary democracies of "liberal" states. Any organization not controlled by the party was denied not only free speech but also the very right to exist. This was true as well for any centers of intellectual activity that asserted an independence from the party.

Nevertheless, even if the public debate was a monologue, it does not follow that there was no political discussion or disagreement. However, the debates were strictly private, limited to a handful of individuals. The occasional rumblings of the population, which sometimes placed some limits on political decision making, was the only form of popular expression.

The dictatorship claimed legitimacy by virtue of the fact that the state and the party "represented" the working class. What was the reality? To be sure, many leaders had been workers in their youth, no doubt a larger number than in other states in the world-system. But once they became members of the ruling class, these persons became "bourgeoisified" and constituted the notorious *Nomenklatura*.

It was also no doubt true that among ordinary people, skilled workers tended to earn as much, even more than schoolteachers or an average "intellectual worker." This constituted a reversal of the usual wage hierarchy. But reversing a wage hierarchy is not the same as abolishing it.

At the work site, the worker had no way of exercising trade-union rights vis-à-vis management. In fact, the worker had fewer possibilities of making demands than he had in nonsocialist states. The workers did nonetheless have one great compensation: social security (especially job security) and the implicit right to a low level of productivity. But these social advantages depended in fact on overall state revenue, and when the states got into serious financial difficulties, provoked in part by low levels of productivity, the social safety net suffered. The so-called socialist states could no longer fulfill their promises, and this resulted in a social crisis. Out of this crisis emerged Solidarność and all the subsequent developments.

Despite all the official speeches, almost no one thought they were really living in a workers' state. At the very most, they believed they lived under a regime seeking an improvement in the living conditions of the workers—in other words, in a reformist state.

When the few advantages these states offered declined, the regimes lost their social bases.

* *The socialist state constituted a necessary stage on the universal, correct route of progress, leading to the communist utopia.*

This was the Leninist (or, to be more exact, the Stalinist) version of the theory of progress, itself the legacy to Marxism (as well as to liberalism) from the Enlightenment, which was in turn, by a sort of *Aufhebung* (sublation), a secularized version of Christian eschatology.

The theory of stages, founded on an unshakable belief in progress, justified everything. By affirming that everything the party (infallible guarantor of progress) did was correct, this theory provided moral and rational underpinnings not only to the first three theses but also to any deviations from the paths that Marxist tradition had laid out.

Since each stage followed the rules of social evolution, there theoretically could not be a regression. Furthermore, since these historical stages had been specified by the party, each party member became by definition an apostle of progress. Finally, given the fact that the workers were now in power, the state could not fail to progress infallibly. The theory of progress permitted, indeed required, that newer revolutionary states be under the protection of more advanced revolutionary states—a system of a hierarchy of elders presumed to prevail within the family of Marxist-Leninist states (and even of all progressive states). What some described as imperialism, others called natural duty. As long as public opinion had reason to believe in the reality of progress, this right of the strongest did not seem too shocking. But stagnation, exacerbating latent conflicts, aroused anti-imperialist sentiments against the Soviet Union, and thus led not only to the dislocation of Marxist-Leninist states but also to the breakdown of the "world" of socialist states, a geopolitical concept that has now dissolved.

★ *To make the transition from the stage of socialism (the party in power) to the stage of communism, it was necessary to "construct socialism," that is, to pursue national development.*

Communist parties came to power in sovereign, independent (but besieged) states. Whereas Marx predicted that the first revolutions would occur in the most technologically advanced countries, the successive seizures of power actually occurred in peripheral and semiperipheral zones of the world-economy.

Thereby the "construction of socialism" underwent a great metamorphosis. It became the process by which semiperipheral (and even peripheral) states would catch up with the core zones of the capitalist world-economy. There were three basic elements in this program.

The first was planning, which entailed very heavy bureaucratic structures. These structures did rather well during the period of "primitive accumulation." But as the infrastructure became more modern, the planning apparatus had to take on much more complex tasks, and this was hampered by the role of the party. Planning eventually became a kind of negotiation process among economic caids, who were constantly revising the plans retrospectively to make them accord with the real results. This was clearly a formula for failure.

The second element in the construction of socialism was all-out industrialization, as autarkic as possible. This objective overlooked the fact that industrialization was more than building plant machinery—that it involved considerations of profitability, which in turn were dependent on the constantly evolving worldwide spread of technology. In point of fact, as technological progress diffused across the world (itself furthered in great part by the "construction of socialism"), the industries in the socialist states became less and less competitive and therefore less and less able to contribute to catching up with advanced countries.

The third element was a commodification so unbridled that it is hard not to view it with much irony, so counter was it to all the rhetoric about a communist society. Still, to support planning and industrialization, labor and everything else had to be subject to market transactions, even if these transactions were strictly controlled centrally.

At the outset, national development seemed to be the great achievement of the socialist countries. Rates of growth were high and optimism was the order of the day. But the economic stagnation of the 1970s and 1980s proved these states to be just as peripheral and semiperipheral as the other Third World states. It was a tremendous letdown for these states, which had boasted of their rapid national development.

In sum, one after the other, each of the five theses of the Marxism of the parties (really existing Marxism) came to be viewed skeptically by the very persons who had sustained these regimes. In getting rid of Marxism-Leninism, they thought they were getting rid of Marx himself. But it is not so easy. Thrown out the front door, Marx threatens to sneak in the window. For Marx has not exhausted (quite the contrary) either his political relevance or his intellectual potential. It is to this we now turn.

MARX'S THOUGHT CONTAINS FOUR KEY IDEAS (IDEAS THAT ARE largely but not exclusively Marxian) that seem to me still useful, even indispensable, to the analysis of the modern world-system. Despite all the negative experiences of Marxist-Leninist movements and states in the twentieth century, these ideas still illuminate the political choices we have to make.

CLASS STRUGGLE

"It is fairly clear that the identity of Marxism depends entirely on the definition, import and validity of its analysis of class and class struggle. Without this analysis, there is no Marxism . . ." (Balibar, 1991, 156).

Let us not forget first of all that a large part of the internal opposition to the Marxist-Leninist party-states was the expression of class conflict, the conflict of ordinary workers against that new, somewhat peculiar, variety of bourgeoisie, the *Nomenklatura*. (Marx would have had as delicious a time analyzing the *Nomenklatura* in the Polish situation of 1980–81 as he had in his analysis of the class struggle in France between 1848 and 1851).

The concept that different classes have different, indeed antag-onistic, interests is not an idea that Marx invented. It was in the air in Western Europe in all the major discussions from 1750 to 1850. It wasn't even a left-wing concept originally. But Marx and Engels gave it great notoriety in the *Communist Manifesto*, and it has been virtually the defining concept of workers' movements ever since.

There have been two major objections to this concept. The first is a moral, hence a political, objection. It goes like this: Yes, there are class conflicts here and there, but they are neither inevitable nor desirable. This amounts to saying that class struggle is merely a political option (and hence a voluntary choice), and therefore its moral and rational character is open to debate. Persons (usually on the political Right) who make this argument are in effect preaching to the working class a policy of negotiation, reconcilia-tion, and collaboration.

However efficacious such a policy may be, such recommenda-tions are alien to Marxist analysis. Although there is undeniably a certain characteristic tone of moralizing in Marx's writing, Marx always disclaimed being a preacher or a prophet. Rather he claimed to be an analyst, a scientific analyst. Hence, anyone who wishes to refute Marx must place himself at the same level of analysis. Marx did not call on workers (or anyone else) to start a class struggle; he observed that they were fighting one, often without even being fully aware of it.

Marx based his argument on two widely (if not universally) accepted premises. The first was that all people seek to improve their material conditions and struggle therefore against those who exploit them or take advantage of their difficulties. This claim is a strong one, hard to deny. The fact that the exploited are often weak, resigned, and afraid, and rarely strong, determined, and bold is perhaps true. But it is merely a comment on the tactical probabil-ities of the class struggle, not a refutation of its existence.

The second premise upon which Marx based his argument was that people who are in objectively parallel or similar situations tend to act in similar ways, such that we can talk of group responses (in this case of class responses), although of course no group is ever totally homogeneous or monolithic. Furthermore, if one refuses to analyze the actions of social groups, it becomes impossible to explain social reality. Once again, Marx was merely underlining the historic reality of class struggle. In order to argue against this premise, we must show empirically that such struggles do not occur, which is surely very hard to do. Or, one must argue, somewhat more plausibly, that the observation about class struggles is correct but overstated. In this view, the importance of class struggles is less than Marxists suggest, because other forms of struggle loom larger. This is a frequent objection, and not only from the Right. Throughout the world, analysts underline the importance of nationalist, racial, ethnic, religious, and gender struggles. It is clear such struggles exist and are important, and it must be admitted that Marxists (including Marx himself) tended for a long time to neglect, denigrate, ignore, even denounce them, for one simple reason: They were haunted by the fear of a divided working class, and thus tried in every way to overcome these divisions. This led them deliberately to understate the theoretical importance of any social cleavage other than that of class.

The inadequacy of Marxist analysis of nationalist, racial, ethnic, or gender struggle has been widely noted for at least two decades now—that is to say, long before the collapse of the Communisms in 1989. Shall we, however, therefore conclude that all these social struggles are equally important? Marx himself tried to show in *The Eighteenth Brumaire* how the struggles of small peasant proprietors were in the end a form of working-class struggle.

The thesis that class struggles are inevitable and fundamental is not at all disproved by the outbreak of other forms of struggle, for it is always possible to argue that the latter were masked forms of the former (see Wallerstein, 1991a, 1991b). Indeed, Marx's thesis is greatly strengthened to the degree that one can argue persuasively that many class struggles are conducted under the label of struggles between "peoples." Of course, we must spell out why and how this should be so. But once done, we have a firmer understanding of the ups and downs of modern history. Needless to say, however, it then becomes impossible to exalt the merits of a single, all-encompassing organized party.

POLARIZATION

Marx places great importance on the phenomenon of polarization, in two senses. On the one hand, Marx insists on a tendency toward economic polarization, immiserization, by which he means that the poor are getting poorer and the rich, richer. On the other hand, he also seeks to analyze a social polarization, by which he means that everyone is becoming either bourgeois or proletarian, and all intermediate and hard-to-categorize groups are disappearing.

The thesis of immiserization has long come up against strong resistance on the grounds that, for at least a century, the real income of the working class in industrialized countries has been rising. The conclusion drawn was that there was no absolute polarization, and even relative polarization had declined due to the redistributions of the welfare state. Thus, Marx was quite mistaken, it is argued.

It is certainly true that the real income of the working classes (or more exactly of skilled workers) has been rising, such that an absolute polarization between the bourgeoisie and the proletariat has not occurred (although it is less clear what we can say about relative polarization). But in taking each industrialized state separately, we are committing the same theoretical error made by both the Marxists of the parties and the classical liberals. In reality, the countries in question are part and parcel of the capitalist world-economy, and it is within the latter that the processes described by Marx occur. As soon as one takes the capitalist world-economy as the unit of analysis, one sees two things.

First, immiserization is constant at the level of the world-economy. It is not only relative (even the World Bank accepts this) but it is also absolute (as witnessed, for example, by the growing inability of peripheral zones to provide enough basic foodstuffs for their populations).

Second, the observation about the rising real revenues of the working class in industrialized countries is distorted by too narrow a perspective. We tend to forget that all these countries (originally mainly the United States, but today all of them) are countries of immigration, receiving a steady flow of immigrants from peripheral zones, and that these immigrants are not the beneficiaries of these rising real revenues. This is another way of reminding us about the relation of class struggles to struggles of "peoples," a point made previously.

The "working class" whose real revenues *are* rising is largely composed of the local "indigenous" or ethnically dominant groups. The lower stratum is, however, primarily a stratum of first- or second-generation immigrants, for whom economic polarization remains a reality. Not being of "local" origin, they tend to conduct their class struggles under the banner of race or ethnicity. One can deny social polarization only by giving to the true bourgeoisie and proletariat definitions that are far too narrow (reflecting primarily the social situation of the nineteenth century). If, however, we use a more useful definition—persons living essentially on current incomes, which are, however, polarized—then we see that Marx was quite right. An even larger proportion of the world's population falls into one or the other of these categories. They live neither on their property or their rents, but on the income they derive from their current insertion in the real economic processes of the world.

IDEOLOGY

Marx was a materialist. He believed that ideas do not come out of nowhere and that they are not simply the product of the musings of intellectuals. Our ideas, our sciences reflect the social reality of our lives, he said, and in this sense all our ideas derive from some specific ideological climate. Many have taken pleasure in pointing out that this logic must apply as well to Marx himself and to the working class, which Marx had placed in a special category, as he considered it the universal class. To be sure, this criticism is valid, but it merely enlarges the field to which Marx's arguments apply.

Today, at a time when the entire nineteenth-century intellectual heritage of history and the social sciences has been reopened for discussion, thinking about the social bases of our ideas and our thinkers seems more necessary than ever. Obviously Marx was not the inventor of the thesis of the social determination of ideas, even though this thesis has come to be linked to his worldview. It's generally considered to be a Marxian thesis. There is therefore no reason to underestimate either the importance of an analysis of ideologies (including of Marxism) or the importance of Marx's contribution to this analysis.

ALIENATION

The concept of alienation is less familiar than the others because it was less frequently utilized by Marx himself. This is so much the case that some analysts attribute the concept only to the "young Marx" and therefore discard it. This would be a pity, since it seems to me a concept essential to Marx's thought.

Viewing alienation as incarnating the evils of capitalist civilization, Marx saw its demise as the greatest achievement of a future communist society. For, according to Marx, alienation is the malady that, in its principal incarnation—property—destroys the integrity of the human person. To struggle against alienation is to struggle to restore to people their dignity.

The only way to contest this thesis is to argue that alienation is an inevitable evil (a sort of original sin), and that there is nothing that can be done about it, except to diminish over time its most pernicious expressions. It would nevertheless be difficult to deny that it is alienation that underlies the great social angers of our times.

Marx offers us the possibility of imagining another kind of social order. No doubt he has often been reproached for not having spelled out his utopias, but in that case it is up to us to do so. His thought is there. Who, or what, would be served by ignoring it completely?

BIBLIOGRAPHY

BALIBAR, ETIENNE. 1991. "From Class Struggle to Classless Struggle?" In *Race, Nation, Class*, ed. E. Balibar and I. Wallerstein. London: Verso. 153–184.

LEFEBVRE, HENRI. 1980. Marxism exploded. *Review*. 4:19–32.

WALLERSTEIN, IMMANUEL. 1991a. "Class Conflict in the Capitalist World-Economy." In *Race, Nation, Class*, ed. E. Balibar and I. Wallerstein. London: Verso. 115–124.

———. 1991b. "Social Conflict in Post-Independence Black Africa: The Concepts of Race and Status-group Reconsidered." In *Race, Nation, Class*, ed. E. Balibar and I. Wallerstein. London: Verso. 187–203.

CHAPTER THIRTEEN

THE COLLAPSE OF LIBERALISM

The years 1989–1991 mark a decisive turning point in contemporary history. On that almost everyone seems to agree. But turning from what to what? The year 1989 is the year of the so-called end of the so-called Communisms. The years 1990–91 are the immediate time boundaries of the so-called Persian Gulf War.

The two events, intimately linked, are nonetheless entirely distinct in character. The end of the Communisms marks the end of an era. The Persian Gulf War marks the beginning of an era. The one closes out; the other opens out. The one calls for reevaluation; the other for evaluation. The one is the story of hopes deceived; the other of fears still unfulfilled.

Yet, as Braudel reminds us, "events are dust," even big events. Events make no sense unless we can insert them in the rhythms of the *conjonctures* and the trends of the *longue durée*. But that is less easy to do than it sounds, since we must then decide which *conjonctures* and which structures are most relevant.

Let us start with the end of the Communisms. I have called it the end of an era, but which era? Shall we analyze it as the end of the postwar epoch 1945–1989, or as the end of the Communist epoch 1917–1989, or as the end of the French Revolutionary epoch 1789–1989, or as the end of the ascension of the modern world-system, 1450–1989? It can be interpreted as all of these.

Let me put aside, however, the last of these interpretations for a while, and start by analyzing this period as the end of the epoch 1789–1989, with its two key world revolutionary movements, 1848 and 1968. Note well, not for the moment that of 1917. How may we characterize this period: that of the industrial revolution? that of the bourgeois revolution(s)? that of the democratization of political life? that of modernity? All of these interpretations are commonplace, and all have some (even much) plausibility.

A variation on these themes, one that would perhaps be more precise, might be to call the era 1789–1989 the era of the triumph and domination of liberal ideology; in this case 1989, the year of the so-called end of the Communisms, would in fact mark the downfall of liberalism as an ideology. Outrageous and implausible, with the revival of the faith in the free market and the importance of human rights, you say? Not all that much. But, in order to appreciate the argument, we must begin at the beginning.

In 1789, in France, a political upheaval occurred to which we have given the name French Revolution. As a political event it passed through many phases, from the initial phase of uncertainty and confusion to the Jacobin phase, and then, via the interim of the Directory, to a Napoleonic phase. In a sense we can argue it was continued subsequently in 1830, in 1848, in 1870, and even in the Resistance during the Second World War. Through it all, it had as its slogan "Liberty, equality, fraternity"—a clarion call of the modern world that has proved to be superbly ambiguous.

The balance sheet of the French Revolution in terms of France itself is very uneven. There were irreversible changes that were real changes, and there were many seeming changes that changed nothing. There were continuities from the Ancien Régime via the revolutionary process, as Tocqueville showed long ago, and there were decisive ruptures. This balance sheet for France is not, however, our concern here. The bicentennial and its platitudes are over.

It is rather the impact of the French Revolution (interpreted widely) on the world-system as a whole that is the theme I wish to explore. The French Revolution transformed mentalities and established "modernity" as the Weltanschauung of the modern world. What we mean by modernity is the sense that the new is good and that it is desirable, because we live in a world of progress at every level of our existence. Specifically, in the political arena, modernity means the acceptance of the "normality" of change, as opposed to its "abnormality," its transitory character. At last, an ethos consonant with the structures of the capitalist world-economy had become so widely diffused that even those who were uncomfortable with this ethos had to take it into account in public discourse.

The question became what to do about the "normality" of change in the political arena, since those who leave power are always reluctant to cede it. The differing views about how to handle the "normality" of change comprise what we have come to call the "ideologies" of the modern world. The first ideology on the scene was "conservatism," the view that change should be retarded as long as possible, and its scope impeded as much as possible. But note that no serious conservative ideologue has ever suggested total immobility, a position that was possible to assert in previous eras.

The response to "conservatism" was "liberalism," which saw the break with the Ancien Régime as a definitive political rupture and the end of an era of "illegitimate" privilege. The political program incarnated by liberal ideology was the perfection of the modern world by means of the further "reform" of its institutions.

The last of the ideologies to make its appearance was "socialism," which rejected the individualistic presumptions of liberal ideology and insisted that social harmony would not come about merely by unleashing individuals from all the constraints of custom. Rather, social harmony had to be socially constructed, and for some socialists it could only be constructed after a further historical development and a great social battle, a "revolution."

All three ideologies were in place by 1848 and have conducted noisy battles with each other ever since, throughout the nineteenth and twentieth centuries. Political parties have been created everywhere, ostensibly reflecting these ideological positions. To be sure, there has never been an uncontested, definitive version of any of these ideologies, and there has also been a lot of confusion about the dividing lines between them. But in both learned and popular political discourse it has been generally accepted that these ideologies exist and represent three different "tonalities," three different styles of politics with respect to the normality of change: the politics of caution and prudence; the politics of constant rational reform; and the politics of accelerated transformation. Sometimes we call this the politics of the Right, the Center, and the Left.

There are three things to note about the ideologies in the period following 1848. I say following 1848, because the world revolution of 1848—which combined the first appearance of a conscious workers' movement as a political actor with the "springtime of the peoples"—set the political agenda for the next century and a half. On the one hand, the "failed" revolution(s) of 1848 established clearly that political change was not likely to be as rapid as the accelerators wanted but neither would it be as slow as the cautious hoped. The most plausible prediction (prediction—not wish) was constant rational reform. Thus the liberal center triumphed in the core zones of the world-economy.

But who was to effectuate these reforms? This is the first anomaly to address. In the initial blossoming of the ideologies, between 1789 and 1848, all three ideologies situated themselves in positions that were firmly antistate in the antinomy State-Society. The centrality of this antinomy in political thought was equally a consequence of the French Revolution. Conservatives denounced the French Revolution as an attempt to use the state to undermine and negate the institutions thought to be basic to society—the family, the community, the Church, the monarchy, the feudal orders. Liberals, however, also denounced the state as the structure that prevented each individual—the actor considered to be basic to the constitution of society—from pursuing his or her own interests as he or she saw fit, in what Bentham called the "calculus of pleasure and pain." And socialists as well denounced the state on the grounds that it reflected the will of the privileged, rather than the general will of society. For all three ideologies, then, the "withering away of the state" seemed an ideal devoutly to be wished.

Yet—and this is the anomaly we are noting—despite this unanimously negative view of the state in theory, in practice (especially after 1848) the exponents of all three ideologies moved in multiple ways to strengthen state structures. Conservatives came to see the state as a substitute mechanism for constraining what they considered to be the disintegration of morality, given the fact that traditional institutions could no longer do it, or could no longer do it unaided by the state police institutions. Liberals came to see the state as the only efficient, only rational mechanism by which the pace of reform could be kept steady and oriented in the right direction. Socialists after 1848 came to feel that they would never

be able to overcome the obstacles to their fundamentally transforming society without their obtaining state power.

The second great anomaly was that, although everyone said there
were three distinct ideologies, in political practice each ideological party tried to reduce the political scene to a duality, claiming
that the other two ideologies were basically alike. For conservatives,
both liberals and socialists were believers in progress who wished
to utilize the state to manipulate the organic structures of society.
For socialists, conservatives and liberals represented mere varia-
tions on a defense of the status quo and the privileges of the upper
strata (old aristocracy and new bourgeoisie combined). For liberals, both conservatives and socialists were authoritarian opponents of the liberal ideal, the flourishing of individuals in all their
potentialities. This reduction of three ideologies to a duality (but
in three different versions) was in part no doubt mere passing political rhetoric. More fundamentally, however, it reflected the constant
reconstruction of political alliances. In any case, over the course
of 150 years, this repeated reduction of the trinity to dualities
created a great deal of political confusion, not least of all in the
meaning of these labels.

But the greatest anomaly of all was that in the 120 years after
1848—that is, at least until 1968—under the guise of three
ideologies in conflict with each other, we really had only one, the
overwhelmingly dominant ideology of liberalism. To understand
this, we have to look at what the concrete issue under debate was
during the entire period, the fundamental social problem that
required a solution.

The great "reform" that was called for, if the capitalist
world-system were to remain politically stable, was the integration of the working classes into the political system, thereby transforming a domination based merely on power and wealth into a
domination of consent. This reform process had two main pillars.
The first was the according of suffrage, but in such a way that,
although everyone would vote, relatively little institutional change
would occur as a result. The second was transferring a part of the
global surplus value to the working classes, but in such a way that
the largest part remained in the hands of the dominant strata and

the system of accumulation remained in place.

The geographical zone in which such social "integration" was required most urgently was that of the core states of the capitalist world-economy—Great Britain and France above all, but the United States, other states in Western Europe, and the White settler states as well. We know that this transformation was steadily implemented in the period 1848–1914, and that by the time of the First World War, the patterns of both universal suffrage (albeit still only manhood suffrage in most places) and the welfare state were in place, even if not yet fully realized in all these states.

We could say simply that the liberal ideology had realized its objective and we could leave it at that, but that would be insufficient. We must also notice what happened to both conservatives and socialists in the process. The leading conservative politicians turned themselves into "enlightened conservatives," that is, virtual competitors with official liberals in the process of the integration of the working classes. Disraeli, Bismarck, and even Napoleon III stand as good examples of this new version of conservatism, what might be termed "liberal conservatism."

At the same time, the socialist movement in the industrialized countries, including its most militant exemplars such as the German Social-Democratic Party, became the leading parliamentary voice for the achievement of the liberal reforms. Through their parties and their trade unions, the socialists exerted "popular" pressure for achieving what the liberals wanted, the taming of the working classes. Not only Bernstein but Kautsky, Jaurès, and Guesde as well, not to speak of the Fabians, became what we might call "liberal socialists."

By 1914, the political work of the industrialized countries was largely divided between "liberal conservatives" and "liberal socialists." In the process, purely liberal parties began to disappear, but this was only because all significant parties were de facto liberal parties. Behind the mask of ideological conflict stood the reality of ideological consensus.

The First World War did not break this consensus. Rather, it confirmed it and extended it. The year 1917 was the symbol of this extension of the liberal consensus. The war started with an assassination in a peripheral zone of the world-economy, Bosnia-Herzegovina. The moment had come for the core states to go beyond the narrower objective of integrating their own working classes to think about the integration of that larger segment of the world's working classes, those that lived in the peripheral and semiperipheral zones of the world-system. In the language of today, the issue had now become the taming of the South in ways parallel to the taming of the working classes inside the core zones.

There were two versions of how to resolve North-South issues. The one was put forward by that herald of the renewal of liberalism on a world scale, Woodrow Wilson. Wilson asked the United States to enter the First World War "to make the world safe for democracy." After the war, he called for the "self-determination of nations."

To which nations was Wilson referring? Obviously not to those of states in the core zone. The process of the construction of effective and legitimate state machineries in France and Great Britain, even Belgium and Italy, had long since been completed. Wilson was talking of course of the nations or "peoples" of the three great empires in process of dissolution: Russia, Austria-Hungary, and the Ottomans—all three comprising peripheral and semiperipheral zones of the world-economy. In short, he was talking of what we today call the South. After the Second World War, the principle of the self-determination of nations was to be extended to all the remaining colonial zones—in Africa, Asia, Oceania, and the Caribbean.

The principle of the self-determination of nations was the structural analogy at the world level of the principle of universal suffrage at the national level. Just as each individual was to be considered politically equal and have one vote, so each nation was to be sovereign and thus politically equal and therefore have one vote (a principle today incarnated in the General Assembly of the United Nations).

Nor did Wilsonian liberalism stop there. The next step after suffrage at the national level was the institution of the welfare state, that is, a redistribution of a part of the surplus value via governmental income transfers. The next step at the world level after self-determination was to be "national (economic) development," the program put forth by Roosevelt, Truman, and their successors after the Second World War.

Needless to say, conservative forces reacted with their usual prudence and distaste to the Wilsonians' clarion call for global reform. Needless to say as well, after the disruptions caused by the Second World War, conservatives began to see the merits in this liberal program, and Wilsonian liberalism in practice became after 1945 a liberal-conservative thesis.

But 1917 had, of course, a second significance. It was the year of the Russian Revolution. Wilsonianism was hardly born when it was faced with a great ideological opponent, Leninism. Lenin and the Bolsheviks appeared in the political arena in protest primarily against the transformation of socialist ideology into what I have called liberal socialism (the same thing as Bernstein's revisionism, to which Lenin attached the Kautsky position as well). Leninism therefore was proposing a militant alternative, initially by its opposition to workers' participation in the First World War, and then by the seizure of state power in Russia by the Bolshevik Party.

We know that in 1917, socialists everywhere, including Russia, expected the first socialist revolution to occur in Germany; for several years the Bolsheviks awaited the fulfillment of their own revolution by one in Germany. We know the German revolution never came and that the Bolsheviks had to decide what to do.

The decision they took was twofold. On the one hand, they decided to build "socialism in one country." They thus entered a path in which the primary demand of the Soviet state vis-à-vis the world-system became the political integration of the Soviet state as a great power into the world-system and its economic development via rapid industrialization. This was Stalin's program, but it was that of Khrushchev, Brezhnev, and Gorbachev as well. Thus the program was, in practice, one of the Soviet state's demanding its "equal rights" on the world scene.

What then of world revolution? Lenin initially founded the Third International ostensibly to pursue in militant ways the tasks that the Second International had in effect renounced. The Third International soon turned, however, into a mere foreign policy adjunct of the U.S.S.R. The one thing it never did was stimulate real insurrections of the working classes. Instead, the focus of activity shifted, beginning with the Baku Congress of the Peoples of the East in 1921, to which Lenin invited not merely Communist parties but also all sorts of nationalist and national liberation movements.

The program that emerged from Baku, and that became in reality the program of the world Communist movement, was the program of anti-imperialism. But what was anti-imperialism? It was a translation of the Wilsonian program of the self-determination of nations into more aggressive and impatient language. In the period after the Second World War, as one after the other of these national liberation movements came to power, what program did they put forward? It was the program of national (economic) development, usually relabeled socialist development. Leninism, the great opponent of liberal-socialism at the national level, was beginning to look suspiciously like liberal-socialism at the world level.

In the period 1848–1914, the liberal program was the taming of the working classes in core zones via universal suffrage and the welfare state. It was implemented by a combination of socialist militancy and sophisticated conservative astuteness. In the period 1917–1989, the liberal program at a world scale was the taming of the South. It was being implemented by a combination of socialist militancy and sophisticated conservative astuteness.

The second world revolution of 1968, just like the first world revolution of 1848, transformed the ideological strategies of the capitalist world-economy. Whereas the revolution of 1848, via its successes and its failures, ensured the triumph of liberalism as an ideology and the eventual transformation of its two rivals— conservatism and socialism—into mere adjuncts, the revolution of 1968, via its successes and its failures, undid the liberal consensus. The revolutionaries of 1968 launched a protest from the Left against this consensus, and above all against the historic transformation of socialism, even Leninist socialism, into liberal-socialism. This took the form of a resurgence of various anarchist themes, but also, perhaps above all, of Maoism.

In the wake of the breaching of the worldwide liberal consensus by the so-called New Left, conservative ideology was also renewed for the first time since 1848, and it became once again politically aggressive rather than defensive. Sometimes this was given the name of neoconservatism, but sometimes it was called neoliberalism, reflecting the fact that its program was primarily designed to remove constraints on the market, thereby to regress on welfare state reallocations, the first such significant regression in a century.

How can we account for the world revolution of 1968 and its consequences for ideological strategies? In terms of the structure of the world-system as a whole, we can say that the politics of liberalism—the taming of the world's working classes via suffrage/sovereignty and welfare state/national development—had reached its limits. Further increases of political rights and economic reallocation would threaten the system of accumulation itself. But it had reached its limits before all sectors of the world's working classes had in fact been tamed by being given a small but significant part of the benefits.

The majority of the populations of the peripheral and semi-peripheral zones were still excluded from the operations of the system. But so were a very significant minority of the populations of the core zones, the so-called Third World within. In addition, the world's women became conscious of their profound permanent exclusion, at all class levels, from true political rights, as well as, for the most part, from equal economic rewards.

What 1968 represented, therefore, was the beginning of the reversal of the cultural hegemony that the world's dominant strata had, with great assiduity, been creating and strengthening since 1848. The period from 1968 to 1989 saw the steady crumbling of what remained of the liberal consensus. On the Right, conservatives increasingly sought to destroy the liberal center. Compare the statement of Richard Nixon—"we are all Keynesians now"—with the campaign of George Bush in 1988 against the "L-word" ("L" for liberal). Witness the virtual coup d'état in the British Conservative Party, where Margaret Thatcher ended the tradition of enlightened conservatism that went back beyond Disraeli to Sir Robert Peel in the 1840s.

But the erosion was even greater on the Left. It took the form most tellingly of the disintegration of the liberal-socialist regimes. In peripheral and semiperipheral zones alike, even the most "progressive" and rhetorically militant among these regimes were patently unable to achieve national development to any significant degree; in response, one after the other, each with a glorious past of national liberation struggle, lost its popular legitimacy. The culmination of this process was the so-called collapse of the Communisms—the advent of Gorbachevism in the U.S.S.R., of "special economic zones" in the People's Republic of China, and the fall of the one-party Communist systems in all the countries of Eastern Europe.

In 1968, those who were frustrated with the liberal consensus turned against the liberal-socialist ideology in the name of anarchism and/or Maoism. In 1989, those frustrated with the liberal consensus turned against the quintessential exponents of liberal-socialist ideology, the Soviet-style regimes, in the name of the free market. In neither case was the alternative proposed one to be taken seriously. The alternative of 1968 quickly proved meaningless, and the alternative of 1989 is in the process of doing the same. But, between 1968 and 1989, the liberal consensus and the hope it offered for gradual improvement in the lot of the world's working classes were fatally undermined. But if they were undermined, then there can be no taming of these working classes.

The true meaning of the collapse of the Communisms is the final collapse of liberalism as a hegemonic ideology. Without some belief in its promise, there can be no durable legitimacy to the capitalist world-system. The last serious believers in the promise of liberalism were the old-style Communist parties in the former Communist bloc. Without them to continue to argue this promise, the world's dominant strata have lost any possibility of controlling the world's working classes other than by force. Consent is gone, and consent has gone because bribery had gone. But force alone, we have known since at least Machiavelli, cannot permit political structures to survive very long.

II

Thus we come to the meaning of the Persian Gulf crisis, the beginning of the new era. In this era, the only effective weapon of the dominant forces is becoming force. The Persian Gulf War, unlike all other North-South confrontations in the twentieth century, was an exercise in pure realpolitik. Saddam Hussein started it in this fashion, and the United States and the coalition it put together responded to it in the same way.

Realpolitik was not absent, of course, from previous conflicts. It informed the Congress of Baku in 1921 as well as the arrival of the Chinese Communist Party at Shanghai in 1949. It was part and parcel of the Bandung declaration of 1955, of the Vietnam War, and of the Cuban confrontation of 1962. It was always an integral part of the strategy of the antisystemic movements—witness Mao's maxim, "Political power comes out of the barrel of a gun"—but force was always an adjunct to the central organizing motifs of antisystemic ideology. The South, the peripheral zones, the world's working classes fought their battles under the banner of an ideology of transformation and hope, an ideology in which there was a clear appeal to popular power.

We have been arguing that the forms this ideological struggle of the world's antisystemic movements took were less militant than they either seemed or claimed. We have said that the world's antisystemic forces had in fact been pursuing, in large part unwittingly, the liberal ideological objective of homogenizing integration into the system. But, in so doing, they at least offered hope, even exaggerated hope, and invited adherence to their cause on the basis of these hopes and promises. When the promises were finally seen to be unfulfilled, there was first fundamental uprising (1968) and then the anger of disillusionment (1989). The uprising and the disillusionment were directed more against the presumably antisystemic liberal-socialists than against the pure vintage liberals. But no matter, since liberalism had achieved its objectives via these liberal-socialists (and to be sure the liberal-conservatives as well), and had always been unable to be effective alone.

Saddam Hussein drew the lesson of this collapse of the liberal ideological carapace. He concluded that "national development" was a lure and an impossibility even for oil-rich states like Iraq. He decided that the only way to change the world's hierarchy of power was through the construction of large military powers in the South. He saw himself as the Bismarck of an eventual pan-Arab state. The invasion of Kuwait was to be the first step in such a process, and would have had as a side benefit the immediate solution to Iraq's debt crisis (elimination of a main creditor plus a windfall of looted capital).

If this was an exercise in pure realpolitik, then we must look at the calculations. How must Saddam Hussein have evaluated his risks and therefore his chances of success? I do not believe he miscalculated. Rather I believe he reasoned in the following manner: Iraq had a fifty-fifty chance of winning in the short run (if the United States hesitated to respond), but if Iraq moved, the United States would find itself in a no-win situation, where it had a one hundred percent chance of losing in the middle run. For a player of realpolitik, these are good odds.

Saddam Hussein lost his short-run fifty–fifty gamble. The United States reacted with the use of its maximal military strength and was of course unbeatable. Iraq, as a country, emerged much weakened from the war, albeit less so than the United States thought it would be. But the political situation in the Middle East is fundamentally unchanged from that of 1989, except that the political responsibility of the United States has increased considerably without any significant increase in its political ability to defuse the tensions. Whatever the short-run developments, the continued erosion of the U.S. middle-run political role in the world-system will continue unabated, given the continuing erosion of the U.S. competitive position in the world market vis-à-vis Japan and the European Community.

The question that is open for the long run is not what developments will occur in the North, which are fairly easy to predict. When the next long upturn of the world-economy occurs, the likely poles of strength will be two: a Japan-U.S. axis, to which China will be attached, and a pan-European axis, to which Russia will be attached. In the new expansion and new rivalry among core powers, each pole concentrating on developing its principal semi-peripheral zone (in the one case, China, in the other case, Russia, or the restructured U.S.S.R.), the South will in general be further marginalized, with the exception of enclaves here and there.

The political consequence of this new economic expansion will be intense North-South conflict. But if the North has lost its weapon of ideological control of the situation, can the antisystemic forces—in the South and those elsewhere who support the South (that is, in older language, the world's working classes)—reinvent an ideological dimension to their struggle?

As the ideological themes of yesteryear, those incarnated in socialist and anti-imperialist doctrines, have used themselves up, three principal modes of struggle have emerged. Each has created enormous immediate difficulties for the dominant strata of the world-system. Not one seems to pose a fundamental ideological challenge. One is what I would call the neo-Bismarckian challenge, of which Saddam Hussein's thrust has been an example. The second is the fundamental rejection of the Enlightenment *Weltanschauung*; we have seen this in the forces led by the Ayatollah Khomeini. The third is the path of individual attempts at socio-geographical mobility, whose major expression is the massive, unauthorized, ongoing migration from South to North.

Two things stand out about these three forms of struggle. First, each is likely to increase manyfold in the fifty years to come, and will consume our collective political attention. Second, the world's Left intellectuals have reacted in extremely ambiguous fashion to each of these three forms of the struggle. Insofar as they seem to be directed against the dominant strata of the world-system and seem to cause the latter discomfort, Left intellectuals have wanted to support these struggles. Insofar as each is void of ideological content, and hence potentially reactionary rather than progressive in middle-run political consequence, Left intellectuals have taken their distance, even considerable distance, from these struggles.

The question is what choice left forces have. If 1989 represents the end of a cultural era that ran from 1789 to 1989, what will be, what can be, the new ideological themes of the present era? Let me suggest one possible avenue of analysis. The themes of modernity, the era just past, were the virtue of newness and the normality of political change. These themes led, as we have tried to argue, steadily and logically to the triumph of liberalism as an ideology, that is, to the triumph of the political strategy of conscious, rational reform in the expectation of the inevitable perfecting of the body politic. Since, within the framework of a capitalist world-economy, there are (unrecognized) inbuilt limits to the "perfecting" of the body politic, this ideology reached its limits (in 1968 and 1989), and has now lost its efficacity.

We are now into a new era, an era I would describe as an era of disintegration of the capitalist world-economy. All the talk about creating "a new world order" is mere shouting in the wind, believed by almost no one, and in any case most improbable to realize.

But what ideologies can exist if we are faced with the prospect of disintegration (as opposed to the prospect of normal progressive change)? The hero of liberalism, the individual, has no significant role to play, since no individual can survive very long amidst a disintegrating structure. Our choice as subjects can only be to form groups large enough to carve out corners of strength and refuge. It is therefore no accident that the theme of "group identity" has come to the fore to a degree unknown before in the modern world-system.

If the subjects are groups, these groups are in practice multiple in number and overlapping in very intricate ways. We are all members (even very active members) of numerous groups. But it is not enough to identify the theme of the group as subject. In the 1789–1989 era, both conservatives and socialists sought, albeit unsuccessfully, to establish the social primacy of groups. Conservatives sought the primacy of certain traditional groupings; socialists sought the primacy of the collectivity (the people) as a singular group. We must, in addition, put forward an ideology (that is, a political program) based on the primacy of groups as actors.

There seem to me only two ideologies one can conceivably construct, although at this point neither has in fact been fully constructed. One can put forth the virtue and legitimacy of the "survival of the fittest" groups. We hear this theme announced in the new aggressivity of proponents of neoracist themes, which are often clothed in meritocratic garb rather than the garb of racial purity. The new claims are no longer necessarily based on old narrow groupings (such as nations or even skin-color groups), but rather on the right of the strong (however ad hoc their grouping) to hold onto their loot and protect it within their fortress localities.

The problem with the neo-Bismarckian and the anti-Enlightenment thrusts in the South is that they are inclined eventually to come to terms with their compeers in the North, thereby becoming merely one more fortress locality of the strong. We see this clearly in the politics of the Middle East of the last fifteen years. Faced with the threats represented by Khomeini, Saddam Hussein was supported and strengthened by all sectors of the world's dominant strata. When Saddam Hussein moved to grab too large a share of the loot, these forces turned against him, and Khomeini's successors were happy to rejoin the dominant pack. This easy switching of alliances says something about the politics of the dominant strata (and the hypocrisy of their cant about concern with human rights), but it says something as well about Khomeini and his group and about the Baathist party under Saddam Hussein as well.

Starting from the primacy of groups in an era of disintegration, there is an alternative ideology to that of the "survival of the fittest" groups. It is one that recognizes the equal rights of all groups to a share in a reconstructed world-system while simultaneously recognizing the nonexclusivity of groups. The network of groups is intricately crosshatched. Some Blacks, but not all Blacks, are women; some Moslems, but not all Moslems, are Black; some intellectuals are Moslem; and so on ad infinitum. The real space for groups necessarily implies the space within groups. All groups represent partial identities. Defensive frontiers between groups tend to have the consequence of creating hierarchies within groups. And yet, of course, without some defensive frontiers, groups cannot exist.

This, then, is our challenge—the creation of a new Left ideology in a time of disintegration of the historical system within which we live. It is not an easy task, nor is it one that can be accomplished overnight. It took many, many decades to construct the ideologies of the post-1789 era.

The stakes are high, for when systems disintegrate, something eventually replaces them. What we now know of systemic bifurcations is that the transformation can go in radically divergent directions because small input at that point can have great consequences (unlike eras of relative stability such as the modern world-system enjoyed from circa 1500 to recently, when big inputs had limited consequences). We may emerge from the transition from historical capitalism to something else, say circa 2050, with a new system (or multiple systems) that is (are) highly inegalitarian and hierarchical, or we may emerge with a system that is largely democratic and egalitarian: It depends on whether or not those who prefer the latter outcome are capable of putting together a meaningful strategy of political change.

We can now turn to the question, Who excludes whom? In the capitalist world-economy, the system worked to exclude the majority (from benefits) by including in the work-system, in a layered hierarchy, all the world's potential work force. This system of exclusion via inclusion was infinitely strengthened by the diffusion in the nineteenth century of a dominant liberal ideology that justified this exclusion via inclusion, and managed to harness even the world's antisystemic forces to this task. That era, happily, is over.

Now we must see if we can create a very different world-system, one that will include everyone in its benefits, and it may do this by the very exclusions involved in the construction of self-conscious groups that nonetheless recognize their interlacing.

The definitive formulation of a clear antisystemic strategy for an era of disintegration will take at least two decades to develop. All one can do now is put forward some elements that might enter into such a strategy; however, one cannot be sure how all the pieces fit together, and one cannot assert that such a list is complete.

One element must surely be a definitive break with the past strategy of achieving social transformation via the acquisition of state power. While assuming governmental authority can be useful, it is almost never transformatory. The assumption of state power should be regarded as a necessary defensive tactic to be used under specific circumstances in order to keep out ultra-Right repressive forces. But state power should be recognized as a *pis aller* that always risks a relegitimation of the existing world order. This break with liberal ideology will undoubtedly be the hardest step to take for antisystemic forces, despite the collapse of liberal ideology I have been analyzing.

A total unwillingness to manage the difficulties of the system is what is implied in such a rupture with past practice. It is not the function of antisystemic forces to solve the political dilemmas that the increasingly strong contradictions of the system impose upon the dominant strata. The self-help of popular forces should be seen as quite distinct from a negotiation of reforms in the structure; virtually all antisystemic forces, even the most militant ones, were led into this trap during the liberal ideological era.

Instead, what antisystemic forces should be concentrating on is the expansion of real social groups at community levels of every kind and variety, and their grouping (and constant regrouping) at higher levels in a nonunified form. The fundamental error of antisystemic forces in the previous era was the belief that the more unified the structure, the more efficacious it was. To be sure, given a strategy of the priority of conquering state power, this policy was logical and seemingly fruitful. It is also what transformed socialist ideology into liberal-socialist ideology. Democratic centralism is the exact opposite of what is needed. The basis of solidarity of the multiple real groups at higher levels (state, region, world) has to be subtler, more flexible, and more organic. The family of antisytemic forces must move at many speeds in constant reformulation of the tactical priorities.

Such a coherent, nonunified family of forces can only be plausible if each constituent group is itself a complex, internally democratic structure. And this in turn is possible only if, at the collective level, we recognize that there are no strategic priorities in the struggle. One set of rights for one group is no more important than another set for another group. The debate about priorities is debilitating and deviating and leads back to the garden path of unified groups ultimately merged into a single unified movement.

The battle for transformation can only be fought on all fronts at once.

A multifront strategy by a multiplicity of groups, each complex and internally democratic, will have one tactical weapon at its disposal that may be overwhelming for the defenders of the status quo; it is the weapon of taking the old liberal ideology literally and demanding its universal fulfillment. For example, when faced with the situation of mass unauthorized migration from South to North, is not the appropriate tactic to demand the principle of the unlimited free market—open frontiers for all who wish to come? Faced with such a demand, liberal ideologues can only shed their cant about human rights and acknowledge that they do not really mean freedom of emigration since they do not mean freedom of immigration.

Similarly, one can push on every front for the increased democratization of decision making, as well as the elimination of all pockets of informal and unacknowledged privilege. What I am talking about here is the tactic of overloading the system by taking its pretensions and its claims more seriously than the dominant forces wish them to be taken. This is exactly the opposite of the tactic of managing the difficulties of the system.

Will all of this be enough? It is hard to know, and probably not, by itself. But it will force the dominant forces into more and more of a political corner and therefore into more desperate countertactics. Still, the outcome would still be uncertain, unless the antisystemic forces can develop their utopistics—the reflection and the debate on the real dilemmas of the democratic, egalitarian order they wish to build. In the last period, utopistics was frowned upon as diversion from the priority of gaining state power and then of national development. The net result has been a movement based on romantic illusion; hence it is subject to angry disillusionment. Utopistics are not utopian reveries but the sober anticipation of difficulties and the open imagining of alternative institutional structures. Utopistics have been thought to be divisive. But if antisystemic forces are to be nonunified and complex, then alternative visions of possible futures are part of the process.

The year 1989 represented the agonizing end of an era. The

so-called defeat of antisystemic forces was in fact a great liberation. It removed the liberal-socialist justification of the capitalist world-economy and thus represented the collapse of the dominant liberal ideology.

The new era into which we have entered is nonetheless even more treacherous. We are sailing on uncharted seas. We know more about the errors of the past than about the dangers of the near future. It will take an immense collective effort to develop a lucid strategy of transformation. Meanwhile, the disintegration of the system goes on apace, and the defenders of hierarchy and privilege are wasting no time in finding solutions and outcomes that will change everything in order that nothing change. (Remember that Lampedusa said this as a judgment of Garibaldian revolution.)

There is no reason for either optimism or pessimism. All remains possible, but all remains uncertain. We must unthink our old strategies. We must unthink our old analyses. They were all too marked with the dominant ideology of the capitalist world-economy. We must do this no doubt as organic intellectuals, but as organic intellectuals of a nonunified worldwide family of multiple groups, each complex in its own structure.

CHAPTER FOURTEEN

THE AGONIES OF LIBERALISM:
WHAT HOPE PROGRESS?[60]

We meet on a triple anniversary: the twenty-fifth anniversary of the founding of Kyoto Seika University in 1968; the twenty-fifth anniversary of the world revolution of 1968; the fifty-second anniversary of the exact day (at least on the U.S. calendar) of the bombing of Pearl Harbor by the Japanese fleet. Let me begin by noting what I believe each of these anniversaries represents.

The founding of Kyoto Seika University is a symbol of a major development in the history of our world-system: the extraordinary quantitative expansion of university structures in the 1950s and 1960s.[61] In a sense, this period was the culmination of the Enlightenment promise of progress through education. In itself, this was a wonderful thing, and we celebrate it here today. But, as with many wonderful things, it had its complications and its costs. One complication was that the expansion of higher education produced large numbers of graduates who insisted on jobs and incomes commensurate with their status, and there came to be some difficulty in answering this demand, at least as promptly and as fully as it was made. The cost was the social cost of providing this expanded higher education, which was only one part of the cost of providing welfare in general for the significantly expanding middle strata of the world-system. This increased cost of social welfare would begin to lay a heavy burden on state treasuries. In 1993 we are discussing throughout the world the fiscal crises of the states.

This brings us to the second anniversary, that of the world revolution of 1968. This world revolution started in most countries (but not all) within the universities. One of the issues that served as tinder for the fire was no doubt the sudden anxiety of these prospective graduates about their job prospects. But, of course, this narrowly egoistic factor was not the principal focus of the revolutionary explosion. Rather it was merely one more symptom of the generic problem—the real content of the whole set of promises contained in the Enlightenment scenario of progress, promises that, on the surface, had seemed to have been realized in the period after 1945.

This brings us to the third anniversary, the attack on Pearl Harbor. It was this attack that brought the United States into the Second World War as a formal participant. In fact, however, the war was not a war primarily between Japan and the United States. Japan, if you will pardon my saying so, was a second-rank player in this global drama, and its attack was a minor intervening event in a long-standing struggle. The war was primarily a war between Germany and the United States, and had been de facto a continuous war since 1914. It was a "thirty years' war" between the two principal contenders for succession to Great Britain as the hegemonic power of the world-system. As we know, the United States would win this war and become hegemonic, and thereupon would be the one to preside over this worldwide surface triumph of Enlightenment promises.

Hence, I shall organize my remarks in terms of this set of themes, which in fact we mark by these anniversaries. I shall discuss first the era of hope and struggle for Enlightenment ideals, 1789–1945. Then I shall seek to analyze the era of Enlightenment hopes realized, but falsely realized, from 1945 to 1989. Third, I shall come to our present era, the "Black Period" that began in 1989 and will go on for possibly as much as a half-century. Finally, I shall talk of the choices before us—now, and also soon.

THE FIRST GREAT POLITICAL EXPRESSION OF THE ENLIGHTEN-ment, in all its ambiguities, was of course the French Revolution. What the French Revolution was about has itself become one of the great ambiguities of our era. The 1989 Bicentennial in France was the occasion of a very major attempt to substitute a new interpretation of the revolution for the long-dominant "social interpretation," now asserted to be outmoded.[62]

The French Revolution itself was the end point of a long process, not in France alone but in the entire capitalist world-economy as an historical system. For, by 1789, a goodly part of the globe had already been located inside this historical system for three centuries. And during those three centuries, most of its key institutions had been established and consolidated: the axial division of labor, with a significant transfer of surplus value from peripheral zones to core zones; the primacy of reward to those operating in the interests of the endless accumulation of capital; the interstate system composed of so-called sovereign states, which, however, were constrained by the framework and the "rules" of this interstate system; and the ever-growing polarization of this world-system, a polarization that was not merely economic but social as well, and was on the verge of becoming demographic, too.

What this world-system of historical capitalism still lacked, however, was a legitimating geoculture. The basic doctrines were being forged by the theoreticians of the Enlightenment in the eighteenth century (and indeed earlier), but they were to be socially institutionalized only with the French Revolution. For what the French Revolution did was to unleash public support for, indeed clamor for, the acceptance of two new worldviews: political change was normal and not exceptional; sovereignty resided in the "people," and not in a sovereign. In 1815, Napoleon, heir and world protagonist of the French Revolution, was defeated, and there followed a presumed "Restoration" in France (and wherever else the Anciens Régimes had been displaced). But the Restoration did not really, could no longer really, undo the widespread acceptance of these worldviews. In order to deal with this new situation, the trinity of nineteenth-century ideologies—conservatism, liberalism, and socialism—came into being, providing the language of subsequent political debates within the capitalist world-economy.

Of the three ideologies, however, it was liberalism that emerged triumphant, as early as what might be thought of as the first world revolution of this system, the revolution of 1848.[63] For it was liberalism that was best able to provide a viable geoculture for the capitalist world-economy, one that would legitimate the other institutions both in the eyes of the cadres of the system and, to a significant degree, in the eyes of the mass of the populations, the so-called ordinary people.

Once people reached the point of thinking that political change was normal and that they in principle constituted the sovereign (that is to say, the decider of political change), anything was possible. And this, of course, was precisely the problem that faced those who were powerful and privileged within the framework of the capitalist world-economy. The immediate focus of their fears was to some extent the small but growing group of urban industrial workers. But, as the French Revolution amply demonstrated, rural nonindustrial workers could be quite as troublesome or fearsome from the perspective of the powerful and privileged. How were these "dangerous classes" to be kept from taking these new norms too seriously, and thereupon interfering with the process of capital accumulation by undermining the basic structures of the system? This was the political dilemma that was posed acutely to the governing classes in the first half of the nineteenth century.

One obvious answer was repression. And repression was amply used. The lesson of the world revolution of 1848, however, was that simple repression was not ultimately very efficacious; it provoked the dangerous classes, worsening tempers rather than calming them. It came to be realized that repression, to be effective, had to be combined with concessions. On the other hand, the putative revolutionaries of the first half of the nineteenth century also learned a lesson. Spontaneous uprisings were not very efficacious either, since they were more or less easily put down. Threats of popular insurrection had to be combined with conscious long-term political organization if they were to speed up significant change.

In effect, liberalism offered itself as the immediate solution to the political difficulties of both Right and Left. To the Right, it preached concessions; to the Left, it preached political organization. To both, it preached patience: in the long run, more will be gained (for all) by a via media. Liberalism was centrism incarnate, and its siren was alluring. For it was not a mere passive centrism that it preached but an active strategy. Liberals put their faith in one key premise of Enlightenment thought: rational thought and action was the path to salvation, that is, to progress. Men (it was rarely a question of including women) were naturally rational, were potentially rational, were ultimately rational.

It followed that "normal political change" ought to follow the path indicated by those who were most rational—that is, most educated, most skilled, therefore most wise. These men could design the best paths of political change to pursue; that is, these men could indicate the necessary reforms to undertake and enact. Rational reformism was the organizing concept of liberalism, which therefore dictated the seemingly erratic position of liberals concerning the relation of the individual to the state. Liberals could simultaneously argue on the one hand that the individual ought not to be constrained by state (collective) dictates and, on the other hand, that state action was necessary to minimize injustice to the individual. They could thus be in favor of laissez-faire and factory laws at the same time. For what mattered to liberals was neither laissez-faire nor factory laws per se, but rather measured deliberate progress toward the good society, which could be achieved best, perhaps only, via rational reformism.

This doctrine of rational reformism proved in practice to be extraordinarily attractive. It seemed to answer everyone's needs. For those of conservative bent, it seemed as though it might be the way to dampen the revolutionary instincts of the dangerous classes. Some rights to suffrage here, a little bit of welfare state provisions there, plus some unifying of the classes under a common nationalist identity—all this added up, by the end of the nineteenth century, to a formula that appeased the working classes while maintaining the essential elements of the capitalist system. The powerful and the privileged lost nothing that was of fundamental importance to them, and they slept more peacefully at night (fewer revolutionaries at their windows).

For those of a radical bent, rational reformism seemed to offer a useful halfway house. It provided some fundamental change here and now, without ever eliminating the hope and expectation of more fundamental change later. Above all, it provided living men with something in their lifetimes. And these living men then slept more peacefully at night (fewer policemen at their windows).

I do not wish to minimize 150 years or so of continuous political struggle—some of it violent, much of it passionate, most of it consequential, and almost all of it serious. I do, however, wish to put this struggle in perspective. Ultimately, the struggle was fought within rules established by liberal ideology. When the fascists, who rejected those rules fundamentally, arose, they were put down and eliminated—with difficulty, no doubt; but they were put down.

There is one other thing we must say about liberalism. We have asserted that it was not fundamentally antistatist, since its real priority was rational reformism. But, if not antistatist, liberalism was fundamentally antidemocratic. Liberalism was always an aristocratic doctrine; it preached the "rule of the best." To be sure, liberals did not define the "best" primarily by birth status; they defined it rather by educational achievement. The best were thus not the hereditary nobility but the beneficiaries of meritocracy. But the best were always a group smaller than the whole. Liberals wanted rule by the best—aristocracy—precisely in order not to have rule by the whole—democracy. Democracy was the objective of the radicals, not of the liberals; or at least it was the objective of those who were truly radical, truly antisystemic. It was to prevent this group from prevailing that liberalism was put forward as an ideology. And when liberals spoke to those of conservative bent who were resistant to proposed reforms, the liberals always asserted that only rational reformism would bar the coming of democracy, an argument that ultimately would be heard sympathetically by all intelligent conservatives.

Finally, we must note a significant difference between the second half of the nineteenth century and the first half of the twentieth century. In the second half of the nineteenth century, the main protagonists of the demands of the dangerous classes were still the urban working classes of Europe and North America. The liberal agenda worked splendidly with them. They were offered universal (male) suffrage, the beginning of a welfare state, and national identity. But national identity against whom? Against their neighbors to be sure; but more importantly and profoundly, against the non-White world. Imperialism and racism were part of the package offered by liberals to the European/North American working classes under the guise of "rational reformism."

Meanwhile, however, the "dangerous classes" of the non-European world were stirring politically—from Mexico to Afghanistan, from Egypt to China, from Persia to India. When Japan defeated Russia in 1905, it was regarded in this entire zone as the beginning of the "rollback" of European expansion. It was a loud warning signal to the "liberals," who were of course primarily Europeans and North Americans, that now "normal political change" and "sovereignty" were claims that the peoples of the entire world, not just the European working classes, were making.

Hence, liberals turned their attention to extending the concept of rational reformism to the level of the world-system as a whole. This was the message of Woodrow Wilson and his insistence on the "self-determination of nations," a doctrine that was the global equivalent of universal suffrage. This was the message of Franklin Roosevelt and the "four freedoms" proclaimed as a war aim during the Second World War, which was later to be translated by President Truman into "Point Four," the opening gun of the post-1945 project of the "economic development of underdeveloped countries," a doctrine that was the global equivalent of the welfare state.[64]

The objectives of liberalism and of democracy were once again, however, in conflict. In the nineteenth century, the proclaimed universalism of liberalism was made compatible with racism by "externalizing" the objects of racism (putting them outside the boundaries of the "nation") while "internalizing" the de facto beneficiaries of universal ideals, the "citizenry." The question was whether global liberalism of the twentieth century could be as successful in containing the "dangerous classes" in what came to be called the Third World or the South as national-level liberalism in Europe and North America had been in containing their national "dangerous classes." The problem, of course, was that, at a world level, there was no place to which one could "externalize" racism. The contradictions of liberalism were coming home to roost.

STILL, IN 1945, THIS WAS FAR FROM EVIDENT. THE VICTORY OF the Allies over the Axis powers seemed to be the triumph of global liberalism (in alliance with the U.S.S.R.) over the fascist challenge. The fact that the last act of the war was the dropping of two atomic bombs by the United States on the only non-White Axis power, Japan, was scarcely discussed in the United States (or indeed in Europe) as perhaps reflecting some contradiction of liberalism. The reaction, needless to say, was not the same in Japan. But Japan had lost the war, and its voice was not taken seriously at this point.

The United States was now by far and away the strongest economic force in the world-economy. And, with the atomic bomb, it was the strongest military force, despite the size of the Soviet armed forces. It would within five years be able to organize the world-system politically by means of a fourfold program: (a) an arrangement with the U.S.S.R. guaranteeing it control over a corner of the world in return for remaining in its corner (not of course rhetorically, but in terms of real policy); (b) an alliance system with both Western Europe and Japan, which served economic, political, and rhetorical objectives as well as military ones; (c) a modulated, moderate program to arrive at the "decolonization" of the colonial empires; (d) a program of internal integration within the United States, amplifying the categories of real "citizenship," and sealed with a unifying ideology of anti-Communism.

This program worked, and worked remarkably well, for some twenty-five years, that is, precisely up to our turning point of 1968. How, then, shall we evaluate those extraordinary years, 1945–1968? Were they a period of progress and the triumph of liberal values? The answer has to be: very much yes, but also very much no. The most obvious indicator of "progress" was material. The economic expansion of the world-economy was extraordinary, the largest in the history of the capitalist system. And it seemed to occur everywhere—West and East, North and South. To be sure, there was greater benefit to North than to South, and the gaps (both absolute and relative) grew in most cases.[65] Since, however, there was real growth and high employment in most places, the era had a rosy glow. This was all the more so in that greatly increased expenditures on welfare went along with growth, as we've already mentioned, in particular expenditures on education and health.

Second, there was peace once again in Europe. Peace in Europe, but not, of course, in Asia, where two long, wearing wars were fought in Korea and Indochina. And not, of course, in many other parts of the non-European world. The conflicts in Korea and Vietnam were not, however, the same. Rather, the Korean conflict is to be paired with the Berlin Blockade, the two occurring in fact almost in conjunction with each other. Germany and Korea were the two great partitions of 1945. Half of each country fell within the military-political sphere of the United States on one side and the U.S.S.R. on the other. In the spirit of Yalta, the lines of division were supposed to remain intact, whatever the nationalist (and ideological) sentiments of Germans and Koreans were.

In the period 1949–52, the firmness of these lines was put to the test. After much tension (and in the case of Korea, enormous loss of life) the outcome was in fact the maintenance of boundary status quo, more or less. Thus, in a real sense, the Berlin Blockade and the Korean War concluded the process of the institutionalization of Yalta. The second outcome of these two conflicts was the further social integration of each camp, institutionalized by the establishment of strong alliance systems: NATO and the U.S.-Japan Defence Pact on the one side, the Warsaw Pact and the Soviet-Chinese accords on the other. Furthermore, the two conflicts served as a direct stimulus of a major expansion in the world-economy, heavily fueled as it was by military expenditures. European recovery and Japanese growth were two immediate major beneficiaries of this expansion.

The war in Vietnam was a quite different type from the one in Korea. It was the emblematic site (but far from the only one) of the struggle of national liberation movements throughout the non-European world. While the Korean War and the Berlin Blockade were part and parcel of the cold war world regime, the Vietnamese struggle (like the Algerian and many others) were protests against the constraints and structure of this cold war world regime. They were therefore in this elementary and immediate sense the product of antisystemic movements. This was quite different from the struggles in Germany and Korea, where the two sides were never at peace but only at truce; that is, for each, peace was faute de mieux. The wars of national liberation, were, on the contrary, one-sided. None of the national liberation movements wanted wars with Europe/North America; they wanted to be left alone to pursue their own paths. It was Europe/North America that was unwilling to leave them alone, until eventually it was forced to do so. The national liberation movements were thus protesting against the powerful, but they were doing so in the name of fulfilling the liberal agenda of the self-determination of nations, and the economic development of underdeveloped countries.

This brings us to the third great accomplishment of the extra-ordinary years, 1945–1968: the worldwide triumph of the antisystemic forces. It is only an apparent paradox that the very apogee of U.S. hegemony in the world-system and the global legitimation of liberal ideology was also the moment when all those movements whose structures and strategies had been formed as antisystemic movements in the period 1848–1945 came to power. The so-called Old Left in its three historic variants—Communists, Social-Democrats, and national liberation movements—achieved state power, each variant in different geographic zones. Communist parties were in power from the Elbe to the Yalu, covering one-third of the world. National liberation movements were in power in most of Asia, Africa, and the Caribbean (and their equivalents in much of Latin America and the Middle East). And social-demo-cratic movements (or their equivalents) had come to power, at least rotating power, in most of Western Europe, North America, and Australasia. Japan was perhaps the only significant exception to this global triumph of the Old Left.

Was this a paradox? Was this the result of the juggernaut of social progress, the inevitable triumph of popular forces? Or was this a massive co-optation of these popular forces? And is there a way to distinguish intellectually and politically between these two propositions? These were the questions that were beginning to create unease in the 1960s. Whereas the economic expansion, with its clear benefits in living standards around the world, rela-tive peace in large zones of the world, and the seeming triumph of popular movements, all lent themselves to positive and optimistic appraisals of world developments, a closer look at the real situation revealed major negatives.

The cold war world regime was one not of the expansion of human freedom but of great internal repression by all the states, whose justification was the presumed seriousness of the highly choreographed geopolitical tensions. The Communist world had purge trials, gulags, and iron curtains. The Third World had one-party regimes and dissenters in prison or exile. And McCarthyism (and its equivalents in the other OECD countries), if less overtly brutal, was quite as effective in enforcing conformity and breaking careers, where necessary. Public discourse everywhere was allowed only within clearly delimited parameters.

Furthermore, in material terms, the cold war world regime was one of growing inequality, both internationally and nationally. And while antisystemic movements often moved against old inequalities, they were not shy about creating new ones. The *Nomenklaturas* of the Communist regimes had their parallels in the Third World and in Social-Democratic regimes in the OECD countries.

In addition, it was quite clear that these inequalities were not randomly distributed. They were correlated with status-group (whether coded as race, religion, or ethnicity), and this correlation held both at the world level and within all states. And they were of course correlated with gender and age-group, as well as with a number of other social characteristics. In short, there were groups left out, many such groups, groups adding up to considerably more than half the world's population.

It was thus the realization of long-standing hopes in the years between 1945 and 1968, hopes that came to be thought of as hopes falsely realized, that underlay and accounted for the world revolution of 1968. That revolution was directed first of all against the whole historical system—against the United States as the hegemonic power of this system, against the economic and military structures that constituted the pillars of the system. But the revolution was directed just as much, if not more, against the Old Left —against the antisystemic movements considered insufficiently antisystemic; against the U.S.S.R. as the collusive partner of its ostensible ideological foe, the United States; against the trade unions and other workers' organizations that were seen as narrowly economistic, defending the interests primarily of particular status-groups.

Meanwhile, the defenders of the existing structures were denouncing what they regarded as the antirationalism of the revolutionaries of 1968. But, in fact, liberal ideology had hung itself by its own petard. Having insisted for over a century that the function of the social sciences was to advance the boundaries of rational analysis (as a necessary prerequisite of rational reformism), they had succeeded only too well. As Fredric Jameson points out:

> [M]uch of contemporary theory or philosophy . . . has involved a prodigious expansion in what we consider to be rational or meaningful behavior. My sense is that, particularly after the diffusion of psychoanalysis but also with the gradual evaporation of "otherness" on a shrinking globe and in a media-suffused society, very little remains that can be considered "irrational" in the older sense of "incomprehensible. . . ." Whether such an enormously expanded concept of Reason then has any further normative value . . . in a situation in which its opposite, the irrational, has shrunk to virtual nonexistence, is another and an interesting question.[66]

For if virtually everything had become rational, what special legitimacy was there any longer in the particular paradigms of Establishment social science? What special merit was there in the specific political programs of the dominant elites? And most devastating of all, what special capacities did the specialists have to offer that ordinary people did not have, did dominant groups have that oppressed groups did not have? The revolutionaries of 1968 spotted this logical hole in the defensive armor of the liberal ideologues (and in its not-so-different variant of official Marxist ideology) and jumped into the breach.

As a political movement, the world revolution of 1968 was no more than a brushfire. It flamed up ferociously, and then (within three years) it was extinguished. Its embers—in the form of multiple, competing pseudo-Maoist sects—survived another five to ten years, but by the end of the 1970s, all these groups had become obscure historical footnotes. Nonetheless, the geocultural impact of 1968 was decisive, for the world revolution of 1968 marked the end of an era, the era of the automatic centrality of liberalism, not merely as the dominant world ideology but as the only one that could claim to be unremittingly rational and hence scientifically legitimate. The world revolution of 1968 returned liberalism to where it had been in the period 1815–1848, merely one competing political strategy among others. Both conservatism and radicalism/socialism were in that sense liberated from the magnetic field force of liberalism that had kept them in check from 1848 to 1968.

The process of demoting liberalism from its role as geocultural norm to mere competitor in the global marketplace of ideas was completed in the two decades that followed 1968. The material glow of the 1945–1968 period disappeared during the long Kondratieff-B downturn that set in. This is not to say that everyone suffered equally. Third World countries suffered first and worst. The OPEC oil price rises were a first mode of trying to limit the damage. A large part of the world surplus was funneled through the oil-producing states to OECD banks. The immediate beneficiaries were three groups: the oil-producing states who took a rent; the states (in the Third World and the Communist worlds) who received loans from OECD banks with which to restore their balance of payments; the OECD states who thereby could still maintain exports. This first attempt collapsed by 1980 in the so-called debt crisis. The second mode of trying to limit the damage was Reagan's military Keynesianism, which fueled the speculative boom of the 1980s in the United States. This collapsed in the late 1980s, pulling the U.S.S.R. down with it. The third attempt was that of Japan, plus the East Asian dragons and some surrounding states, to benefit from the necessary and inevitable production relocations of a Kondratieff-B period. We are witnessing the limits of this effort in the early 1990s.

The net result of twenty-five years of economic struggle was a worldwide disillusionment with the promise of developmentalism, a keystone in the offerings of global liberalism. No doubt East and Southeast Asia have been spared this sense of disillusion thus far, though this may be merely a time lag. Elsewhere, however, the consequences have been great, and particularly negative for the Old Left—first the national liberation movements, then the Communist parties (leading to the collapse of the Communist regimes of Eastern Europe in 1989), and finally the social-democratic parties. These collapses have been celebrated by liberals as their triumph. It has rather been their graveyard. For liberals find themselves back in the pre-1848 situation of a pressing demand for democracy—for far more than the limited package of parliamentary institutions, multiparty systems, and elementary civil rights—this time for the real thing, a genuine egalitarian sharing of power. And this latter demand was historically the bugbear of liberalism; to counter it, liberalism offered its package of limited compromises combined with seductive optimism about the future. To the extent that today there is no longer a widespread faith in rational reformism via state action, liberalism has lost its principal politico-cultural defense against the dangerous classes.

THUS IT IS WE HAVE ARRIVED AT THE PRESENT ERA, WHICH I think of as the Black Period before us. It can be said to have begun symbolically in 1989 (the continuation of 1968[67]) and will go on for at least twenty-five to fifty years.

I have emphasized thus far the ideological shield that dominant forces constructed against the claims insistently put forward by the "dangerous classes" after 1789. I have argued that this shield was liberal ideology, and that it operated both directly and, even more insidiously, via an edulcorated socialist/progressive variant that traded the essence of antisystemic claims for a substitute of limited value. And finally I have argued that this ideological shield was largely destroyed by the world revolution of 1968, of which the collapse of the Communisms in 1989 was the final act.

Why, however, did this ideological shield collapse after 150 years of such efficacious functioning? The answer to that question lies not in some sudden insight by the oppressed into the falsity of ideological claims. The awareness of the speciousness of liberalism had been known from the outset and asserted frequently with vigor throughout the nineteenth and twentieth centuries. Nonetheless, the movements in the socialist tradition did not conduct themselves in ways that were consistent with their rhetorical critiques of liberalism. Quite the opposite, for the most part!

The reason is not hard to find. The social base of these movements—movements that all claimed grandly to speak in the name of the mass of humanity—was in fact a narrow band of the world's population, the less well-off segment of the "modernist" sector of the world-economy as it was structured between, say, 1750 and 1950. These included the skilled and semiskilled urbanized working classes, the intelligentsias of the world, and the more skilled and educated groups in those rural areas in which the functioning of the capitalist world-economy was more immediately visible. This added up to a significant number, but not at all to the majority of the world's population.

The Old Left was a world movement supported by a minority, a powerful minority, an oppressed minority, but nonetheless a numerical minority of the world's population. And this demographic reality limited its real political options. Under the circumstances, it did the only thing it could. It opted for being a spur to speed up the liberal program of rational reformism, and at this it succeeded very well. The benefits it brought to its protagonists were real, if only partial. But, as the revolutionaries of 1968 proclaimed, a lot of people had been left out of the equation. The Old Left had talked a univeralist language, but had practiced a particularist politics.

The reason that these ideological blinkers of specious universalism were tossed aside in 1968/1989 was that the underlying social reality had changed. The capitalist world-economy had pursued the logic of its ceaseless accumulation of capital so unremittingly that it was approaching its theoretical ideal, the commodification of everything. We can see this reflected in multiple new sociological realities: the extent of the mechanization of production; the elimination of spatial constraints in the exchange of commodities and information; the deruralization of the world;

the near exhaustion of the ecosystem; the high degree of monetization of the work process; and consumerism (that is, the enormously expanded commodification of consumption).[68]

All these developments are well known, and they are indeed the subject of continuous discussion worldwide. But consider what they mean from the point of view of the endless accumulation of capital. They mean first of all, most of all, an enormous limitation on the rate at which capital can be accumulated. And the reasons are fundamentally sociopolitical. There are three central factors. The first is a factor long recognized by analysts, but whose full realization is only being reached now. The urbanization of the world and the increase in both education and communications have engendered a degree of worldwide political awareness that both renders political mobilization easy and makes it difficult to obscure the degree of socioeconomic disparities and the role of governments in maintaining them. Such political awareness is reinforced by the delegitimization of any irrational sources of authority. In short, more people than ever demand the equalization of reward and refuse to tolerate a basic condition of capital accumulation, low remuneration for labor. This is manifested both in the significant worldwide rise of the level of "historical" wages, and in the very high and still growing demand on governments to redistribute basic welfare (in particular, health and education) and to ensure steady income.

The second factor is the greatly increased cost to governments of subsidizing profit via the construction of infrastructure while permitting enterprises to externalize costs. This is what journalists refer to as the ecological crisis, the crisis of rising health costs, the crisis of the high costs of big science, etc. The states cannot at one and the same time continue to expand subsidies to private enterprise and continue to expand welfare commitments to the citizenry. One or the other must give to an important degree. With a more aware citizenry, this essentially class struggle promises to be monumental.

And the third strain is the result of the fact that political awareness is now worldwide. Both global and state-level disparities are racial/ethnic/religious in distribution. Hence, the combined result of political awareness and the fiscal crises of the states will be a massive struggle that will take the form of civil warfare, both global and state-level.

The multiple strains on the system will have as their first victim the legitimacy of state structures and, therefore, their ability to maintain order. As they lose this ability, there will be economic as well as security costs, which in turn will render more acute the strains, which will in turn further weaken the legitimacy of the state structures. This is not the future; it is the present. We see it in the enormously increased feeling of insecurity—concern about crime, concern about random violence, concern about the impossibility of securing justice in court systems, concern about the brutality of police forces—that has multiplied manyfold during the last ten to fifteen years. I am not contending that these phenomena are new, or even necessarily much more extensive than earlier. But they are perceived as new or worse by most people, and certainly they are perceived as far more extensive. And the major result of such perceptions is the delegitimization of state structures.

This kind of escalating, self-reinforcing disorder cannot go on forever. But it can go on for twenty-five to fifty years. And it is a form of chaos in the system, caused by the exhaustion of the systemic safety valves, or, to put it another way, by the fact that contradictions of the system have come to the point where none of the mechanisms for restoring the normal functioning of the system can work effectively any longer.

OUT OUT OF CHAOS WILL COME A NEW ORDER, AND THIS THEN brings us to the last issue: the choices before us—now and also soon. Because it is a time of chaos, it does not mean that during the next twenty-five to fifty years we will not see in operation the major basic processes of the capitalist world-economy. People and firms will continue to seek to accumulate capital in all the familiar ways. Capitalists will seek support from state structures as they have done in the past. States will compete with other states to be major loci of the accumulation of capital. The capitalist world-economy will probably enter into a new period of expansion, which will further commodify economic processes worldwide and further polarize effective distribution of reward.

What will be different in the next twenty-five to fifty years will be far less the operations of the world market than the operations of the world's political and cultural structures. Basically, the states will lose steadily their legitimation and therefore will find it difficult to ensure minimum security, internally or among themselves. On the geocultural scene, there will be no dominant common discourse, and even the forms of cultural debate will be a matter of debate. There will be little agreement on what constitutes rational or acceptable behavior. The fact that there will be confusion, however, does not mean that there will be no purposive behavior. Indeed, there will be multiple groups seeking to achieve clear, limited objectives, but many of these will be in acute direct conflict with each other. And there may be a few groups with clear long-term concepts of how to construct an alternative social order, even if there is little chance that these concepts will in fact serve as useful heuristic guides to action. In short, everyone will be acting somewhat blindly, even if they do not think they are.

Nonetheless, we are condemned to act. Therefore, we must first be clear about what has been deficient in our modern world-system, about what it is that has made so large a percentage of the world's population angry, or at least ambivalent as to its social merits. It seems quite clear to me that the major complaint has been the great inequalities of the system, which means the absence of democracy. This was no doubt true of virtually all known prior historical systems. What was different under capitalism is that its very success as a creator of material production seemed to eliminate all the justification for the inequalities, whether manifested materially, politically, or socially. These inequalities seemed all the worse because they divided not merely a very tiny group from everyone else, but as much as one-fifth or one-seventh of the world's population from all the rest. It is these two facts—the increase of total material wealth and the fact that more than a mere handful of people, but far less than the majority, could live well— that have so exasperated the sentiments of those who have been left out.

We can contribute nothing to a desirable resolution of this terminal chaos of our world-system unless we make it very clear that only a relatively egalitarian, fully democratic historical system is desirable. Concretely we must move actively and immediately on several fronts. One is the active undoing of the Eurocentric assumptions that have permeated the geoculture for at least two centuries now. Europeans have made great cultural contributions to our common human enterprise. But it is simply not true that over ten thousand years they have made much greater ones than other civilizations, and there is no reason to assume that there will be fewer loci of collective wisdom in the millenium to come. The active replacement of the current Eurocentric bias by a more sober and balanced sense of history and its cultural evaluation will require acute and constant political and cultural struggle. It calls not for new fanaticisms but for hard intellectual work, collectively and individually.

We need, in addition, to take the concept of human rights and work very hard to make it apply equally to "us" and to "them," to citizens and to aliens. The right of communities to protect their cultural heritage is never the right to protect their privilege. One major battleground will be in the rights of migrants. If indeed, as I foresee for the next twenty-five to fifty years, a very large minority of the residents of North America, Europe, and, yes, Japan, will in fact be recent migrants or the children of such migrants (whether or not the migration will have occurred legally), then we all need to struggle to make sure such migrants have truly equal access to economic, social, and, yes, political rights in the zone into which they have migrated.

I know that there will be enormous political resistance to this on the grounds of cultural purity and of accumulated property rights. The statesmen of the North are already arguing that the North cannot assume the economic burden of the entire world. Well, why not? The North's wealth has in very large part been the result of a transfer of surplus value from the South. It is this very fact that, over several hundred years, has led us to the crisis of the system. It is a question not of remedial charity but of rational reconstruction.

These battles will be political battles, but not necessarily battles at the level of the state. Indeed, precisely because of the process of delegitimizing the states, many of these battles (perhaps most of them) will go on at more local levels, among the groups into which we are reorganizing ourselves. And since these battles will be local and complex among multiple groups, a complex and flexible strategy of alliances will be essential, but it will be workable only if we keep in the front of our minds the egalitarian objectives.

Finally, the struggle will be an intellectual one, in the reconceptualization of our scientific canons, in the search for more holistic and sophisticated methodologies, in the attempt to rid ourselves of the pious and fallacious cant about the value neutrality of scientific thought. Rationality is itself a value judgment if it is anything, and nothing is or can be rational except in the widest, most inclusive context of human social organization.

You may think that the program I have outlined for judicious social and political action over the next twenty-five to fifty years is far too vague. But it is as concrete as one can be in the midst of a whirlpool. I have said essentially two things about life in a whirlpool. First, know to which shore you want to swim. And second, make sure that your immediate efforts seem to be moving in that direction. If you want greater precision than that, you will not find it, and you will drown while you are looking for it.

NOTES

1 Immanuel Wallerstein, "The Three Instances of Hegemony in the History of the Capitalist World-Economy," in *The Politics of the World-Economy: The States, the Movements, and the Civilizations* (Cambridge: Cambridge University Press, 1984), 37–46.

2 Each of the points here summarized briefly has been elaborated at greater length in many essays written over the past fifteen years, a good collection of which is included in Immanuel Wallerstein, *Geopolitics and Geoculture: Essays in a Changing World-System* (Cambridge: Cambridge University Press, 1991).

3 See *inter alia* W. Brian Arthur, "Competing Technologies, Increasing Returns, and Lock-in by Historical Events," *Economic Journal* XLIX, no. 394 (Mar. 1989), 116–131; and W. Brian Arthur, Yu. M. Ermoliev and M. Kaniovski, "Path-Dependent Processes and the Emergence of Macro-Structure," *European Journal of Operations Research* XXX (1987), 292–303.

4 A more detailed exposition of this effort and its failure is expounded in two other essays in this collection: "The Concept of National Development, 1917–1989: Elegy and Requiem" and "The Collapse of Liberalism."

5 Ideologies were only one of three ways of coping. The other two were the social sciences and the antisystemic movements. I discuss this in detail and seek to specify the interrelations between the three modes in "The French revolution as world-historical event," in *Unthinking social science: The limits of nineteenth-century paradigms* (Cambridge: Polity Press, 1991), 7–22.

6 The Charter conceded by Louis XVIII was politically crucial to his "restoration." In his declaration at St.-Ouen, the future king announced that he was determined to "adopt a liberal constitution," which he designated as a "charter." Bastid (1953, 163–164) observes that "the term Charter, whose meanings in former times had been multiple and varied, above all brought to mind the memory of communal liberties." He adds that, "for those of liberal bent, it evoked quite naturally the English Magna Carta of 1215." According to Bastid, "Louis XVIII would never have been able to win public acceptance had he not satisfied in some way the aspirations for liberty." When, in 1830, Louis-Philippe in turn also proclaimed a Charter, this time it had to be one that was "assented to"

(*consentie*) rather than one that was "bestowed" (*octroyée*) by the king.

7 "It is to mankind as a whole that liberals have, without major exception, addressed themselves" (Manning, 1976, 80).

8 In *The Charterhouse of Parma*, the revolutionary Ferrante Palla always introduces himself as a "free man."

9 Plamenatz argues that, although there were four factions among those opposed to the July Monarchy that one might designate as being on the "Left" and who later supported the Revolution of 1848, the term used to refer to them collectively was not "socialists" but "republicans" (1952, 47 and *passim*).

10 As Tudesq notes (1964, 235) : "The Legitimist opposition to the July Monarchy was an opposition of notables to established authority. . . ." Were the Legitimists not thus contradicting Bonald's dictum that "the true nature of society . . . is what society, public society, is presently"?

11 See the discussion of Bonald's views in Nisbet (1944, 318–319). Nisbet uses "corporation" in the sense of "associations based on occupation or profession."

12 "Both Saint-Simonism and economic liberalism evolved in the direction of what we call today economic rationalisation" (Mason, 1931, 681).

13 Halévy quotes an article that appeared in the *Quarterly Review* of April 1835 (vol. LIII, p. 265), entitled *Sir Robert Peel's Address*: "When before did a Prime Minister think it expedient to announce to the *People*, not only his acceptance of office, but the principles and even the details of the measures which he intended to produce, and to solicit—not from parliament but from the people—that they would so far maintain the prerogative of the king as to give the ministers of his choice not, indeed, an implicit confidence, but a fair trial?" (1950, 178, fn. 10).

14 As Leninism reconstructed itself from being a program for the revolutionary overthrow of the governments by the organized working class to being a program for national liberation followed by national development (of course a "socialist" one), it was in fact following a parallel path to Wilsonianism, which was the official version of liberal ideology. See "Liberalism and the Legitimation of Nation-States: An Historical Interpretation," in this collection.

15 See most particularly "The French Revolution as a World-Historical Event," in *Unthinking Social Science* (Cambridge: Polity Press, 1991), 7–22.

16 "By the 1830s, romantic revolutionaries were speaking almost routinely of *le peuple, das Volk, il popolo,* or *lud* as a kind of regenerative life force in human history. The new monarchs who came to power, after the Revolution

of 1830, Louis Philippe and Leopold I, sought the sanction of 'the people' as king 'of the French' and 'of the Belgians,' rather than of France or Belgium. Even the reactionary Tsar Nicholas I, three years after crushing the Polish uprising of 1830–1831, proclaimed that this own authority was based on 'nationality' (as well as autocracy and Orthodox)—and his word *narodnost*, also meaning 'spirit of the people,' was copied from the Polish *narodowosc*." James H. Billington, *Fire in the Minds of Men: Origins of Revolutionary Faith* (London: Temple Smith, 1980), 160.

17 An excellent discussion of the blurred field for the July Monarchy in France is to be found in John Plamenatz, *The Revolutionary Movement in France, 1815–1879* (London: Longman Green, 1952), 35–62.

18 "[B]y 1840 the characteristic social problems of industrialization—the new proletariat, the horrors of uncontrolled breakneck urbanization—were commonplace of serious discussion in Western Europe and the nightmare of the politician and the administrator." Eric J. Hobsbawm, *The Age of Revolution, 1789–1848* (New York: World, 1962), 207.

19 I have spelled this out in greater detail in "Three Ideologies or One? The Pseudobattle of Modernity" in this collection.

20 "The Legitimist opposition to the July Monarchy was an opposition of notables to the established order . . ." André-Jean Tudesq, *Les grands notables en France (1840–1849)* (Paris: Presses Univ. de France, 1964), 1, 235.

21 Lord Hugh Cecil, *Conservatism* (London: Williams and Northgate, 1911), 192.

22 Philippe Beneton has caught the dilemma quite precisely: "Traditionalism was in fact the greatest weakness of conservatism. Conservatives were faced with contradictions whenever the tradition whose defenders they were was interrupted for a long period and/or gave way to other (non-conservative) traditions . . .

"These contradictions explain . . . certain oscillations in conservative political thought . . . between fatalism and *a radical reformism*, between the rule of a limited state and the appeal of a strong state." *Le conservatisme* (Paris: Presses Univ. de France, 1988), 115–116.

23 Although few liberals were as consequent as Bentham, Brebner shows how, starting with an individualist antistate position one can arrive at a collectivist position. The conundrum is how society arrives at knowing the sum of individual interests. As Brebner says, for Bentham, the answer is that "individual interest must be *artificially* identified or made one by the omnipotent lawmaker, employing the felicific calculus of 'the greatest happiness of the greatest number.'" Thus, Brebner concludes: "What were Fabians but latter-day Benthamites?" J. Bartlett Brebner, "Laissez-Faire and State

Intervention in Nineteenth-Century Britain," *The Tasks of Economic History* (Supplement VIII, 1948), 61, 66.

24 L. T. Hobhouse, *Liberalism* (London: Oxford University Press, 1911), 146. It is this Benthamite/Hobhouse conclusion from liberal ideology that explains why a Ronald Regan fulminates against "liberalism" while in fact professing a version of liberal ideology. Are Bentham and Hobhouse typical? They are closer to the practice of liberals than other liberal ideologues. As Watson says: "No political party in nineteenth-century England can be shown to have believed in [the night-watchman doctrine of the state] or to have attempted to practice it." George Watson, *The English Ideology: Studies in the Language of Victorian Politics* (London: Allan Lane, 1973), 68–69.

25 J. Salwyn Schapiro, *Liberalism and the Challenge of Fascism* (New York: McGraw Hill, 1949), vii.

26 I discuss this issue in some detail in my essay "The National and the Universal: Can There Be Such a Thing as World Culture?" in *Geopolitics and Geoculture* (Cambridge: Cambridge University Press, 1991), 184–199.

27 The case for this is argued in G. Arrighi, T. K. Hopkins, and I. Wallerstein, "1989: The Continuation of 1968," *Review* 15, no. 2 (Spring 1992), 221–242.

28 Sir W. Ivor Jennings, *The Approach to Self-Government* (Cambridge: At the University Press, 1956), p. 56.

29 The literature is abundant. For two overviews, see Joseph L. Love, "Theorizing Underdevelopment: Latin America and Romania, 1860–1950," *Review* 11, no. 4 (Fall 1988), 453–496; and Bipan Chandra, "Colonial India: British versus Indian Views of Development," *Review* 14, no. 1 (Winter 1991), 81–167.

30 I develop this discussion of the meaning of 1968 in more detail in "1968, Revolution in the World-System," in *Geopolitics and Geoculture: Essays in the Changing World-System* (Cambridge: Cambridge Univ. Press, 1991), 65–83.

31 See the more detailed argument in my article "The French Revolution as a World-Historical Event," in *Unthinking Social Science: The Limits of Nineteenth-Century Paradigms* (Cambridge: Polity Press, 1991), 7–22.

32 This argument is elaborated in "Liberalism and the Legitimation of Nation-States: An Historical Interpretation," in this collection.

33 Benjamin Disraeli, Earl of Beaconsfield, *Sybil, or the Two Nations* (1845; reprint, London: John Lane, The Bodley Head, 1927).

34 Ibid., 641.

35 See "The Concept of National Development, 1917–1989," in this collection.

36 For a fuller analysis of the world revolution of 1968, see my essay "1968, Revolution in the World-System," in *Geopolitics and Geoculture: Essays in the Changing World-System* (Cambridge: Cambridge Univ. Press, 1991), 65–83.

37 For an excellent account, see Jerry L. Avorn et al., *Up Against the Ivy Wall: A History of the Columbia Crisis* (New York: Atheneum, 1968).

38 See note 27.

39 See my longer explication of this in "The Collapse of Liberalism," in this collection.

40 See R. Kasaba and F. Tabak, "The Restructuring of World Agriculture, 1873–1990," in *Food and Agricultural Systems in the World-Economy*, ed. P. McMichael (Westport, CT: Greenwood Press, 1994), 79–93.

41 For the implications of this for social analysis, see the special issue, "The 'New Science' and the Historical Social Sciences," *Review* 15, no. 1 (Winter 1992).

42 A discussion of the debates surrounding the adoption of this text is to be found in Marcel Gauchet, "Rights of Man," in *A Critical Dictionary of the French Revolution*, ed. F. Furet and M. Ozouf (Cambridge: Harvard Univ. Press, Belknap Press, 1989), 818–828. For the original text, see J. Tulard et al., *Histoire et dictionnaire de la Révolution française, 1789–1799* (Paris: Robert Laffont, 1987), 770–771. The English text is reprinted in I. Brownlie, ed., *Basic Documents on Human Rights* (Oxford: Clarendon Press, 1971), 8–10, without, however, the Preamble.

43 U.N. General Assembly Resolution 217 A(III).

44 U.N. General Assembly Resolution 1514(XV). On the development of a "decolonization norm" in the post-1945 world-system, see the brief comments of G. Goertz and P. F. Diehl, "Towards a Theory of International Norms," *Journal of Conflict Resolution* 26, no. 4 (Dec. 1992): 648–651.

45 Entry "Droit des gens" in J. Tulard et al., *op. cit.*, 770.

46 I have elaborated this argument previously and will not repeat it here. On the normality of political change, see "The French Revolution as a World-Historical Event," in *Unthinking Social Science* (Cambridge: Polity Press, 1991), 7–22. On the sovereignty of the people, see "Liberalism and the Legitimation of Nation-States: An Historical Interpretation," *Social Justice* 19, no. 1 (Spring 1992): 22–33.

47 *The Modern World-System*, vol. 3, *The Second Era of Great Expansion of the Capitalist World-Economy, 1730–1840s* (San Diego: Academic Press, 1989), 52.

48 See Arthur Schlesinger, Jr., *The Vital Center: The Politics of Freedom* (Boston: Houghton Mifflin, 1949).

49 I have developed these two themes too at length elsewhere. See, most particularly, "Three Ideologies or One? The Pseudobattle of Modernity," in this collection. I have only summarized them most briefly here in order to allow me to discuss my present theme—the role of the ideas of human rights and the rights of peoples in the politics of the modern world.

50 The literature is voluminous. For a sample, see Raphael Samuel, ed., *Patriotism: The Making and Unmaking of British National Identity*, 3 vols. (London: Routledge, 1989); Eugen Weber, *Peasants into Frenchmen: The Modernization of Rural France, 1870–1914* (Stanford, CA: Stanford Univ. Press, 1976); Seymour Martin Lipset, *The First New Nation: The United States in Historical and Comparative Perspective* (New York: Basic Books, 1963).

51 William McNeill, "Introductory Historical Commentary," in *The Fall of Great Powers: Peace, Stability, and Legitimacy*, ed. Geir Lundestad (Oslo: Scandinavian Univ. Press, 1994), 6–7.

52 Edward Said, *Orientalism* (New York: Pantheon, 1978), 207, 254.

53 See *The Congress of the Peoples of the East*, translated and annotated by Brian Pearce (London: New Park Publishers, 1977).

54 See note 30.

55 Indeed, as of 1993, Médecins du Monde is publishing a political journal whose title is *Ingérances: Le Désir d'Humanitaire*.

56 See my essay, "Development: Lodestar or Illusion? in *Unthinking Social Science* (Cambridge: Polity Press, 1991), 104–124.

57 It is worth noting in passing that the editorial group of seven persons and the Advisory Committee of eighteen (there was some overlap) were composed, as far as I can make out, without exception, of U.S. scholars—a commentary on world social science in 1953.

58 I have discussed this at length in a paper, "Culture as the Ideological Battleground of the Modern World-System," in *Geopolitics and Geoculture* (Cambridge: Cambridge Univ. Press, 1991), 158–183. See also the other essays in Section II, Geoculture: The Underside of Geopolitics.

59 V. G. Kiernan, "Revolution," in *A Dictionary of Marxist Thought*, 2d rev. ed., ed. T. Bottomore (Oxford: Blackwell, 1991), 476.

60 Lecture at 25th Anniversary of the Founding of Kyoto Seika University, December 7, 1993, Kyoto International Conference Hall (cosponsored by *Asahi Shimbun*, Tokyo).

61 See John W. Meyer et al., "The World Educational Revolution, 1950–1970," in *National Development and the World System: Educational Economic, and Political Change, 1950–1970*, ed. J. W. Meyer and M. T. Hannan (Chicago: Univ. of Chicago Press, 1979), 37–55.

62 For a magnificent and quite detailed account of the intellectual debates surrounding the Bicentennial in France, see Steven Kaplan, *Adieu 89* (Paris: Fayard, 1993).

63 The process by which liberalism gained center stage and made its two contestants, conservatism and socialism, into virtual adjuncts instead of opponents, is discussed in "Three Ideologies or One? The Pseudobattle of Modernity" in this collection.

64 The nature of the promises made by liberalism at the world level and the ambiguity of the Leninist response to global liberalism are explored in my essay "The Concept of National Development, 1917–1989: Elegy and Requiem," in this collection.

65 See a summary of the data in John T. Passé-Smith, "The Persistence of the Gap: Taking Stock of Economic Growth in the Post–World War II Era," in *Development and Underdevelopment: The Political Economy of Inequality*, ed. M. A. Seligson and J. T. Passé-Smith (Boulder, CO: Lynne Reiner, 1993), 15–30.

66 *Postmodernism, or the Cultural Logic of Late Capitalism* (Durham, NC: Duke Univ. Press, 1991), 268.

67 See note 27.

68 These points are elaborated in "Peace, Stability, and Legitimacy, 1990–2025/2050," in this collection.